National
College *of*
Ireland

Situated in the heart of Dublin's Docklands, the National College of Ireland is committed to widening participation in third level education, and providing its students with the skills and knowledge they need to meet Ireland's changing social and economic circumstances.

To achieve this, the College works in partnership with its students and a diverse range of stakeholders, including their families, employers and communities. Through its School of Community Studies, the College deliberately engages with parents/guardians to create an interest in and excitement about learning, as well as raising educational aspirations. We believe that if parents are empowered to become involved in supporting their children at home and at school, they can create a culture of educational achievement within their own families and, by ripple effect, within their wider communities.

This book examines the involvement of parents in their children's education, and how as parents they are influenced by the changing society in which they live.

About the Author

Margaret Josephine Bleach has been Director of the Early Learning Initiative at the National College of Ireland since 2008. Previously she worked as a primary school teacher and Home School Community Liaison Co-ordinator in Darndale, North Dublin. She was involved in the development and delivery of the Early Start Pre-School Intervention Programme, and subsequently worked as a facilitator with the School Development Planning Support Service (Primary) of the Department of Education and Science.

Having completed a Masters of Studies in Education (Hons) with Trinity College Dublin in 2003, Josephine's four children encouraged and inspired her to undertake a PhD in Education which she completed in 2008 and upon which this book is based.

PARENTAL INVOLVEMENT IN PRIMARY EDUCATION IN IRELAND

Margaret Josephine Bleach

The Liffey Press

Published by
The Liffey Press
Ashbrook House, 10 Main Street
Raheny, Dublin 5, Ireland
www.theliffeypress.com

A catalogue record of this book is
available from the British Library.

ISBN 978-1-905785-79-7

Printed in the UK by MPG Biddles.

This book is dedicated to the following:

- Ann Fitzgibbon and Don Herron, my PhD supervisors at Trinity College

- The Boards of Managements, principals and parents who took part in the research

- Management and colleagues in the School Development Planning Support Service (Primary)

- Michele Ryan and the School of Community Studies, National College of Ireland

- David Givens of The Liffey Press

- My family and friends, in particular my husband John and children Shane, Ben, Margaret and Frances.

Thank you all for your encouragement and support throughout the process.

CONTENTS

LIST OF TABLES AND FIGURES

List of Tables

List of Figures

Chapter One

INTRODUCTION

Introduction

The last two decades have seen an intense period of discussion and negotiation at national level on the future direction of Irish education. One of
the key aims of this dialogue was to 'maximise parent involvement and
choice' in their children's education (Ireland, 1992, p. 27). Not only
were parents to be kept informed of their own children's learning, but
they were to be involved in decision-making at all levels within the
school. This lengthy consultation process culminated in the following
legislation, namely the *Education Act 1998,* and the *Education Welfare
Act 2001,* and the *Primary School Curriculum 1999* (Department of
Education and Science [DES], 1999a), which outline the national policy
of parental involvement.

As a parent of four children, a teacher and a School Development
Planning Support (SDPS) facilitator, I had an interest in how the policy
was being implemented on the ground. From my observations, there appeared to be a discrepancy between the actual policy of parental involvement at national level and the 'policy-in-use' (Crump, 1992, p.
419) at local level. Schools, while they depended on the voluntary support of parents, did not have the time or the interest to involve parents.
Parents, on the other hand, focused more on the home curriculum and
their investment in the human capital of their children (Schultz, 1973).
While parents were happy to send their children to school and help out if
necessary, they showed little enthusiasm for getting involved in their
children's schools. This research aims to evaluate the implementation of
the national policy of parental involvement in their children's education
and schools, using the following questions:

- How are parents involved in their children's education both at home and in school?

- What is their relationship with their children's schools?

- What type of communication system exists between home and school?

The Irish State combines universal benefits with a targeted approach in favour of those most in need (Daly and Yeates, 2002, p. 88). In general it prefers its citizens to purchase the welfare services they require and contribute either financially and/or by volunteering to the provision of services to those who can not afford to pay privately. In line with this preference, the policy of parental involvement is implemented differently in schools with disadvantaged status. 'Educational disadvantage' is defined in the *Education Act 1998* as the impediments to education arising from social or economic disadvantage which prevent students from deriving appropriate benefit from education in schools (Ireland, 1998). The parents of children attending these schools are more likely to have lower levels of education, be unemployed and live in local authority housing. Under the DEIS action plan (DES, 2005d), these schools receive additional resources including a home-school coordinator through the Home School Community Liaison (HSCL) Scheme. These schools will be referred to throughout the research as disadvantaged schools. Schools, which are not designated as disadvantaged by the DES, will be referred to as middle class schools. The parents in these schools are more likely to have higher levels of education, own their own houses and be in full-time employment. These schools get no additional resources from the DES for home-school liaison. Therefore, this study will attempt to answer the following questions:

- What are the differences between middle class and disadvantaged parents in their involvement in their children's education both at home and at school?

- Are there other variables, such as family status, religion, age, gender, which impact on parental involvement to far greater degree than social class?

Policy implementation involves an extremely complex set of interacting elements over time. Irish society has changed tremendously over the last twenty years since the introduction of the HSCL Scheme in 1990 and the publication of the Green Paper *Education for a Changing World* (Ireland, 1992). As partnership is a key element of the educational discourse in Ireland, this research asks:

- How is the national policy of partnership between parents, the school, the State and the Catholic Church in supporting and planning for the best possible education for children at home and at school being implemented?

This chapter explores the background to the policy. Section one examines the parental roles, which influence their involvement in their children's education. In section two, variables, such as gender, citizenship, religion, social class and family forms, are explored. These have an impact on the identities and practices of parents. The changes in society, which have influenced their values and prompted the introduction of the partnership policy paradigm, are also highlighted. Section three examines partnership at national level. The partners include the Catholic Church, the State, teachers and parents. As the dynamics of power infuses all aspects of parental involvement (Reay, 1998, p. 71), the relationship between these stakeholders is highlighted. In section four, the implications and challenges of partnership for both parents and schools at local level is outlined. Finally, the term 'partnership' itself is explored.

Family-school relationships are socially-constructed and historically variable (Lareau, 1997, p. 704). Chapter Two outlines how the national policy of parental involvement was developed. The policy as agreed in the relevant official documents is reviewed. The overall thrust and emphasis of these documents, along with their gaps and inconsistencies, is highlighted. Using the main points in these documents, indicators, which were used to evaluate how the policy was being implemented in the schools in this study, were devised.

The research methodology is outlined in Chapter Three. A case study involving five Catholic primary schools was used to explore the different ways parents are involved with their children's education and schooling. Three schools are in a middle class area, while the other two have been designated under DEIS as Urban Band 1. This means that they are two of the 150 Irish primary schools with the highest concentration of disadvantage (DES, 2005d). Participant observation, questionnaires, interviews, focus groups and documentary analysis were the research methods used.

Chapters Four and Five outline the research findings. The home curriculum and the ways parents support the school at home is examined in Chapter Four. These results are discussed in Chapter Six. Chapter Five describes parental involvement in the education system at both national and local level. Participants' perceptions and knowledge of the stakeholders, policy, legislation and curriculum at national level is probed along with their relationship with the school. These findings are explored in Chapter Seven. The final chapter explores the themes from the literature review and evaluates the implementation of the national policy of home-school partnership.

Parental Involvement in Their Children's Education

Parental involvement or investment in their children's education begins with the birth of their children and appears to be never ending. Bourdieu (1974; 1977a) suggested that its form will depend on the cultural capital of the family. This consists of parental values and attitudes towards education, the amount of cultural resources such as books, art materials, computers etc. available in the home, along with the educational qualifications obtained by their extended family (Bourdieu, 1997, p. 47). These will influence both the home curriculum and parental involvement in their children's school. In the literature many labels are used to describe the role parents play in their children's education but for the purposes of this research, they have been summarised under four broad headings: educator, consumer, welfare recipient and supporter. In reality, these roles are intertwined as parents pragmatically adopt the one they perceive as most suited to their children's needs.

The terms 'educator', 'consumer', 'welfare recipient' and 'supporter' were chosen because they appeared to be more relevant to this research than the terms 'involved' and 'uninvolved', which were used by Ryan (1994) and Conaty (2002) to describe parents in the HSCL Scheme. Research suggests that the vast majority of parents are both concerned with and involved in their children's education (Reay 1998 p. 64; Furstenberg et al., 1999, p. 217). However, there can be considerable variations between parents. Whereas some parents, like those in Lopez's (2001, p. 14) research, perceive 'involvement as primarily attending to the immediate economic/financial needs of their families', others have the social and economic capital to focus on the long-term educational and development needs of their children. This section explores the roles parents can play in their children's education and their influence on home-school relationships.

Educator

Under the Constitution of Ireland (1937), parents are considered to be the primary educators of their children. While traditionally they were only responsible for their children's basic physical needs, parental responsibilities have increased to include nurturing a learning environment, co-operating with and supporting the school and fulfilling their special role in their children's development (DES, 1995, p. 9; 1996, p. 14). In addition, the necessity for advanced educational qualifications in modern societies demands a vast amount of emotional and educational labour from parents and requires them to have a strong orientation towards the future (De Regt and Weenink, 2005). In today's society, parents are expected to proactively lead and manage their children's education, both at home and at school, and are considered responsible for all aspects of their children's development.

Due to this social-constructivist theory of learning and developmental psychology, the State and the school have altered their expectations of parents in relation to their children's education. Out-of-school learning is perceived as providing a fundamental basis for in-school advance (Bourdieu, 1974; 1977a; Macbeth and Ravn, 1994, p. 6). Parents are expected to do a lot of 'educational' work both before and after children come to school (David, 1993). This home curriculum consists of the activities and conversations that parents and children engage in from birth onwards. It involves not only the social, cultural and intellectual development of children but the formulation and transmission of values, including their attitudes towards education, learning and career aspirations (Bourdieu, 1974, p. 34; DES, 2000a). Parents also have to provide their children with what they need in terms of social interaction and/or educational opportunities (Bell and Ribbens, 1994, p. 243). This involves monitoring their children's development and reinforcing the school curriculum at home (Lareau, 1997, p. 704).

Most parents, the Commission on the Family noted (1998, p. 85), learn as they go along, influenced by the way they were brought up, by what they have read and their observations of others. Many access expert knowledge through consulting books, magazines and other media (Vincent, 1996, p. 152; Coleman, 1998, p. 43) and networking with other parents (Bell and Ribbens, 1994). The Internet gives parents access to information from many sources. Type 'education + parents' into Google and you get 3,040,000 websites. These sites ranged from information, courses, quizzes, and advice to 'activities and resources for parents who want their children to excel in school' (www.eduplace.com/parents, 2004). As a result of this global traffic in ideas about Western educational thought and egalitarian individualism (Fahey, 1998, p. 386) more parents are aware of the importance of their role as educators of their children.

Parental involvement in the school is just an extension of this role. They are expected to plan ahead, find the right school, get to know the teachers and the curriculum, join the Parents Association and support their children's learning (Ward, 2007). In addition, parents are required to attend school events and activities (DES, 2000a) and get involved in the Board of Management (BOM) and policy working groups (SDPS, 2004). Familiarity with the schools' routines gives parents information about the workings of the school and provides a useful check on whether their children are moving towards the proper levels of independence and responsibility (Heightman, 1992, p. 21). It helps them move from a longitudinal, biographical focus to an age graded normative perspective (Graue et al., 2001, p. 478). In addition, it gives parents the cultural capital (Bourdieu, 1977a) and confidence to act as advocates for their children, when teachers failed to recognise a child's individual needs or even misjudge a child's abilities or intentions (Coleman, 1998, p. 24; Garanzine, 2000, p. 245).

Parents in this study who consider that they have a primary responsibility for the education of their children will be considered 'educators'. These parents will be proactive about their role, actively seeking support to enhance their children's educational opportunities and their own skills as parents. Vincent (2001, p. 349) described them as 'risk managers'.

'Educators' are not willing to leave education to the school and take very few chances where their children's educational prospects were concerned. They are more likely to initiate contact with the school over achievement, welfare and more systematic issues.

Supporter

The term 'supporter' has been widely used by parents, teachers and the DES to describe the relationship between parents and the school (Department of Education, 1995; Hyland, 1995; Commission on the Family 1998, p. 284). Depending on the parent, this support may be active or silent. Active supporters may be very involved with the school but they do not question or challenge the authority of the school. Silent supporters help their children at home but do not get directly involved with the school. They are, however, quite willing to attend meetings and events when required and contribute financially to their children's education. This role is based on traditional patriarchal familism (Fahey, 1998, p. 386).

Parents' rights are acknowledged but are perceived to be in harmony with the interests of the school and the teachers. They are accountable for providing food, clothing and sleep for their child, along with ensuring school attendance and suitable homework conditions (Macbeth, 1994, p. 82; National Educational Welfare Board [NEWB], 2004). In addition, parents must demonstrate an interest in and reinforce the child's schoolwork at home and ensure that the child respects and obeys their teachers (Cullingford, 1996a, pp. 11-2; NEWB, 2004). Compliance with the school norms of deferential and positive parental involvement is expected (Lareau and McNamara Horvat, 1999, p. 49). Parents' unpaid labour is thereby used to increase the effectiveness of the education system.

Most parents have no wish to be in control of teachers or the school (Coleman, 1998, p. 147). They are conscious of the difficulties teachers face daily. Relying on the expertise and disinterested concern of teachers, the majority of parents respect and support their children's teachers. The formal educational requirements of their children are, in most parents' opinion, best left to the professional expertise of the teachers. Irish parents appear to be similar, preferring to work with teachers rather than against them (Hyland, 1995, p. 42; DES, 2000b).

Parents in this research who perceive the school and the teacher as having primary responsibility for the education of their children will be described as 'supporters'. Their role is to support the work of the school and teachers by caring for their children, helping with homework and providing financial and/or other assistance as necessary. 'Supporters' monitor, perhaps question, but do not challenge the teacher in any sustained fashion (Vincent, 2001, p. 351). This support, which includes not only time and interest but also moral education and actual teaching, should not be defined as passive (Cullingford, 1996a, p. 11). In fact, it can be an extension of parents' role as educators. By gaining the trust of teachers and access to important institutional information, 'supporters' ensure that the school will be answerable to them when problems arise (Graue et al., 2001, p. 485).

Consumer

While parents themselves may not favour the term 'consumer' in relation to their children's education (Cullingford, 1996b; Gorad, 1997), the DES describes them as 'customers' and 'clients' (DES, 1998a, p. 3). While the Irish government does not encourage market forces in education to the same extent as other Western governments such as Great Britain and the United States, the DES conforms to the market based model of public management (DES, 1998b, 2005c). This influences their relationship with schools and parents. Consumerism has also increased in Irish society with individualism and extravagant expenditure on the home and children replacing traditional collective values (Keohane and Kuling, 2004, p. 158). This market-let approach has been encouraged by the forces of globalisation (Smith, 2004, p. 514) and will impact on parenting practices and home-school partnership.

Consumerism implies choice of public goods with no necessary involvement in their production or quality (Munn, 1998, p. 383). A consumer pays another person for the service, has a number of suppliers to choose from, has the legal right to expect a certain quality of product or service and is normally not obligated to the seller in any way other than paying the amount of money asked for the product or service (Bottery, 2005, p. 280). It can lead to adversarial, self-interested, fragile relationships with few responsibilities on the part of the consumer. Parents today live in a globalised consumer society. In this fast-paced and impersonal society, they, like most others, want to get on with their business without any unnecessary personal relationships. Many of their parenting tasks are outsourced to others. They purchase the services of day-care, after-school care and recreation centres as well as babysitters and nannies (Dennis, 2002, p. 112). To many parents the school may be just another service provider.

Consumers are expected to pay for the services that they receive, with the best services going to the consumer who can pay the most (Bottery, 2005, p. 284). Some schools receive substantial financial assistance from parents (Organisation for Economic Co-operation and Development [OECD], 1991, p. 45) and the additional costs of education can be a major issue for many families (Commission on the Family, 1998, p. 286; Society of St Vincent De Paul, 2003, p. 2). The lengthy lists of school costs includes voluntary contributions, school transport, examination fees, lockers, photocopies, books, uniforms, materials, outings, games and extra-curricular activities. The hidden and often unexpected nature of these costs increases the financial burden on parents.

In addition, consumers can be expected to perform unpaid tasks (Ritzer, 2004, p. 61) in order to improve organisational efficiency. Similarly, schools ask parents to help with reading, homework and to provide additional resources for their children's education. With parents helping out on school trips, in the classroom, at concerts and sporting events along with painting the school, parental involvement may be a ruse to obtain voluntary labour from parents.

Consumers need skills and knowledge if they are to make informed choices (Levin, 2004, p. 179). The imbalance of power between vendor and buyer, the lack of alternatives, along with the capacity of individuals to make choices may limit their options (Mintzberg, 1996, p. 77). There is a lack of accurate, profound and clear information about schools (Oplatka, 2004, p. 153). The information that parents can gather is limited to the visible, image-based organisational structures of the school rather than classroom practices. In Ireland, parents can access the DES's website for a school's Whole School Evaluation (WSE) Report. As it is in its infancy stages, there is not a report available on all schools. Each year, newspapers publish league tables of second level schools based on the number of students who received places in third level institutions. Getting involved with the school may be the only way parents can access information about schools (Graue et al., 2001, pp. 481-3) and thus make informed decisions about their children's education.

While in theory the customer is always right, all organisations, including schools, have ways to control their customers (Foucault, 2000, p. 18). They provide cues that indicate to customers what is expected of them as well as a variety of structural constraints that lead their customers to behave in a certain way. Finally, they ensure that customers internalise and follow taken-for-granted norms. Parents are strongly influenced by the collective norms and values of society and the social class to which they belong (Bourdieu, 1974, pp. 33-5). With the societally agreed model of a good school so rooted in our society it is unlikely that there will be any strong desire to seek alternative kinds of schools or change the existing structures of schools.

Central to consumerism, according to Gewirtz et al. (1995, p. 21) is the assumption that parents will invest a great deal of energy in ensuring that they have made the right choice of school for their child. However, economic capital gives a wide choice to some parents, and much less choice or sadly none to others (Commission on the Family, 1998, p. 548; Lynch and Lodge, 2002, p. 183). Cultural capital, which is linked to economic capital (Bourdieu, 1997, p. 49), is even more crucial in the decoding of schools, the interpretation of information and in the matching of child to school. While opportunity, nostalgia, tradition and convenience often make school choice a far from rational process, parents may also behave differently depending upon their children's birth order, age or gender (Gorard, 1997, p. 189). Research using different samples suggested that, in general, the reputation and atmosphere of the school, good discipline and academic results, along with proximity to home and their children's wishes were the influential factors in parental choice of school (Hunter, 1991, p. 38; Hughes et al., 1994, p. 204; Bosetti, 2004, p. 398). Many parents preferred schools that appeared to offer similar experiences to their own traditional-style schooling. Most were happy with their children's schools and felt that teachers were doing a good job.

Consumerism emphasises the rights of the individual over the collective responsibilities of all citizens (Hantrais, 2004, pp. 197-8; Bottery,

2005, p. 278). 'Consumers' focus on the education of their own children rather involvement in their schools. They actively choose their children's schools and extra-curricular activities and are prepared to supplement the State's provision, whenever necessary. They are aware of the quality and cost of the service provided and will complain if it is not delivered as promised.

Welfare Recipient

Ireland is considered a liberal welfare State. All Irish parents are 'welfare recipients' in that all parents receive a children's allowance, which is a universal monthly non-means tested payment from the State. They are also entitled to avail of the public health, education and other social services. Education, with its emphasis on maintaining social order and developing human capital (Schultz, 1977), is perceived as an integral part of the welfare state. In recent years, the school has become an agent for a variety of groups. These include the NEWB, Special Needs Education Board, National Educational Psychological Service, Health Board and the Gardaí. Increasingly, it is seen as a focal point for the delivery of a range of health and social services for children and their families (Heeney, 2006). These include prevention, screening and treatment services, the delivery of parenting support programmes and after-school activities. This, according to educational experts, yields the double advantage of supporting the intellectual development of all children while alleviating pressure on working mothers (Macbeth, 1995, p. 52; Commission on the Family, 1998, p. 48; Esping-Anderson, 2002b, p. 50).

Traditionally, parents were seen as being responsible for the socialisation, moral training and leisure activities of children, while teachers were responsible for their education and academic progress (Wyness, 1996, p. 55). Both were dependent on the other to take their responsibilities seriously and do a good job. As the welfare state has developed, the school's role has expanded. They now provide breakfast clubs, homework clubs and after-school activities. With the introduction of Social, Personal and Health Education (SPHE), teachers have taken on more of the parental role, especially in the moral area (OECD, 1997, p. 25). Parents increasingly look to the school and experts for support and guidance to help them cope with the modern methods of childrearing (Franklin and Madge, 2000, p. 43; De Regt and Weenink, 2005).

Schools and society can perceive parents who are different from the norm as obstacles to their children's learning and educational achievement (Wolfendale, 2000, p. 9; Zappone, 2002, p. 50). Consequently, these parents are singled out for parent education programmes. The HSCL scheme is an initiative which aims to enhance the educational attainment and achievement of children from disadvantaged backgrounds (Archer and Shortt, 2003, p. 43). It promotes home-school cooperation as a means of alleviating the 'adverse factors arising from inadequate home support' (Ireland, 1992, p. 88) in both literacy and numeracy. The HSCL teachers target marginalised families (Conaty, 2002). The DEIS Action Plan (DES, 2005d), which targets disadvantaged schools, renews the emphasis on the involvement of parents in meeting children's educational needs (Hanafin, 2006, p. 1).

Two parental traits emerge as crucial for children's success in education. One is the 'cultural capital' (Bourdieu, 1997, p. 47), where parents have the knowledge and economic resources to make the best use of the school system and to compensate for any inadequacies it may have. It enables them to be aware of and take advantage of educational changes and opportunities. The other is having the self-confidence and ability to deal with system (Coleman, 1998). Being an effective advocate for your children, being able to mediate between the child and school and intervene when appropriate, is an essential parenting skill, particularly when 'parental interest' is usually measured by teachers' perceptions of such interest and the number of times parents visit the school rather than the level of interest itself (Drudy and Lynch, 1993, pp. 154-5).

'Welfare recipients' are those who lack the cultural capital and sense of entitlement (Bourdieu, 1997, p. 47; Vincent, 2001, p. 360), which allows them to successfully negotiate their children's journey through the education system. They are dependent on the professional expertise of teachers and the school.

Questions

The roles parents play in their children's education influence the type of home curriculum they provide and their relationship with their children's school. Using labels described above, this research will explore how parents are involved in their children's education. Are they educators, advocating for and leading their children's learning as they progress through the education system? Do they support the school by helping with homework and supplementing the work of the school with a varied home curriculum and extra-curricular activities? Are they active supporters of the school, involved in fundraising, school events, classroom and extra-curricular activities? Do they operate as consumers – choosing an educational service that will meet the learning needs of their child? Or are they welfare recipients, who are dependent on the school and the State to help them to meet their children's educational and socialisation needs?

Influence of Parental Identities and Values

Just as parenting practices are influenced by the beliefs and identities of parents, education policies are influenced by the values and norms of the society in which they evolve. In Ireland, the dominant 'status group' (Collins, 1977, p. 125) is white, Catholic and Irish. This ethnic majority is given a structured superior status within the Constitution (Ireland, 1937) and Irish society. Others, like members of other religions, the travelling community, migrant workers and refugees, who do not share the social and cultural values of the nation are marginalised.

This section highlights the normative practices which underpin Irish society and the education system. These include citizenship, gender, social class, religion and family forms. Their impact on parenting practices and the education system, in particular the policy of parental involvement in their children's education, will be considered. In addition, the links between education and other State policies are explored.

Citizenship

Democracy is a central principle in the Irish Constitution (Ireland, 1937). All adult citizens, irrespective of gender and social class, have political rights. Politics is organised on the model of a liberal democracy (Peillon, 1995, p. 365) with political competition making the parties responsive to the needs and claims of as wide a range of interests as possible. The catch-all nature of the main political parties makes them reluctant to define their ideals and policies. However, the relationship between a general sense of economic well-being and the electoral popularity of the incumbent parties (Mair, 1992, p. 376) ensures that they focus more on economic and social politics than in most other western European party systems. This has resulted in a marked expansion in State intervention (O'Connell and Rottman, 1992, p. 206), with the electorate being treated like consumers (O'Halloran, 2004, p. 23), whose vote can be bought by gimmicks and stunts.

'Partnership', which allows organised socio-economic interest groups to be involved in the process of public decision-making, is firmly embedded within the Irish political psyche (Taylor, 2005, p. 50). It has formed the cornerstone of government strategy since the beginning of the 1990s and is perceived as having contributed significantly to Ireland's economic regeneration. Cooperative approaches to policy-making and implementation are now considered superior to the traditional systems. As a result, the Irish State uses social partnership to develop policy in all areas, including education. However, this process is not without its problems. The need to achieve a wide consensus often prevents clear policy choices (O'Donnell and Thomas, 2002, p. 181) and limits decisions to the parameters decided by the interest groups (Compston, 2002, p. 313). In addition, the government retains ultimate responsibility for decision making (Department of the Taoiseach, 2006, p. 74) and continues to maintain strategic control along with defining the roles and spheres of influence of the different partners (Connelly, 2007).

The policy processes used by the Irish State are illuminating. The formal process begins with public consultations, which may include public meetings, displays in public buildings and requests for written submissions from the general public through advertisements in the newspapers. Reports are then written and published. Negotiations with related interest groups or social partners take place. Finally, after a highly publicised passage through both houses of the Oireachtas or the local council, the law, plan or regulation is passed. Persistence, one's organisational power base along with an effective use of the media appears to determine the amount of influence one has over these changes.

One of the remarkable features of Irish life is the involvement of people in community groups, resident groups and lobbying campaigns of all kinds (McManus, 2004, p. 80). However, the number of people offering their services as volunteers has dropped (Molloy, 2005, p. 136). People are too busy, too stressed and too exhausted to find the time. They are also devoting more time to self-advancement and career-based study rather than community involvement (O'Mahony and Prunty, 2007, p. 9).

The pervasiveness of the clientelistic networks in Irish politics (Mair, 1992, p. 395; O'Halloran, 2004, p. 19) reflects the priority that is given to individual interests. The politician's role can be described as both that of a messenger and a legislator. Citizens have easy access to them at both national and local level through their constituency clinics. At their bequest, politicians raise issues with the appropriate minister or public servant. This system has the advantage of providing a two-way communication between citizens and legislators, where individual grievances are addressed. However, the disadvantage is that politicians can focus entirely on helping individuals to circumvent policies (O'Malley, 2004, p. 103) instead of collective concerns. By promoting individualism over the common good, it erodes citizenship (O'Halloran, 2004, p. 22) and limits public debate to immediate concerns rather long-term policy issues (Kelleghan and McGee, 2005, p. 23).

As *de facto* citizenship is impossible without social and economic rights, the welfare State was created to provide individuals with the opportunity to be become full and pro-active members of society (Walters, 1997, p. 222). It has enabled the change from private to public patriarchy (Walby, 1994). When necessary, it becomes the 'good parent' (Pinkney, 2000, p. 116), who supplements or replaces poor and inadequate parents. However, the right of parents as citizens to lead their lives in accordance with their own convictions appears to limit the State's right to intervene in family life. In addition, the Irish State prefers to sponsor market solutions, encourage private welfare provision as the norm and to limit public responsibilities to acute market failures (Esping-Anderson, 2002a, p. 15). The HSCL scheme and DEIS Action Plan (DES, 2005d) are part of these preventative measures.

In recent years there has been a major revision of the substance of Irish identity. As represented by the Celtic Tiger, consumerism and economic growth now vie with Catholicism and nationalism as the basis of collective identity (Keohane and Kuhling, 2004). There has been a transformation in the status of women, work practices and household forms.

Increasing prosperity has meant that more citizens than ever before have a stake in the economy through well-paid jobs, their homes and other personal assets. Modern communication systems, such as the Internet and satellite television, allow unprecedented access to the global flow of ideas, information and cultural products. Membership of the EU (European Union) provides a bench mark against which the competence of the State can be judged. The European 'average' and the OECD league tables enables citizens to see their national policies within a broader context and highlights their government's ability to deliver key services (Leonard, 2005, pp. 94-5).

Gender

Traditionally gender influenced the role parents played in their children's lives. Mothers were responsible for housework and childcare, while fathers supported the family financially. The Constitution (Ireland, 1937) is based on this paradigm of patriarchal familism, or the male breadwinner model (Scannell, 1988). It conferred power and status on men in the public spheres of work, politics and religion, confined women to the private sphere of the home and protected marriage as an institution. This resulted in discrimination against both fathers and mothers. Mothers were denied their rights as individual equal citizens, while fathers' rights were dependent on their relationship with the child's mother (Commission on the Family, 1998). This model of the mother-child relationship, rather the triangular mother-child-father relationship, is the paradigm that tends to dominate contemporary social science, child psychology and psychoanalysis (McKeown et al., 1998, p. 50). In recent years, there has been a move towards egalitarian individualism, which protects the personal rights of individual citizens (Fahey, 1998).

There has also been a move towards the 'adult worker' model in which paid work is a central principle of self-sufficiency and responsibility for both men and women (Williams, 2004, p. 6). As a result, more mothers are working outside the home. While this may limit their involvement with their children's school, it does not have to limit their involvement in their children's education. Once mothers have conquered the time and space challenges, they may use home learning, their support network and workplace to monitor and support their children's education

(Weiss et al., 2003). In addition, with the increase in their responsibilities, they may perceive paying for private tuition and tutors as far more beneficial to their children's learning than they themselves getting personally involved in providing unpaid labour and fund raising for their children's school.

Keeping fathers stuck in their traditional role, McKeown et al. (1998, p. 208) argued, prevents them from developing to their full potential as fathers. Gender bias in society ignores the domestic and childcare work of fathers and tries to discourage them from getting involved with children at all. At birth the father is treated as the secondary supporting parent. They are expected by their employers to work long hours, which limits their involvement with their children (Williams et al., 1998). In women-centred venues, such as play groups, playgrounds and schools, they feel out of place and uneasy, especially when mothering networks keep a suspicious 'watchful eye' on them (Doucet, 2006). In the legal sphere, mothers have more rights and are perceived to control the father-child relationship. Non-resident fathers are expected to pay maintenance even if their access to the children is restricted. State services and supports treat parenting as synonymous with mothering and either ignores fathers or fails to make the necessary contacts with them (McKeown, 2001).

With more mothers working outside the home, there is evidence that fathers are taking more responsibility for childcare (Williams et al., 1998, p. 494). Both Andrews (2005, p. 64) and Osnowitz (2005) found that fathers were as emotionally responsive and nurturing of children as mothers and had no problems undertaking the visible responsibilities typically associated with motherhood, such as school related activities and medical appointments. Recent research has highlighted the positive impact of father involvement on educational attainment (Flouri and Buchanan, 2004, pp. 149-150) and decision making (Brooks, 2004).

Despite the trend towards egalitarian individualism, parental involvement in schools tends to be a gendered activity (Abrahamson et al., 2005, p. 47). While the mothers' role has been extended to include both traditional male and female responsibilities, fathers continue to be absent or shadowy figures in their children's education. Despite asking for both parents' participation, it was mainly mothers who agreed to be interviewed in Graue et al.'s (2001, pp. 475-6) study. They observed that while fathers attended official school functions, mothers predominated in the face-to-face interactions at the school. In Lareau's (1997, p. 711) study, only a few fathers had very specific information about the school. Most depended on their wives to collect and store this information. However, Brooks (2004, p. 501) argued that it would be wrong to assume that there was a correlation between the level of involvement and the level of influence on educational decision making. Fathers played an important role in their children's higher education choices as a result of their access to particular forms of social capital. While mothers may have access to better information about the schools, fathers may have more information about the qualifications and skills necessary to succeed in the workplace.

At its core, being a parent involves taking responsibility for one's children. Behaviours by fathers, which impact on children, are no different to those of mothers. While childcare remains primarily a women's responsibility, with the majority of 'educational work' being carried out by mothers, fathers are both able and willing, if required, to assume the role of 'labourer of educational choice' (Brooks, 2004, p. 512). Geist (2005, p. 30) found that the domestic division of labour depended on the gender ideology of men and women, the number of hours they worked and their relative financial resources.

Social Class

While social class influences the identity of parents, there is disagreement about its influence on their involvement in their children's education. Some would suggest that it is the parents' commitment to (Coleman 1998 p. 10) and interest in (Drudy and Lynch, 1993, pp. 154-7) education rather than their social class, which makes the difference. The social capital (Putnam, 2000, p. 296) of the parents, along with their sense of 'entitlement' (Vincent, 2001, p. 348) as regards their children's education, is also influential. However, Bourdieu (1977a, p. 497) found that 'a very pronounced correlation may be observed between academic success and the family's cultural capital measured by the academic level of the forbears over two generations on both sides of the family'. He (p. 48) suggested that the domestic transmission of cultural capital, which is inextricably linked to social class and economic capital, is 'the best hidden and socially most determinant educational investment'. Other studies have also shown that education is a proxy for privilege or middle class values (Putnam, 2000, p. 95) and it is educated parents who are normally most active in fostering the human capital development of their children (Craig, 2006, p. 563).

Lynch and Lodge (2002, p. 63) suggest that social class is a silent subject where euphemistic language, such as good, bad, disadvantaged, marginalised, is used to describe the problem. They suggested (p. 183) that inequality works at two levels. Firstly, national policies create serious economic inequalities between classes. As a result, low income working class households are seriously disadvantaged as they lack the money, transport, time and sometimes even the knowledge to discriminate between schools. Middle class families, because of their social, cultural and economic capital, are able to take full advantage of the system and make the freest choices. The State needs to recognise how much parental success is interwoven in to a system of opportunity and equality of life chances that are set by economic and political priorities (Zappone, 2002, p. 41).

Being an advocate for your child at school is one of the most important roles a parent plays in the education system. The sense of 'entitlement' (Vincent, 2001, p. 348) of disadvantaged parents was such that they assumed that they had neither the capacity nor the right to intervene in school matters and reacted with either anger or resigned acceptance (McNamara Horvat et al., 2003, p. 14). They felt constantly under pressure to demonstrate that they were 'good' parents by caring for their children, valuing education and turning their children out clean and tidy (Carlen et al., 1992, pp. 165-6). Due to their own low levels of educational attainment, some disadvantaged parents lacked confidence in their ability to help their children (Lareau, 1997, p. 710). Middle class parents, on the other hand, believed that they possess similar or superior educational skills and prestige to the teachers (Ibid., p. 708). They use their cultural capital and social networks to contest the school's official view of their child's abilities, influence the behaviour and selection of teachers, strategically customise their child's school career and locate professional advice and expertise (McNamara Horvat et al., 2003, p. 14). Depending on the circumstances, middle class parents react either collectively or as individuals and will use their networks to link with others who have the necessary information, expertise or authority to compel the school to follow a preferred course of action.

Cultural capital (Bourdieu, 1997) is an important asset to parents. The middle class mothers in Reay's (1998, p. 70) study were engaged in an extensive systematic programme of generating cultural capital for their children. The upper middle class respondents in De Regt and Weenink's (2005, p. 71) research, who felt unable to force their lazy, unwilling or unruly child to attend school and complete homework, used their economic and cultural capital to procure an alternative route in the educational process for their children. Many disadvantaged parents, Furstenberg et al. (1999, p. 226) found, did not have adequate knowledge of what it takes to achieve in the middle class world. Not having the cultural and economic resources to subcontract to those who did, these disadvantaged parents tended to focus on the here and now, believing that the future would take care of itself if they managed to keep their children in school and out of trouble. While agreeing with the need for education, they found it difficult to prevent their children dropping out of school. While both sets of parents were similar in their feelings of powerlessness around the behaviour of their children, the disadvantaged parents felt powerless in their relationship with the school and welfare authorities. As a result, they tended to adopt a resigned fatalism about the outcomes of their children's education (Gewirtz et al., 1995, p. 44).

According to standard measures, the ill health, emotional and behavioural problems of children of parents in poor environments/poverty were not much higher than the population as a whole, which suggests that these parents were managing to care for their children well (Furstenberg et al., 1999, p. 217; Quinton, 2004, p. 59). In the second of the two Annual Parent Surveys for an Early Intervention Strategy Project in eleven Scottish urban authorities, characterised by extensive social disadvantage and educational underachievement, the picture of the educational life in these, often hard pressed, families was encouragingly upbeat and positive (Bastiani, 2000, p. 20). A majority provided regular encouragement and practical support for their children's school learning and were actively engaged as a family in a wide range of educational activities, both in the home and throughout the wider community. In its review of the implementation of the revised curriculum, the National

Council for Curriculum and Assessment (NCCA) (2005, pp. 207-8) found that the parents in disadvantaged schools were much more involved in their children's learning at school than those in middle class schools. Similarly, the working class parents in Reay's (1998, p. 62) study talked in terms of regular involvement spanning curricular as well as social issues. However, absenteeism is higher in the most disadvantaged urban schools with almost a quarter missing twenty days or more in the school year 2004-05 (NEWB, 2005, p. 27). In comparison only 7 per cent of students in the least urban disadvantaged schools missed twenty days or more.

The policy of parental involvement is implemented differently in middle class and disadvantaged schools. In disadvantaged areas, schools have the benefit of the HSCL programme, which is a specific intervention to help the disadvantaged access the educational and cultural advantages of the middle classes. This is further discussed in Chapter Two. Parental involvement in middle class schools is entirely dependent on the awareness of the BOM of its responsibilities towards parents, the goodwill of the principal and the voluntary activities of the Parents Association and individual parents. While parental involvement in their children's education in middle class and disadvantaged schools will be compared in this research, Furstenberg et al. (1999, p. 224) found that resourceful parents, who have at their command an array of family management practices, are more likely to succeed regardless of where they live.

Religious Values

For many parents, religion is a key influence on their identity and values. Not only does their religion support their spiritual beliefs, but it encourages the development of their social capital. Putnam (2000, p. 66) found that faith communities, in which people worshipped together, provided an important incubator for civic skills and norms. In Ireland, it appears to be similar with church-goers more likely to volunteer (Taskforce on Active Citizenship, 2007b, p. 14; CSO, 2007b, p. 29).

For historical reasons, there has been a close identification between Irish citizenship and Catholicism (Herbert, 2003, p. 11). The Catholic Church was the dominant interest group in the State up to the late 1950s. By providing legitimacy, external recognition and stability to the newly established republic (Hornsby-Smith, 1992, p. 275), it played an important role in the formation and development of the State. Through its monopoly over morality and the acceptable standards of behaviour, the Catholic Church formed a collective orthodoxy, which permeated the Constitution (Ireland, 1937) along with civil society and the interest groups within it (Inglis, 2000, p. 50). Together with the State, it controlled and dominated most aspects of people's lives (Hilliard, 2003). While the majority passively accepted the situation, others adopted a strategy of deliberate distancing.

In recent years, there has been a major change in the relationship between the Catholic Church and the Irish people. Membership of the EU, the expansion of the welfare state and an increasingly multi-cultural society have altered the status of the Church (NicGhiolla Phádraig, 1995, p. 612). It has been forced to move from a situation of total control and domination to one where it is unsure of its role in a 'status-conventional society' (Waters, 2000, p. 54). The bishops are no longer paternalistic authority figures who can issue diktats which will be obeyed. Politicians are influenced far more by EU policy agendas, social partnership agreements and the demands of the electorate than by the advice or warnings of the bishops. A clear distinction has been drawn between the Church's teaching on morality and State law with both the legislators and the electorate expected to act according to their consciences.

In the past, women played a crucial role in passing on the faith to their children and creating vocations. Both Inglis (1998, p. 24) and Fuller (2002) agreed that the rigorous moral discipline imposed by the Catholic Church on the State could not have been attained without the 'Irish Mother'. She was the Church's representative in the home, supervising the moral conduct of her husband and children. As was seen earlier, the move from patriarchal familism to egalitarian individualism means that parenting is increasingly perceived as joint responsibility. European gender equality legislation, along with the development of feminism and the women's movement, has given women economic and political power. They are no longer dependent on the moral power of the Church. Today, the global media, with their educational and psychological experts, appear to influence mothers and their parenting practices more than the

Church and the 'Irish Mother' can no longer be relied on to inculcate religious values in her children.

According to Lynch and Lodge (2002, p. 142), religion was of little relevance to the young people in their study. Fulton (2000b, p. 161) described the young Catholics in his study as consumers at the supermarket of post-material and spiritual goods. This has been described as '*à la carte* Catholicism' (Pollard, 2001, p. 86), with the Catholic faith being seen as just one possibility in a range of religious options. With individual conscience displacing external authority, the gap between the institutional Church's position on personal morality and the views and practices of most young believers has widened (Fulton, 2000b, p. 169). In addition, the prestige and credibility of the Church has been undermined by a series of scandals that have compromised the role of the bishops as moral guides and the Church's ability to proclaim the gospel. It appears that like in America the decline in religious participation can be attributed mainly to generational differences (Putnam, 2000, p. 72).

While there may be a consistent decline in the number of Catholics, it important to acknowledge that 86.8 per cent of the population described themselves as Roman Catholics in the 2006 Census (CSO, 2007a, p. 31). Catholicism continues to remain part of the Irish identity and a significant source of social interaction. Fahey (1992, pp. 257-9) suggested that convention, social conformity and a stubborn allegiance to the Church, rather than strong personal conviction, underlies some of the devotionalism of Irish Catholics. Due to pressure from extended family and neighbours, parents may find it difficult to break their links with the Church (Fulton, 2000b, p. 164). Religious rituals which incorporate members in to a group (McGuire, 2002 p. 235) remain important secular family and community celebrations. Baptism, First Communion and Confirmation continue to be significant sacramental occasions in the life of a child and their parents.

Social stability, according to Hunt (2002, p. 61), rests on a shared morality. Religion has an important function in enforcing a value consensus and the symbolic 'worshiping' of society. The new 'civil religion' (ibid.) in Ireland, which is perhaps best represented by the celebration of St Patrick's Day, retains many of the symbols and characteristics of Catholicism. While differences in beliefs are acknowledged, they tend to be incorporated into the views of the majority. 'Newcomer' and other minority groups are expected to live by the norms of Irish society (Taskforce on Active Citizenship, 2007c, p. 22).

Family or Lifestyle Factors

Epstein and Seyong (1995, p. 122) argued that time was an important element in the nature and extent of home-school partnership. The age of both parents and children along with family size and form influence parenting practices.

The age of both the parent and their children may impact on parental involvement in their children's education. Volunteering and community involvement is higher among older people (CSO, 2007b, p. 29; Taskforce on Active Citizenship, 2007b, p. 3) with young people the least likely to get involved. They prefer to prioritise the personal and private over the public and collective (Putnam, 2000, p. 259). However, Murphy (2002, p. 90) found that the age of the parent was irrelevant. First time parents were more likely to get involved with those with older children feeling that they had done their share. Other studies were similar. They found that involvement tended to decrease from junior to senior class (Ryan, 1994, p. 26; DES, 2005a, p. 63; NCCA, 2005, p. 208).

The gender of the child also influences the parent-child relationship. Girls were more likely to involve their parents in their education both at home and at school (Edwards and Alldred, 2000, p. 448). They were also more likely to do more family and self care than boys (Evertsson, 2006).

Family size has decreased in Ireland from over four children in the 1960s to less than two in 2006 (CSO, 2007a, p. 20). This will influence parenting practices as fewer children means that parents have more resources to invest in quality per child. Large families create a very high demand for unpaid labour in the home while the costs of childcare are similarly multiplied. They are also more likely to live in social housing than other families with children (Fahey and Russell, 2001, pp. 61-2). Mothers of large families are more likely to be older and have lower education qualifications. While family size may not influence the love and care parents have for their children, it is more difficult to give children individual attention in large families. Children in large families have to learn to share their time, belongings and space with others. In contrast, only children are more likely to have the complete attention of their parents. They tend to be over-indulged, over-praised and mollycoddled (McWilliams, 2006, p. 47).

One of the more recent changes in Irish society has been the growth in lone parent families, headed by women, as a result of marital breakdown and unmarried mothers (CSO, 2007a). These families may find it more difficult to rear their children, while also securing family income. Fifty per cent of the non-attendance cases, in a survey done in Dublin in November 1992, were from one-parent families (Department of Education, 1994, p. 7). The group of parents Ryan (1994, p. 191) in her report on parental involvement in the HSCL Scheme described as 'uninvolved – needs helps' were more likely to be in one-parent families. However, Richardson (2004, pp. 244-8) found that the teenage mothers in her study were concerned and caring about their children and were generally coping well despite the range of difficulties they faced. Most regretted leaving school without qualifications and hoped that their children would remain in education and gain good employment. While studies have found that children in lone-parent families have a lower level of educational attainment compared with children in two-parent families, the education levels of the parents appear to have a far greater impact (Dronkers, 1994, p. 186; Crozier and Davies, 2006, p. 681). Lone parenting is not solely class-related.

Questions

As parental identities and values have such an influence on their parenting practices, this research will examine their impact on home-school partnership. How will participants' perceptions of themselves as citizens influence their relationship with the school? Will there be a difference between how mothers and fathers lead and manage their children's education? Are middle class and disadvantaged parents similar in their attitudes towards child rearing and schooling? How does economic and cultural capital influence parenting practices? What difference will the HSCL scheme make to the involvement of parents in disadvantaged schools? Finally, how will the religious beliefs and life stages of the respondents influence their involvement in their children's education? What impact has the forces of Church paternalism, political clientelism

(O'Sullivan, 1992, p. 464) and egalitarian individualism (Fahey, 1998) on parental involvement in their children's schools?

Partnership at National Level

Culturally prescribed concepts like partnership are invested with considerable power (O'Sullivan, 1989, p. 221). They define the boundaries of normality and demand allegiance for the purpose of meaningful human contact. It is therefore important to analyse not only why and how a concept like partnership is used but whose interests it serves. The development of the national policy of partnership in education is described in further detail in Chapter Two.

The terms 'partners' and 'partnership' in education, according to Sugrue (2004, p. 192) were not widely used before the National Education Convention Report (Coolahan, 1994) and only achieved policy orthodoxy in the White Paper (Department of Education, 1995, p. 9). While these days 'partnership' is firmly rooted in the educational landscape, the views of the partners at national level are illuminating. This section examines those views.

Department of Education and Science (DES)

The Irish education system is highly centralised with curriculum, evaluation and funding all centrally controlled by the DES. This is perceived as vital to the State achieving its goals of economic prosperity, social well-being and a good quality of life for all within a democratically structured society (Department of Education, 1995, p. 4). The capacity to supply a highly skilled and qualified workforce is critical to enhancing the competitiveness of the Irish economy and attracting inward investment. The DES's mission statement reflects these priorities:

> The mission of the Department of Education (1995, p. 193) is to ensure the provision of a comprehensive, cost-effective and accessible education system of the highest quality, as measured by international standards, which will:
>
> - enable individuals to develop to their full potential as persons and to participate fully as citizens in society and
>
> - contribute to social and economic development.

To achieve these goals, the State feels that it must be able to decide on

> the period during which a child must attend school, the length of the school day, the subject matter to be taught and the manner of teaching. Children and parents must abide by the school's regime, subject only to the parents' rights to withdraw their children from religious instruction. The minimum standard of education should be based on expert advice and opinion, best practice in countries with whom Ireland shares similar economic and social conditions and the actual circumstance which prevail in society (Ibid., p. 5).

It appears that parents' role as the primary educators of their children is limited by the norms of the DES and its educational experts. This is in keeping with the government's retention of the ultimate responsibility for policy decision-making (Department of the Taoiseach, 2006, p. 74). Partnership is defined as consulting the social partners on policy proposals and the design of implementation arrangements.

The DES considers 'raising awareness of the importance of families and communities in providing encouragement and the right setting for effective learning' as one of the challenges facing the education system (DES, 2005d, p. 13). To this end and as part of its responsibility to provide for those children whose parents have neglected their duty (Ireland, 1937), the DES, in conjunction with various voluntary and statutory agencies, provides a range of preventative initiatives, which target disaffected and marginalised pupils and their families. Schools with disadvantaged status have DES funded programmes such as the Early Start Pre-School Intervention Programme, the HSCL and the SCP. These have been integrated under DEIS, the DES's action plan for social inclusion (DES, 2005d), which aims to enhance the educational achievement of pupils and to promote their retention in the education system.

By providing children with pre-school and after-school meals, homework support, along with extra-curricular sporting and cultural activities, these schools are becoming an extension of the home (Heeney, 2006, p. 148). While home-school partnership is a theme running though the documentation, these programmes are often devised without dialogue or consultation with the parents who will be most affected by them (Hanafin and Lynch, 2002, p. 37). As their emphasis is on increasing children's chances of educational success along with the capabilities and skills of their parents, they tend to concentrate on parent information and education programmes rather than parental involvement in decision-making and governance.

Middle class parents, on the other hand, are an important lobby and are perceived by the government as a key sounding board for educational policy (Kilfeather, 2003, p. 243) and a source of electoral support. Media recommendations (Reid, 2004, p. 3) to a newly appointed Minister for Education included the advice that policies, which upset parents, especially middle class voting ones, are best avoided. However, despite parent bodies insisting on equal representation with other educational partners, their role remains both ambiguous and heavily circumscribed. Power remains in the hands of a heavily centralised government department, the patron of the schools and the industrial agreements between the teachers' unions and the State (Tovey and Share, 2003, p. 194).

Irish National Teachers Organisation (INTO)

The INTO, which represents primary school teachers, is among the most powerful white-collar unions in the country. It enjoys direct negotiating rights with the government along with representation on statutory and investigative bodies on various aspects of education (Clancy, 1999, p. 84). With a growing influence within the Irish Congress of Trade Unions in helping to set the agendas of the various national understandings negotiated since the late 1980s, the INTO may prevent certain issues getting on the policy agenda and circumscribe the range of solutions that are considered. It fears that DES's promotion of partnership with parents is an attempt to curtail its power (Walshe, 1999, p. 115) and restrict its professionalism.

The INTO believes that increased parental involvement has the potential to transform schools into organisations where the work of both teachers and parents is recognised, valued and appreciated (INTO, 1997). However, its members are concerned that the increasing parental involvement in schools, particularly to the point of partnership, could be a threat to their professional status and competence. Not only do teachers feel, as professionals, that they should be guiding the agenda, but they also want to remain the final arbiters of professional matters in schools with parental involvement in the classroom at the discretion of the principal and the individual class teacher. It appears that the INTO wishes to limit the parents' position to the traditional role of 'supporter'.

The Catholic Church

The majority of schools (3,104 out of 3,386, 2005 figures) in Ireland are still under the patronage of the Catholic Church (Gaire and Mahon, 2005, p. 15). Traditionally, education was perceived as a means of religious socialisation which would ensure that the Church maintained its influence and moral control over Irish citizens (Hornsby-Smith, 1992, p. 275). The rights of parents and the Church were considered to be complementary (O'Sullivan, 1992, p. 465). It was implicitly understood that the patron or trustee acted on behalf of parents who wished their children to be educated in the Catholic tradition (Coolahan, 1994, p. 24). In reality, the lack of a genuine alternative combined with the social and religious consequences meant that parents had no choice but to send their children to Catholic schools (Tuohy, 2005, p. 120). This allowed the Church to monitor parents and ensure that children were instructed in and imbued with the Church's teaching (Inglis, 1998, p. 57). In turn, children reintroduced institutional adherence among parents who may not wish to contradict what was taught in school.

While acknowledging that much of the protection for Catholic schools derives from the rights of parents as the primary educators of their children and that schools should be open, welcoming and inclusive places for parents, the Catholic Primary School Managers' Association (CPSMA, 2004, p. 17) hold similar views to the INTO. They assert that

> In a spirit of collaboration and trust, the Constitution of the Parents Association will recognise that there are areas of school activity which belong to the professional work of the teachers. There will also be a recognition that certain areas of responsibility (e.g. finance) belong to the Board of Management.

The CPSMA appears to want parents to remain in their traditional role as 'silent partners' (O'Sullivan, 1992, p. 465) or 'supporters'.

National Parents Council Primary (NPCP)

Traditionally, parents were not included in the decision-making processes at either national or local level. During the 1970s a number of parent associations and at least two national associations were established. In 1985 the NPCP was established by the Minister for Education, Gemma Hussey, and the inspectorate as part of the Government Programme for Action in Education (OECD, 1997, p. 146). With its aim to improve the education of children and to support the involvement of parents in their children's education (NPCP, 2007b), the NPCP emphasises partnership and respect for the other parties in education rather than control. Insisting that the principles enshrined in Article 42 of the Constitution must permeate all educational change, they have been fully involved in the development of recent educational policy and have representatives on the primary education committees set up by the DES (Kilfeather, 2003, p. 243). However, its parent body appear to focus more on local issues with the most frequent calls to its helpline being about bullying behaviour in schools (NPCP, 2006, p. 4)

The heterogeneous nature of the parent body and ensuring that spokespersons are truly representative poses difficulties for the NPCP. Casual observation, according to Drudy and Lynch (1993, p. 126), would suggest that Parents Associations are female-dominated and predominately middle class. Their present structures limit the representation and participation of parents nationally. A school needs to have a Parents Association affiliated to the NPCP before its parents can access the NPCP (Kilfeather, 2005, p. 194). It is also dependent on school principals and BOMs to give information to parents. In recent years, the NPCP has been in the process of modernising to meet the identified needs of parents and to make the organisation more flexible, responsive and inclusive (NPCP, 2007a).

In addition to the NPCP, parents, supported by Article 42 and various Catholic fundamentalist groups, have questioned the direction of religious, moral and social education. They have been quite influential in preventing the full implementation of the Relationships and Sexuality Education (RSE) programme and have ensured that SPHE is the only curriculum subject where it is recommended that parents are involved in the development and implementation of the whole school policy (DES,

2003b) and need to be fully informed of the content and teaching approaches (DES, 2000a, p. 38).

In other words, to paraphrase Chomsky (1987, p. 127), partnership is encouraged but within certain parameters defined by the existing power blocks. This means that home-school partnership is perceived solely in terms of the willingness and capacity of parents to support the school and other educational partners. These attitudes appear to limit the constitutional rights of parents as the primary and natural educators of their children (Ireland, 1937) and deny them a genuine role in the process of shaping wider educational purposes.

Partnership at Local Level

A notable feature of school administration in the past was the distancing of parental involvement (Coolahan, 1989, p. 55). The preferred relationship was one of silent partnership, with parents pushing the child to do well at home while maintaining a respectful distance from the teachers. The principal and teachers were responsible for the organisation of school life and the implementation of the curriculum. Parents were responsible for their children outside school hours and for supplementing State aid to schools through voluntary contributions, unpaid labour and other forms of parental involvement (Bloch et al., 2003, p. 12). The relatively recent national policy of home-school partnership challenges these largely taken-for-granted professional and organisational structures.

Many schools treat parents as if they were the estranged partner. They either consider parents a pain because of their interference or a problem because of their indifference (Wyness, 1996). Consequently, parents are dismissed, either explicitly and/or implicitly, from the process of educating their child. There can be substantial resistance from teachers to the idea that parents should be kept informed of their children's progress and/or allowed make crucial decisions about their children's education. This is particularly obvious in the case of parents who appear to hold values which are antithetical to those of the school (Hughes et al., 1994, p. 164).

While appearing to implement the national policy of parental involvement, schools can convert it into an institutionally non-threatening form, which serves to reinforce existing power structures (Simpson and Cieslik, 2002, pp. 119-28). Teachers, especially those concerned about

the parents' power to question their authority and professional competence, may limit their contact with parents (INTO, 1997, p. 17) and use
their professional knowledge and language to keep parents at a distance
(Hargreaves, 2000, p. 220). Requests for help can be laden with the social and cultural experiences of the intellectual and economic elites
(Lareau, 1997, p. 704).

In the so-called partnership between home and school, the home can
be treated as the junior partner, with parents feeling that they are in a no-
win situation with the school (Carlen et al., 1992, p. 138). Despite the
presence of Parents Associations and parent representatives on the BOM,
many parents feel that there are few opportunities for them to voice their
views on issues which are directly affecting their children's lives. The
parents in Hanafin and Lynch's (2002, p. 45) study were particularly resentful of decisions taken at school level over which they had no control
but which cost them money. When they questioned these or other matters
they were made to feel uncomfortable and unwelcome.

There are also question marks over the scope for lay and professional
people to engage in dialogue (Vincent, 2001, p. 347). The current education system is not designed for partnership between parents and teachers.
It can be difficult to find ways to harness home-learning without disrupt-
ing the established system or putting undue pressure on teachers and parents (Macbeth, 1994, p. 79). In addition, providing opportunities for a
more participative role for parents at school level is no guarantee that
they will be taken up or used. Parents may have similar attitudes to many
citizens who, as Irvin and Stansbury (2004, pp. 58-9) found, prefer to
pay people to do the decision making and the work rather than get personally involved. This may be because they are preoccupied with their
personal lives, uninformed and/or apathetic or they prefer to control behaviour by participating in a non-decision making process. The partnership process may be perceived by parents as a system of elite decision
making and public ratification with the political processes providing an
appearance of democratic control that masks where the real power lies
(Held, 1989, p. 61).

Educational goals are rarely disputed in Ireland (Tuohy, 2005, p.
118). The key issue is how schools will implement them. Schools must
balance the demands from the state, society and parents with their long-

term institutional requirements and the needs of their pupils. While schools are free to prioritise using the school development planning process, they must work within the policy framework provided by the State. Circulars from the DES and the patron of the school keep them informed of their duties, with regular inspections ensuring accountability. Schools, through their interactions with parents, will determine the extent to which this national policy of parental involvement will be effective. They will determine whether parents have a voice, get a hearing or are just ignored (Fine, 1997, p. 467). The degree to which the policy differs from the existing status quo in the school the more difficult it will be to implement.

Definition of Partnership

As Chapter Two will outline, the term 'partnership' was an element in both the discourse and documentation on Irish educational legislative and curriculum changes. A 'partnership' is generally viewed as a formal agreement between two or more parties that will provide them with mutual benefits (Levin, 2004, p. 171). However, the term, being part of the symbolic political and social language, embraces a wide range of concepts. Burgos (2004) describes it as a 'floating and empty signifier', a universal value, which means a lot of different things to different people.

Some view partnership as means of making schools more accountable and thereby improving both their performance and the State's human capital (Macbeth and Ravn, 1994, p. 3). Others see it as an ideology to regulate parents in relation to their children's education (Carlen et al., 1992). The OECD (1997, p. 52), while aware of the different meanings and interpretations, described it as 'a *process* (their italics) – learning to work together and valuing what each partner can bring to the relationship'. Concepta Conaty, the National Coordinator of the HSCL scheme, interpreted partnership as follows (Conaty, 2002, p. 71):

> Partnership presupposes equality and implies that the relationship has been formed on the basis that each has an equally important contribution to make to the whole. It implies a commitment to working together, exploring possibilities, planning, decision-making and on-going evaluation.... Partnership as a way of working is challenging and calls for changes in individual and

corporate attitudes, methods of work and structure, particularly
on the part of the school.

Partnership is often viewed as a form of democracy (Heywood, 1997, p.
69). People's definitions of partnership often correspond with their preferred model of democracy and their views on the proper relationship
between the State and its citizens. For those who favour the liberal individualism model, the purpose of democracy is to lay down a framework
of laws within which individuals are allowed to conduct their own lives
and pursue their own interests. On the other hand, there are those who
believe in radical democracy, which allows people to participate in any
decisions, which affect their lives (Ibid.). Partnership, as operated in Ireland, tends to draw from both models. The legislation, curriculum and
official documentation make up the framework of laws, within which
schools and parents have to operate. Parents, through the NPCP, are involved nationally in drawing up these frameworks. They are also supposed to be involved locally through the BOM, Parents Association and
the development of the school plan (Ireland, 1998).

Underlying the national debate on partnership is the question: who
has the ultimate authority as regards the education of the child? The fact
that education and schooling takes place at the intersection of two sets of
rights, those of the family and society, means that there can be tensions
between its public and private benefits and goals. Article 42 (Ireland,
1937) enshrines the principle of parental supremacy in the education of
their children. The role of the State is to protect and promote the constitutional rights of parents along with a limited right to prescribe the attainment of a minimum education (Coolahan, 1981, p. 156). It also has
the duty of providing for those children whose parents have neglected
their duty. However, in the post-industrial era, control of the education
system is vital if the State is to ensure an educated and flexible workforce, which will sustain an efficient, competitive, knowledge-based
economy (Department of Education, 1995, p. 207). In addition, a democratic society has the right to reproduce its most essential political, economic and social institutions through a common schooling experience
(Levin, 2004, p. 172). As a result, there can be a conflict between the
values and norms of the family versus those of the State. National educational policy normally promotes the public interest, while allowing as

much of the private interest as can be accommodated without bringing the two into serious conflict. The result is a tacit partnership between home and school.

However, problems arise because Irish educational policy debate can be quite restricted (O'Sullivan, 1989). Frequently used concepts, like partnership, are rarely elaborated on or analysed sufficiently. Politicians and bureaucrats, according to Williams (2005, p. 100), tend to agree on the public goals for education and avoid contentious topics that could give rise to genuine disagreement. Pragmatic improvements, high profile issues and catch-all slogans appear to be preferable to genuine debates on values and ideology. Sugrue and Gleeson (2004, p. 279) suggest that:

> ... partnership had become little more than an ideological predisposition of key stakeholders in the Irish Education System who use it as a strategy to legitimate their interests and policies. As currently played out, it is flawed and suspect, particularly, from the perspective of maintaining and perpetuating power relations, and a generally cautious and conservative approach to reforms that tend to (re)produce *[their brackets]* rather than transform existing social relations.

Home-school partnership can be perceived as a symbolic policy. Its implementation, particularly the practicalities of how and when it is both appropriate and necessary for schools and parents to collaborate, are rarely addressed at national level (Kellaghan and McGee, 2005, p. 15). For the purposes of this research, educational partnership will be defined as

> The relationship between parents, the school, the State and the Catholic Church in supporting and planning for the best possible education for children both at home and at school.

While the formal alliance and contractual agreement, which Epstein (1992, p. 1140) argued partnership implied, is not always present in these relationships, there is certainly an implicit and informal agreement to work toward shared goals.

Conclusion

Developing and implementing national policy is a complex and dynamic process. This chapter examined the context in which the national policy of home-school partnership was developed. The role parents' play in their children's education will determine their involvement in their children's education and schooling. The terms, educator, supporter, welfare recipient and consumer, were used to illustrate the values of parents, their relationship with the school and their interest and involvement in their children's education. The extent, to which parents are involved in their children education at home and in school, both formally and informally, forms a large part of this study.

Variables, such as citizenship, gender, social class, religion and family forms influence national policies and parenting styles. The impact of the changing cultural values and norms of Irish society parents and their involvement in their children's education is explored in this research.

Partnership has different meanings, connotations and applications depending on who is using the term. National education policy is developed through partnership between the State and the major interest groups in education, using democratic processes and dialogue. Parents and teachers are expected to work in partnership at local level. The issues surrounding the promotion of the concept in Irish education were outlined in this chapter. As the literature suggests that most parents prefer to be silent supporters, it will be interesting to note how many are active partners in their children's education.

Having described the extraneous and personal factors, which impact on parental involvement and national policy, Chapter Two outlines the development and content of national policy and defines the criteria for evaluating its impact on parents. It also outlines key influences, both nationally and locally, which impact on its implementation.

Chapter Two

NATIONAL POLICY OF
PARENTAL INVOLVEMENT

Introduction

From 1950 to 1970 the Irish class structure shifted from one based primarily on property ownership to one based on educational credentials and wage employment (O'Connell and Rottman, 1992, p. 218). The influences of the European Union (EU), Organisation for Economic Cooperation and Development (OECD) and the State's own economic interests led to a questioning of the existing education system and the subsequent adjustments in power relations between the various stakeholders. Traditionally, parents had little or no say in education policy. The introduction of the *Education Act 1998,* the *Education Welfare Act 2000* and the *Primary School Curriculum* (Department of Education and Science [DES], 1999a) gave parents the statutory right to be involved in their children's education and schooling.

Policies, according to Crump (1992, p. 419) exist in three forms. They include the

- Intended policy or what the various interest groups have decided and agreed on

- Actual policy or what is specified in legislation and other official documentation

- Policy-in-use or what has been implemented at school-level.

This chapter looks at the consultation process leading up to the *Education Act 1998,* the *Education Welfare Act 2000* and the *Primary School*

Curriculum (DES, 1999a). The views of the various interest groups and their influence on the development of the national policy of home-school partnership are explored. Particular attention is given to the role of the National Parents Council Primary (NPCP), who represented the views of parents during the process. The details of the policy, as outlined in the various documents, are investigated. These will vary from explicit descriptions of responsibilities and duties to the loose granting of powers that may or may not be used. Implementation is a key aspect of any policy. Issues surrounding implementation, which may impact on the policy-in-use in the schools, are discussed. Particular emphasis will be given to those aspects of the intended and actual policy, which are obscure on key points of implementation. The methods used to convey the policy changes to parents are also highlighted.

Indicators of parental involvement in their children's education and school were developed using the *Education Act 1998*, the *Education Welfare Act 2000*, the *Primary School Curriculum* (DES, 1999a) and other related documentation. These are used to evaluate the involvement of the research participants in their children's education. Finally, using these indicators, the literature on the different types of parental involvement is reviewed.

Policy Formation Process

Apart from the last decade, the educational power structure and system did not change substantially in the twentieth century (O'Buachalla, 1988, p. 316). Monopoly Catholicism made the Church guardian of civil society and its morality (Fulton, 2000a, p. 13). Education was provided by a system of Church-controlled, State-supported national schools. The Episcopal ban on any lay involvement in the management of national schools excluded the emergence of any lay local democratic structure in education. Other groups such as the Department of Education and the Irish National Teachers Organisation (INTO) accepted as normal the Church's dominant role. This section examines the development of the policy from an era when parents were the 'silent partners' (O'Sullivan, 1992, p. 465) in the education system to one where it was hoped that Ireland would have one of the 'most parent-participative systems in the worlds' (OECD, 1997, p. 141).

Policy Formation Pre-1960

Pre-1960s the Department of Education was predominately occupied by political consolidation, cultural rejuvenation and spiritual values (Kellaghan, 1989, p. 191). Being conservative in nature, it took few risks and tended to view innovative proposals with suspicion (Harris, 1989, pp. 7-8). Control was highly centralised within the Department with the Minister for Education making decisions in agreement with the Minister for Finance (Coolahan, 1989, p. 28). The lack of public concern about the education system and the consistent reluctance within the country at large to consider any policy measure that might be seen to challenge the influence of religious bodies, institutions or even individuals (Harris, 1989, p. 8) did not encourage innovation. The role of the State in education was considered a subsidiary one of aiding the Church in the provision of education facilities (Inglis, 1998, p. 57). It adopted the approach of keeping the system ticking over with little or no serious re-appraisal of policy or of the direction in which the system was going.

Traditionally, two consultative processes worked side-by-side. The teachers, managers and the State dealt with lower-level issues relating to the existing system, e.g., resource allocation, curricular issues and working conditions. Higher-level issues, involving the modification of the structural status quo, were confined to the Church and State (O'Buachalla, 1988, p. 334). Parents were not included at either level.

Policy Formation from the 1960s on

From the 1960s on, education became part of the more planned approach to the general economy (Coolahan, 1989, p. 64). The OECD report (1965), *Investment in Education*, was a major modernising force in Irish Education. It was influential in promoting the human capital policy paradigm (Schultz, 1977) and the emerging marketization of education (O'Sullivan, 1992). Education came to be perceived as an investment in people with the parents' consumer rights in relation to their children's education promoted at national level.

With education credentials becoming increasingly important for employment, many parents began to view education as the means to secure their children's competitive edge in the labour market (Fuller, 2002, p. 171). Through the constituency clinics and clientelist relationship they had with politicians, they demanded greater educational provision at post-primary level (O'Sullivan, 1992, p. 455). In addition, educated parents, fully conscious of their constitutional prerogatives, were no longer satisfied with the traditional model of management and policy formation whereby the patron was deemed to 'act on behalf of parents' (Coolahan, 1994, p. 25). During the 1970s, a number of parent associations in various schools and at least two national associations were formed. In 1985 the NPCP was established and has been remarkably successful in focusing and projecting the voice of parents (Hyland, 1995, p. 40).

As a result, the Department of Education became progressively more interventionist in modernising the system (Cussen, 1995, p. 46). The range of educational initiatives caught the public imagination and propelled education to the forefront of public attention (Coolahan, 1989, p. 66). The attention of the media and the vote catching potential of educational reforms, which touched so closely on the daily lives of so many families, was not lost on politicians.

As the education system grew in size and complexity, a succession of reports highlighted its weak administrative and policy making capacity (OECD, 1991). The changes in Irish society led to a strong public desire for new forms of partnership in education. The catalyst for change was Mary O'Rourke, who as Minister for Education announced in August 1990 that she was considering an Education Bill (Walshe, 1999, p. 7). One of her priorities was parental involvement. Circular 24/91, *Parents as Partners in Education* (Department of Education, 1991), which recommended active Parents Associations, clear strategies for parental involvement in all schools and full participation of parent representatives on the Board of Management, was issued to all school. In addition, the HSCL scheme was established in disadvantaged schools.

Home–School Community Liaison (HSCL) Scheme

'Equality of opportunity' became a most attractive and much used political slogan in the 1980s (O'Sullivan, 1989). In 1984 a programme of special measures for schools in disadvantaged areas was introduced. There was a per capita grant for books and materials, and additional home–school community activities. In-service was provided for teachers in disadvantaged areas and concessionary posts and remedial teachers were appointed. The evaluation showed that it had no impact on parental involvement (Conaty, 2002, p. 29).

In 1990 the HSCL Scheme, which was influenced by Catholic social teaching, the United Nations and the EU (Conaty, 2002), was introduced. Through it, the Department of Education wished to develop the parent as the primary educator and promote partnership between teachers and parents in order to help 'at risk' pupils [her apostrophes] (Conaty, 2002, p. 29). The aim of the scheme was to maximise the participation of the children in the education system by promoting active co-operation between home and school and encouraging and helping parents to take an interest in and support their children's education (Ryan, 1994, p. 6). The HSCL scheme was designed as a targeted and focused resource in favour of the most marginalised in designated areas of disadvantage (Conaty, 2002, p. 30). Its thrust was preventative rather than curative (Ibid., p. 72).

The HSCL coordinator is expected to work with and fortify the family so that instances of absenteeism and disruption will be obviated, thus preventing illiteracy, unemployment, drug misuse, jail and psychological collapse (Ibid., p. 75). Classes are provided in personal development along with leisure time and curriculum activities and parents are involved in school-related activities. The aim is to encourage parents away from dependency and enable them to make decisions in relation to their own lives and those of their children (Ibid.).

In 1996, parent and teachers began working together on policy formation (Ibid., p. 98). The first policy to be worked on was HSCL relationships and practices. As a School Development Planning Support (SDPS) facilitator, I would have noticed that, in comparison with mainstream schools, parents were more likely to attend the SDPS planning day in disadvantaged areas. The HSCL coordinator usually helps to ensure that parent participation is built in to the planning process at some stage.

The two evaluations of the HSCL scheme (Ryan, 1994; Archer and Shortt, 2003) have been positive about its impact on home-school relationships. Ryan (1994, p. 134) found that parents were overwhelming positive about the HSCL scheme. Not only had their understanding of the operation of the school increased, but they had developed the self-esteem, self-confidence and skills to help their children. Their fears about school were diminishing and there was an increase of community spirit and pride as a result of the collaborative efforts of schools, parents and community groups. Similarly, Archer and Shortt (2003) found that coordinators and principals believed that the scheme had been successful in achieving its aims of improving home-school cooperation and collaboration. However, the inspectorate, in their evaluation of literacy and numeracy in disadvantaged schools (DES, 2005a, p. 63) found that, despite the HSCL initiative, parental involvement remained poor, particularly in the middle and senior classes. As a result there has been a renewed emphasis on involving parents in their children's education in the DEIS Action Plan (DES, 2005d, p. 40).

Parents who became involved in the HSCL activities were largely female (Ryan, 1994; Conaty, 2002). In addition, the least disadvantaged parents were more likely to become involved in HSCL activities. The reasons why parents did not become involved were varied. They included personal problems, work and family commitments, fear and uncertainty regarding schools and lack of information (Ryan, 1994, p. 135; Purcell, 2006, p. 9). Archer and Shortt (2003, p. 114) recommended that new ways of securing the involvement of previously uninvolved parents were needed.

Policy Formation from 1992-1998

The publication of the Green Paper *Education for a Changing World* (Ireland, 1992) initiated an extraordinary response (Walshe, 1999, p. 31) and an unprecedented consultation process (Clancy, 1999, p. 72). In addition to innumerable seminars and conferences, there were about 1,000 written submissions which reflected the strong business and enterprise thrust of the paper, as well as the growing public interest in education as a vehicle for personal and societal advancement (Fahey, 1995).

A key aim of the Green Paper was to ensure greater openness and accountability throughout the education system and to maximise parental involvement and choice (Ireland, 1992, p. 5). Parents, it stressed, were the primary educators of their children and had a crucial role to play in forming the attitudes of their children towards all facets of life. This task was complemented by the efforts of the State and the school. It identified the lack of openness and sharing of information and power with parents as a major shortcoming in the system. Schools, it argued, must have due regard for the rights and wishes of parents and had an obligation to consult and inform parents on issues affecting their own child and the school generally.

Usually, a Green Paper is followed by a White Paper. However, with the change of government, the then Minister for Education, Niamh Bhreathnach, decided to hold a National Education Convention where 42 interest groups and organisations, including the CPSMA (Catholic Primary School Managers' Association), the INTO and the NPCP, were brought together to discuss Irish educational policy. The aim was to move away from the department's traditional method of negotiating policy changes with each group individually to negotiating 'win-win' solutions through structured multilateral dialogue (Bhreathnach, 1995, p. ix). It was followed by roundtable discussions on the thorny issue of school governance.

The Convention achieved a fair degree of consensus and gave the stakeholders a sense of ownership of the proposals (Walshe, 1999, p. 40). The Convention Secretariat's Report (Coolahan, 1994) formed a major input to the 1995 White Paper *Charting our Education Future* (Department of Education, 1995). It specified that parents, under Article 42 of the Constitution (Ireland, 1937), have the right as individuals to be consulted and informed on all aspects of their child's education. They also have the right as a group to be active participants at school, regional and national level. If the values and beliefs of teachers conflict with the rights of parents, the school should favour the parents' rights with due regard to the principle of democratic justice appropriate to a democratic society. The preservation of the ethos of the school and the rights of the majority of parents were to be balanced with those of the minority of parents, who do not have an option to select a school, which reflects their values. Communication and consultation with parents was emphasised. Parents could participate formally through the NPCP at national level and the Board of Management (BOM) and Parents Associations at local level. Informally, they were to be involved through the development of school policies, the provision of information on school programmes, access to their own child's records and other home-school links.

The White Paper on Education (Department of Education, 1995) set the formulation of educational policy in a European, international and global context and outlined the appropriate legislative and constitutional framework for future educational development. It was felt that its mixture of general principles and detailed guidelines, which would be reinforced by regulations, rules and directives, would allow the policy to develop in a dynamic way (Cussen, 1995, p. 42). The publication of the White Paper led to further dialogue and negotiations culminating in the *Education Act 1998*, the *Education Welfare Act 2000* and other legislation.

Board of Management Reform

Despite the Catholic Church actively supporting the setting up of structures (Hyland, 1995, p. 37) whereby control and management of schools might be shared with parents, no formal management structures were put in place. In 1973, negotiations began between Church interests, teacher union representatives and parents' groups (Coolahan, 1989, p. 56). These negotiations were quite difficult as the various interest groups tried to protect or secure power and influence. Finally, in 1975 new BOMs, comprising of four patron nominees and two parents, were established (Walshe, 1999, p. 89). Initially teachers were excluded but following discussions, arrangements were made for limited teacher representation. In 1980, following the withdrawal of the INTO from participation on BOMs, the number of patrons' nominees were reduced from six to four. The BOMs would consist of four patron nominees, two parents and two teachers. The patron retained the right to appoint the chairperson of the board, who would have a second or casting vote.

BOM regulations were published. These emphasised the administrative and financial responsibilities of the board, which were not to impinge on curricular or formal educational policy (Coolahan, 1989, p. 57). Some parents expressed dissatisfaction at the restricted range of responsibilities of the BOMs and chafed at being cast in the role of local fundraisers without the real power to influence the school's educational policy (Ibid., p. 58).

The structure of the BOM and its role featured strongly in the *Report of the Primary Education Review Body* (1990) and during the consultation process leading up to the *Education Act 1998*. The aim was to bring the governance of schools into line with changed economic, social and political circumstances (Coolahan, 1994, p. 23). Schools needed a more democratic management structure, which would represent all stakeholders and have the necessary authority to perform its management functions effectively (Ireland, 1992, p. 141). In practice, this meant that the patrons/trustees would be ceding many of their powers and functions to the BOM. The bishops and religious were dissatisfied with this and saw it as an attempt by the State to push the Church out of education (Walshe, 1999, pp. 107-9). To safeguard the religious ethos and character of their schools, the patrons wished to appoint majorities on the board and nominate the chairperson. However, both the INTO and the NPCP favoured equal representation. It is interesting that the NPCP's proposals for equal representation of owners/trustees, parents and teachers, who would together nominate two further members, formed the basis for further discussion (Walshe, 1999, p. 110). In 1996 agreement was reached. There would be equal representation on the BOMs in return for written legal guarantees protecting the ethos of the schools.

Education Act 1998

The shift in power relations was highlighted by those organisations the minister chose to consult with prior to publication of the Education Bill 1997. They included the INTO, the NPCP and the Conference of Religious in Ireland (CORI). The Catholic bishops, who once held a veto on all major decisions about education, were excluded. However, there was an unprecedented coalition of religious interests against the Bill and the erosion of the rights of patrons as owners of primary schools (Walshe, 1999, pp. 191-6). The only group which welcomed the Bill was the NPCP, as it contained a section promising a complaints procedure whereby parents and students could appeal school decisions. This caused considerable concern to teachers. A series of amendments to the Bill were proposed with the first one being announced, interestingly enough, by the minister at the parents' conference. The new Education Bill was a much less controversial, more teacher-friendly and, perhaps, less parent-friendly than the previous version (Ibid., p. 208). Lynch (1999, p. 298) maintained that it reflected the interests of the middle and upper classes of society, who are closely integrated, both directly and indirectly, into the educational decision-making machinery of most states.

The *Education Act 1998* placed the education system on a statutory basis. The roles and functions of the various stakeholders were delineated and it gave statutory recognition to the process of negotiating education change through partnership. The Minister for Education was expected to consult with the NPCP and the other educational partners prior to making a decision. Each school had to have a school plan (Ireland, 1998, p. 22). Parents were to be consulted during the development of this plan and entitled to have access to the completed plan. In addition, Section 28 of the *Education Act 1998* outlined a complaints procedure for parents, while Section 29 allows parents to appeal expulsions, suspensions and refusals to enrol students.

Education Welfare Act 2000

Under the *School Attendance Act 1926* attendance at school was made compulsory but, as Article 42.2 made clear, it was not obligatory provided parents made educational provision for their children in their homes. Absenteeism, with or without parental knowledge and consent, has been identified as a major contributory factor to school failure and disadvantage (Department of Education, 1994). Poor attendance and early school leaving, with the associated risks of unemployment and anti-social behaviour, were highlighted as major priorities in the Green Paper on Education (Ireland, 1992).

A review of the *School Attendance Act 1926* and the roles and responsibilities of the various agencies involved was part of the preparatory work for the new legislation in education. The *School Attendance/Truancy Report* (Department of Education, 1994), which specified the problems with the current legislation, led to the development of the *Education Welfare Act 2000*. Its focus was on addressing the underlying causes of school absenteeism through early identification of and support for families whose children may be at risk of developing poor school attendance. The National Educational Welfare Board (NEWB), who would have responsibility for ensuring that each child receives a 'minimum education' (Ireland, 2000, p. 9), was to be established under the Act. It was required to promote in families an appreciation of the benefits of education, and its attendant social and economic advantages. The *School Attendance/Truancy Report* (Department of Education, 1994 pp. 24) suggested that the NEWB could, by cooperating with other agencies, assist parents in becoming more involved in their children's education.

Under the *Education Welfare Act 2000* (Pr.III S.17 (1), p. 16) parents are legally obliged to send their child to school on each school day. Principals must report if a child is absent for twenty days or has been suspended for six days in the school year. The *School Attendance/Truancy Report* (Department of Education, 1994, p. 17) felt that given the Constitutional emphasis on the principle of parental supremacy in relation to the education of their children, parents are culpable not only for their own actions or inaction in respect of the child's non-attendance, but also for any intentional act of the child in not attending school.

While the *Education Welfare Act 2000* largely targeted children whose non-attendance was related to home-based factors such as long-term and intergenerational unemployment, addiction problems and familial conflict, it has also affected middle-class non-attendees whose families take holidays during term time. While Forde Brennan (2003, p. 4), Chairperson of the NPCP, maintained that it was not in keeping with the intentions of the Act that parents would be threatened with the Education Welfare Officer (EWO) if their child has been absent from school, the principal has no choice under the legislation. In fact, the *School Attendance/Truancy Report* (Department of Education, 1994, pp. 13-4) highlighted the non-attendance of children at school for reasons such as family circumstances (minding young children, shopping trips or foreign holidays) or economic necessity (helping with 'selling' at particular times of the year), as a form of parental negligence. However, the parents interviewed in Carlen et al.'s (1992, p. 137) research believed that the law was unrealistic in holding them responsible for their children's failure to attend school regularly. They cited a multitude of social disabilities, such as the overburdening anxieties connected with unemployment, poverty, illness and other family responsibilities, to explain their inability to persuade their child to attend school regularly.

The *Education Welfare Act 2000* was an attempt to address the issue of absenteeism. However, 10 per cent of primary school pupils missed twenty or more days in the school year 2004-5 with the NEWB issuing the first School Attendance Notices (SAN) in 2005 (NEWB, 2005). The SAN resulted in several court cases in various parts of the country in 2006 (NEWB, 2006). These parents had failed over time to co-operate with the

Education Welfare Officers (EWO) and the NEWB felt that the court cases were necessary to uphold these children's right to an education.

The *Education Welfare Act 2000* (Pr.III S.23 (4), p. 21) has also a section on school's Code of Behaviour. It states that prior to registering a student the school must provide the parents with a copy of its Code of Behaviour. Schools may also require the parent to confirm in writing that the code is acceptable to them and that they will make all reasonable efforts to ensure their child complies with the code. It appears that schools are entitled to parental support in this matter.

Primary School Curriculum (DES 1999)

The review of *Curaclam na Bunscoile* (Department of Education, 1971) by the National Council for Curriculum and Assessment (NCCA) began in autumn 1991. While reiterating the objectives of the 1971 curriculum, it also took account of the rapid social, scientific and technological changes and of Ireland's position internationally (Department of Education, 1995, p. 20). Committees which included representatives of all the education partners were established in all subject areas. While the *Primary School Curriculum* (DES, 1999a) has been described as a teachers' curriculum (O'Toole, 1999, p. 3), parents did have an influence on the planning and implementation of the curriculum through their representatives on the NCCA (Kilfeather, 2003, p. 243) and the Implementation Group (Egan, 1998, p. 4). However, they were not part of the Technical Working Group, which consisted of representatives of the DES, the NCCA, the INTO and the Education Centre Network. In addition, parents' low level of representation on the various committees weakened their impact, particularly when the teacher representatives were perceived as 'the experts' [apostrophes in the original] (De Paor, 2003).

Reform efforts and curriculum policymaking are subject to parental pressure. School improvement efforts are often defeated, Hargreaves observed (2000, pp. 225-6), by 'parental nostalgia', which 'drives parents to press teachers to return to and reinstate "real schooling" for their own children'. After analysing the results of school effectiveness studies, Coleman (1998, pp. 16-7) concluded that reform required changing the power relationship between teachers, students and parents to ensure collaborative teaching and learning. Evaluations of the implementation of the *Primary*

School Curriculum (DES, 1999a) have not been encouraging. The evaluators found that the linkage between home and school in children's learning was limited, particularly in the middle and senior classes and in Maths and Visual Arts (DES, 2005a, p. 30; 2005b, p. 49). In addition to schools finding ways to support parental involvement, greater information was needed by parents on the curriculum if they were to support their children's learning in different subjects (NCCA, 2005, p. 246). The NCCA have since produced a DVD to inform parents about their child's learning through the curriculum and to show them how they can support that learning in simple, effective and practical ways at home (NCCA, 2006a, p. 7).

Parental Roles and Responsibilities as Defined by Acts and Curriculum

Duncan (1993, p. 440) suggested that principles relating to parental rights and duties are necessarily expressed in broad terms in legislation. However, the *Education Act 1998* and the *Education Welfare Act 2000* are fairly specific, with the documentation accompanying them even more specific. If laws have surveillance, management and control functions (Giddens, 2001, p. 205), it is interesting to note the similarities, nuances and differences in the descriptions of parental roles and responsibilities in each of the three documents (see Table 2.1).

The *Education Act 1998* gave statutory recognition to the NPCP and enshrined the rights of parents to be consulted and informed on various aspects of school organisation, including their children's records, school plans, policies and accounts. It does not set out the role and responsibilities of parents in relation to their children's education. While no offence or sanction for non-compliance is mentioned in the Act, parents will have recourse to Sections 28 and 29, the complaints and appeals procedures.

The *Education Welfare Act 2000* replaces the *School Attendance Act 1926* and subsequent related pieces of legislation. It places a statutory obligation on parents to ensure their children attend school. There are penalties for parents who do not fulfil their obligations under the Act. Parents must also be involved in the development of the Code of Behaviour and the attendance policy.

The *Primary School Curriculum* (DES, 1999a, pp. 21-2), while rather vague on the parents' role in curriculum implementation, emphasises home-school communication and the active participation of parents in the life of the school. In the *Education Act 1998,* the Minister for Education and Science, on advice from the NCCA, has the right to determine both the content and delivery of the curriculum and may compel the BOM to follow it. Parents may withdraw their children from any subject that is contrary to their conscience but have no right to have any subject inserted in the curriculum. Social, Personal and Health Education (SPHE), which includes Relationships and Sexuality Education (RSE), is the only curriculum subject where schools are expected to involve parents in the development of the curriculum plan (DES 2003b) and keep them fully informed of the content and teaching approaches (DES 2000a p. 38).

Table 2.1: Summary of Acts and Curriculum in Relation to Parents

Education Act 1998	Education Welfare Act 2000	Primary School Curriculum
BOM: • Manage the school for the benefit of students and their parents • Enrolment Policy • Inform/report to parents using school plan • Consult with parents • Access of parents to pupil's records and school accounts **Principal:** • Involve parents • Inform parents of pupil's progress **Parents Association:** Interests of pupil • Advise Principal/BOM • Programme of Activities **Grievance Procedure** **Appeals Procedure**	**Home schooling:** • Register of children not in school • Inspection of their education **Schools:** • Register of children in each school • Attendance or reason for absence • Reporting absences to EWO • School Attendance Strategies • Code of Behaviour • Sign Acceptance **The NEWB:** • Procedures for non-compliance • Duties of the NEWB • Register of young people in employment	School/parents groups are to reach out to help parents to do the following: • Effective partnership and close co-operation • Regular consultation • Involved in organisational planning • Active participation in life of the school • Create and foster positive school spirit • Sense of belonging and interest

The *Education Welfare Act 2000* is looking for compliance on school attendance while the *Education Act 1998* and the *Primary School Curriculum* (DES, 1999a) are more visionary and developmental, articulating the values and future direction of the Irish education system. As the legislation and curriculum are lengthy documents written in legalistic and professional language, information booklets (Table 2.2) for parents were produced by the various agencies responsible for managing and leading the implementation process.

While all three documents emphasise the role of parents in the education system, the content, timing and distribution methods differed quite considerably. The School Development Planning Support (SDPS) document outlines the SDP process and how parents can get involved in decision-making and policy formation in their children's school. The other two documents describe how parents can support the school and get involved with their children's education both at home and at school.

The *Primary School Curriculum: Your Child's Learning: Guidelines for Parents* (DES, 2000a) was sent to schools to distribute to parents. However, three years later some schools had not yet distributed the booklet (Kilfeather, 2003). *Do Not Let Your Child Miss Out* (NEWB, 2004) was sent directly to parents using the children's allowance database. Schools were not informed and did not receive a copy until all were distributed. *School Development Planning at Primary Level: Information for Parents* (SDPS, 2004) was sent to the chairpersons of the Parents Association to distribute. Copies were posted to the principal and chairperson of the BOM and Parents Association prior to the delivery of the leaflets for parents. It was also available in public libraries and citizen advice centres.

As described over the last twenty years, the Irish education system had changed from one where parents had no say in policy formation to one where they are expected to be involved both locally and nationally. With the formation of the NPCP, they were actively involved in the processes which led to the development of the legislation and the curriculum. Parents now have the right to sit on BOMs, form Parents Associations and to be kept informed of their children's progress and all matters relating to the school (Ireland, 1998). This research will note how successful the implementation of the *Education Act 1998*, *Primary School Curriculum 1999* (DES, 1999a) and the *Education Welfare Act*

2000 has been in relation to parents. Is there home-school partnership in supporting and planning for children's education?

Table 2.2: Summary of Documentation Relating to the Acts and Curriculum

School Development Planning at Primary Level Information for Parents	Do not Let Your Child Miss Out	Primary School Curriculum Your Child's Learning Guidelines for Parents
Become active partners by • Election to BOM and Parents Association • Member of policy working groups • Links with child's teachers • Familiar with school plan, booklets and newsletters • Support school policies • Contribute to decisions by giving feedback through questionnaires etc. • Submitting comments or making suggestions	• Know principal and teachers • Read letter and reports • Attend P-T meetings • Ask your child about his/her day • Encourage school activities & sports • Attendance and punctuality • Do not pass on bad experiences • No holidays during term time • Know and discuss the school rules with child • Follow complaint procedures • Unhappy with expulsion/suspension/enrolment contact the DES • 'You can be taken to court if you do not cooperate with the Board to ensure that your child receives an education'	**Help child learn** • Interest in progress • Discuss events/learning • Homework • Expectations and praise • Read/tell stories • Outings/concerts/plays • Different leisure activities • Active and helpful relationship with school • Communication • Participate in and attend school activities **Role of Parents in implementation** • Check school plan • Voice in organisational planning • Visit school to view work & attend events • Help at events, outings, library, involve others • Help child at home in different subjects **Overview of curriculum and activities to do at home to reinforce subject** • SPHE - keep fully informed of content and teaching approaches • Home work • Textbooks (changes) • Assessment (no role mentioned for parents)

Implementation

As the implementation process is more complex, long-term and demanding than devising a policy, strategies are needed at all levels to help mobilize commitment and effective action (Coolahan, 1995, p. 9). Government edict alone cannot produce desired changes. There can be major gaps between the rhetoric of national policy and the reality in schools (Cussen, 1995, p. 51). Human diversity and organisational complexity create implementation difficulties with policies being ignored, resisted or rearticulated to suit local circumstances (Taylor et al., 1997, p. 7).

The Minister for Education and Science has, under the *Education Act 1998,* responsibility to monitor and assess the quality and effectiveness of the education system. Ireland, along with other European countries, is adopting a model of quality assurance. It emphasises school development planning through internal school review by all members of the school community and external evaluation by the Inspectorate. *Looking at our School – An aid to self-evaluation in primary schools (LAOS)* (DES, 2003b) is the framework to be used for both the external and internal evaluations of schools. If schools are to conform to the criteria as outlined in *LAOS* (Ibid.), they should promote the following:

- Open, caring, respectful relationships

- Meaningful home-school communication

- The involvement of parents in their children's learning

- The involvement of parents in the school.

Table 2.3 gives specific details on how these criteria might be implemented in schools. As many are recent innovations, they will be particularly useful in assessing the implementation of the policy.

Parents have to be informed and consulted by the school on all aspects of their children's education. In turn, they have to nurture a learning environment, co-operate with and support the school and other educational partners, and fulfil their special role in the development of the child (Department of Education, 1995, p. 9). As can be seen from Table 2.3, the school plan is an important element in the implementation of this policy on parental involvement. It is also obvious that the State relies on the school for the successful implementation of this policy. All the activities described in the documentation, apart from sending children to school, are voluntary for parents. Neither the State nor the school have direct control over parents in these matters and cannot ensure compliance. Implementation is dependent on parental interest and the school's effort to attract and maintain that interest.

Table 2.3: Criteria and Responsibility for Implementing National Policy

Activities	*Looking at our School – An aid to self- evaluation in primary schools*	Responsibility for Implementation
Inform parents	Ethos Role and responsibilities of the BOM All aspects of the school's operation Code of Behaviour Complaints procedures Safety Statement Content of School Plan School Timetables Implementation of SPHE Programme	BOM, In-school Management, School
Election to the BOM		Patron
Inform parents of pupil's progress	Frequency of parent-teacher meetings Access school records Provision of written reports Encouraged to respond to reports Level and quality of liaison with parents	Principal Teachers
Involve parents	School Review School Plan Monitoring process Review and determination of school's curriculum Determining needs and interests of pupils SPHE and related policies Seek their support and help Joint training for parents and teachers Policy and practice on parental involvement in their children's learning Enable parents to participate fully in the education of their children	School, Principal, Parents groups, Parents Assoc.

Establish a Parents Association		BOM
Grievance Proce-dures/Appeals	Parents are aware of the procedures for processing complaints	In-school Management
Ensure children at-tend or give a reason for absence		Parents EWO
Reporting absences School Attendance Strategies Code of Behaviour	Prepare strategies and measures to ensure school attendance and a Code of Behaviour as required by the *Education Welfare Act 2000*	School, Princi-pal, BOM, parents

Families are not passive recipients of educational norms and policy initiatives. Parents' prime investment is in their own children and families and this takes priority over national policies and expressions of collective parental aspirations. Parents tend to be focused on 'hands-on' practical local concerns rather than far-reaching future orientated 'visionary' changes (Moos and Dempster, 1998, p. 106). In fact, Moos et al. (1998, p. 66) found that parents placed very little emphasis on change and change management. The OECD (1991, p. 60) reported that parents in Ireland wished to see education develop in a concrete and positive way the aptitudes and qualities of the individual child – their own individual child. Wolfendale (1996, p. 35) wondered if the multi-dimensional part parents play in their children's lives conferred a check and a balance to the fullest realisation of parental involvement in their children's schools. They are too busy providing for their children's physical, social, moral, emotional and academic needs at home to give a lot of time to the school's organisational and curriculum needs.

In addition, parents can often resist and disrupt change efforts, especially when they are made without their knowledge or support (Coleman, 1998, p. 157). New approaches need to be made transparent to parents through many different means. Otherwise the result will be confused dissatisfied parents, especially those parents who have not got the 'cultural capital' (Bourdieu, 1997, p. 47) to understand and take advantage of these changes. In addition to the voluntary expense of buying parenting books and attending parenting workshops and courses for oneself, the cost of new textbooks, equipment, additional field trips and events for children will have to be met. While grants are provided by the State, they may not meet the needs of schools and parents if they are to fully implement the *Primary School Curriculum* (DES, 1999a). Fundraising will then become more important than ever, with the INTO (1997, p. 59) observing the difficulties in sustaining parental involvement and interest in the work of the school when they were effectively making up for the shortfall in government spending on primary education.

Indicators for Evaluating National Policy

The evaluation of a national policy poses a number of difficulties. The outcomes may be intended or unintended, wanted or unwanted, direct or indirect. While a policy measure may serve as a catalyst or a trigger for change, it can be difficult to isolate the impact of a particular measure or determine whether a policy in another area is producing the effects observed. It is not enough to note the presence or absence of a particular policy measure. Its impact on the intended recipients also needs to be measured (Hantrais, 2004, p. 198). As Abrahamsom et al. (2005) found in their study of family policy across five EU countries, there can be a mismatch between the official rhetoric and the real-life experience of citizens.

The results of many studies and various efforts to define parental involvement, Epstein (1992, p. 1145) argued, suggested that the following six types of involvement help families and schools to fulfil their shared responsibilities for children's learning and development:

- The basic obligations of families, which included building positive home conditions that support learning and behaviour throughout the school years

- The basic obligations of schools which primarily revolve around home-school communications

- Parental involvement at school particularly the school's encouragement of volunteers and audiences at school events

- Parental involvement in learning activities at home

- Parental involvement in school decision-making, governance and advocacy

- Collaboration with community organisations which includes net-working by families.

These categories were subsequently used by Esptein and Seyong (1995, p. 122) and the OECD (1997, p. 19) in their research on parental involvement in schools. They are reflected in the *Education Act 1998*, the *Education Welfare Act 2000* and the *Primary School Curriculum* (DES, 1999a) and the information booklets which inform parents of the legislative and curricular changes. These classic typologies of parents and education are considered by David (2004, p. 221) to incorporate the normative notions of white middle-class traditional nuclear families. Initially these categories were going to be used as the indicators for the implementation of the goals of national policy. However, after the analysis of my observations as a parent, the pilot data from the questionnaires, interviews and focus groups and further reading and reflection, it was decided that the following indicators were more appropriate in the Irish context:

- Open, caring, respectful relationships

- Home-school communication

- Parental involvement in the home curriculum

- Parental involvement in the school.

These correspond with the overall policy goals as defined above from the White Paper on Education (Department of Education, 1995, p. 9) and *LAOS* (DES, 2003b). The categories, as identified by the literature (Epstein, 1992, p. 1145; Esptein and Seyong, 1995, p. 122; OECD, 1997, p. 19), will be incorporated as subsections (Table 2.4).

These indicators are explored in the next section and research questions, which will be used to inform this research, devised.

In the context of this research, it should be noted that parental involvement at local level existed prior to the *Education Act 1998*, the *Education Welfare Act 2001* and the *Primary School Curriculum* (DES, 1999a) and in many cases may not be solely attributed to these pieces of legislation. Irish parents have always supported the school (Hyland

1995). The lack of base line data prevents a detailed summative evaluation (O'Leary, 2004, pp. 136-7) but the evaluations of the HSCL scheme (Ryan, 1994; Archer and Shortt, 2003) and the OECD (1997) report, *Parents as Partners in Schooling,* which included Ireland, will be used to assess the changes as a result of national policy.

Table 2.4: Indicators for Evaluating the National Policy of Parental Involvement in Their Children's Education and Schooling

Open, Caring, Respectful Relationships		
• Collaboration with community organisations which includes networking by families		
Parental Involvement in the Home Curriculum	**Parental Involvement in the School**	**Home-School Communication**
• The basic obligations of families, which included building positive home conditions that support learning and behaviour throughout the school years • Parental involvement in learning activities at home	• Parental involvement at school particularly the school's encouragement of volunteers and audiences at school events • Parental involvement in school decision-making, governance and advocacy	The basic obligations of schools which primarily revolve around home-school communications. These include • Children's progress • Events and activities • School Plan

Parental Involvement in Their Children's Education

In this research, partnership is defined as the relationship between parents, the school, the State and the Catholic Church in supporting and planning for the best possible education for children both at home and at school. This is in line with the definitions of partnership at national level (DES, 2005c, p. 15; Department of the Taoiseach, 2006, p. 74) with their emphasis on policy development and service delivery. Developing partnership requires an ability to 'overcome inbuilt inertia or resistant to change, conservative attitudes and beliefs, and confusion and lack of understanding about new processes' (National Centre for Partnership and Performance [NCPP], 2003, p. 59). Parents' educational capabilities, their view of the appropriate division of labour between teachers and parents, the information they have about their children's schooling, along with the time, money, and other material resources available in the home will influence their involvement in their children's education and schooling (Lareau, 1997, p. 710). This section examines the literature on parental involvement in their children's education using the indicators described earlier (Table 2.4). The research questions, which are summarised in Chapter Three, are outlined at the end of each section.

Open, Caring, Respectful Relationships

Partnership, like good parenting, is about the quality of relationships rather than techniques or practices. All relationships are negotiated and shaped over time and are influenced by wider forces such as employment, globalisation, social norms and views of what is right and proper (Williams, 2004, p. 17). Parents have to negotiate their relationship with their children as well as their relationship with the school. Both will have a bearing on their involvement with their children's education.

The parents' relationship with their children is very important if the child is to grow in to a well-adjusted independent adult. As can be seen from Chapter One, much of the research highlights the influence of parental characteristics such as social class, race, gender and family composition on their children's success at school. Children are often treated in the policy documentation as if they were the passive recipients of their parents' actions and values (Edwards and Alldred, 2000, p. 440). The opposite may be the case. Children, especially as they grow older, may prefer to limit the involvement of their parents in their education.

Parents' relationship with the school will influence their involvement in their children's schooling. For most parents, their first reading of the school is in terms of how they are treated. The expression 'feel of a school' is used to describe their initial impressions when they walked in the door or visited classrooms – the warmth, the welcome, their impressions (Gewirtz et al., 1995, p. 31). The sense of community, which is established if families feel welcome, may be affected by the rules around visiting and how these rules are enforced. Visiting a school can be very traumatic for non-professional parents who are not conversant with the language of education (Epstein and Seyong, 1995, p. 133). A welcoming environment is rooted in attitude and demeanour of school staff towards parents. It can only be achieved, Lopez found (2001, p. 16), by breaking down the formal and bureaucratic barriers that surround the school. While parents appreciate a more open style of school (Glover, 1992, p. 228), the parents in Cullingford's research (1996a, p. 5) acknowledged that there were some impenetrable factors, be they content, relationship or ethos, that cannot be measured. Even with the most publicly organised parents' evenings, schools presented barriers, with parents' own shyness or unwillingness to intrude in a professional organisation a constraint.

As the parents in Cullingford's research acknowledged, the ethos of the school has an influence on parents' perceptions of how welcome they are in the school. In Catholic schools, the values, practices and perspectives of the Church will be expressed as the cultural and institutional norms (Lodge, 2004, p. 32). No recognition or accommodation of different beliefs and practices may be made, particularly if they impact on school life (Lynch and Lodge, 2002, p. 140). In addition, the emphasis on parental involvement in the life of the school may exert undue pressure on individuals to conform to the norms and values of the school (Hantrais, 2004, p. 192). As a result, parents whose beliefs differ from these norms may decide to remain detached from the school and its view of 'appropriate' parental behaviour (Vincent, 1996, p. 5). They may not feel that they have the same 'sense of entitlement' (Vincent, 2001, p. 348) in challenging the practices or decisions of the school as other parents. Until this power relationship is addressed and schools are prepared to accept parents as critical collaborators, the home-school relationship will be, according to Fine (1995, p. 86), educationally bankrupt.

The parent-community intelligence network (Cullingford, 1996b, p. 76) and the 'parental grapevine' (Bastiani, 1989, p. 41) provide an important source of information and support for parents. While reflecting the dominant local norms, they influence parenting values and practices as well as students' attitudes, behaviours and achievements (Epstein and Seyong, 1995, pp. 119-120). However, this aspect of parental involvement is largely omitted from national policy and the existence, complexity and significance of these networks are often invisible to people who have no direct experience of them (Bell and Ribbens, 1994, p. 252). Networks are the most significant source of information for parents about schools and education (Gorard, 1997, p. 151). For many parents in Lareau's study (1997, p. 712), discussions with other parents at their children's formal after-school activities influenced the way in which they approached their children's schooling. The bus stop, for the participants in Graue et al.'s study (2001 p. 482), was a cultural resource that provided opportunities for parents to congregate and share information about school programmes and events, about teachers and about what other parents were doing. The political organisation of the school was in many ways developed through these bus stop conversations. In Ireland, the schoolyard and gate are similar resources for parents. The NPCP (2004, p. 14) encourages Parents Associations to promote networking among parents by arranging informal and formal events for parents to meet socially. Bosetti (2004, p. 395), however, raised concerns about the accuracy and quality of information parents access through these networks.

Parental Involvement in the Home Curriculum

Parental involvement in the home curriculum is emphasised in the *Education Welfare Act 2001*, the *Primary School Curriculum* (DES, 1999a) and their related information booklets. Parents, as the primary educators of their children, are expected by society to provide 'school-trained' children (Wyness, 1996, p. 141). They must meet the developmental needs of their children for safety, security, routines and rules. As role models for their children, they must demonstrate consistent respect for all other legitimate authorities in the child's life (Garanzine, 2000, p. 249). In other words, parents have the responsibility to prepare their children with the necessary life-skills for functioning in school and society.

Much, if not most, of a child's learning takes place outside school, in the home, in non-school institutions such as sports clubs and in the wider community (Illich, 1973, p. 35; Bourdieu and De Saint-Martin, 1974, p. 345). The home is the prime locus for learning language, social skills, moral values and citizenship (Macbeth, 1994, p. 85). In addition, most children are involved in structured after-school and holiday activities like art, sport, music and drama as well as various community organisations like the scouts (Franklin and Madge, 2000, p. 23). These extra-curricular activities, not only provide educational and cultural benefits (Bourdieu,

1997, p. 47), but are a means of control by keeping children busy and out of trouble (Wyness, 1994, p. 205).

Non-structured activities such as family outings, events and holidays, all contribute to the child's education. On a daily basis, parents informally educate their children about nutrition, hygiene, society, work and relationships. In fact, the children in Tomanović's study (2003, p. 66), portrayed their parents as being preoccupied with schooling. This inevitable and constant home learning includes learning from the mass media, the neighbourhood and community institutions with which the family has contact (Macbeth and Ravn, 1994, p. 7). It can be acquired by accident, deliberately or by copying other members of the family who act as role models. One of the primary influences on students' attitudes towards school, Isherwood and Hammah (1981) found in their study of forty schools in Quebec, was their relationships with their siblings. Those who related to their siblings often and discussed a wide range of issues with them had more positive attitudes towards school.

The parents' role as educators is recognised in both the Constitution (Ireland, 1932) and national policy (DES, 1999a). The DES acknowledges the importance of home learning by encouraging parents to provide 'high quality experiences for their children' (DES, 1999b; 2000a) and by funding preventative initiatives such as the HSCL Scheme (DES, 1999d) and the School Completion Programme (SCP, 2004) in disadvantaged areas. The HSCL schemes aim to raise the capacities and skills of parents to enhance their children's education, particularly in the areas of literacy and numeracy (DES, 1999d; DES, 2005d, p. 40). The SCP provides school meals, after-school and holiday time activities as well as programmes and supports to enable parents to take a greater interest in their children and their education (SCP, 2004). In this way the State fulfils it obligation as the 'good parent' (Pinkey, 2000, p. 116), who compensates for poor or inadequate parents.

Volunteers and Audiences

This aspect of parental involvement in school is emphasised in the *Education Act 1998,* the *Education Welfare Act 2001,* the *Primary School Curriculum* (DES, 1999a) and the information booklets. Fundraising, educational activities including homework and helping in the classroom, support at events, after-school activities, transport for outings and school maintenance were the main activities listed for parental involvement. Formal occasions such as meetings, concerts, sports days, Cullingford found (1996a p. 7), were a way of underlining parental support for the school. Recognising that schools are under resourced and teachers over-stretched, parents are often willing to help out (Commission on the Family, 1998, p. 551). The report on primary school libraries (Library Association of Ireland, 2002, p. 39) found that fundraising by parents provided as many books as the local authority school library service.

Both the HSCL (Ryan, 1994, p. 25) and the OECD (1997, p. 147) reports found that while parents were invited to organised functions and involved in extra-curricular activities, e.g., sports and cultural activities in some schools, there was little involvement in the classroom. Similarly, most of the parents who were interviewed in five locations around the country for the report on primary school libraries knew very little about classroom libraries. They had never or rarely been into their child's classroom for any purpose, never mind familiarising themselves with the library set up (Library Association of Ireland, 2002, p. 53).

Parental involvement in the school does not occur in a vacuum (Vincent, 2001, p. 349). Schools are 'powerful agents of socialisation' (Martin, 1997, p. 67). As children, parents received powerful messages, not only about the various roles and boundaries in school life, but also their role as parents. Parents in Graue et al.'s study (2001, p. 477) used their own experience as students to set expectations and gauge their own child's progress. Traditionally, parents were not involved in Irish schools. Therefore parents today may have few childhood experiences of parental involvement to rely on. In addition, their interactions and relationship with their children's schools may not encourage their involvement. Home-school meetings can be organised to ensure compliance, with opportunities to talk and ask questions limited. The architecture (gates, buzzers, seating arrangements), regulations (parking, access to the class teacher, Code of Behaviour) (Ritzer, 2004, p. 112) and systems of communication (Giddens, 2001, pp. 356-7) of the school confirm to parents the role they are expected to play in their children's education.

Parental involvement is also set within personal work-related and domestic contexts. Most parents cannot and do not participate at the school building (Epstein, 1992, p. 1143). Time constraints, the age or grade levels of students and the life stages of families are important elements in nature and extent of parental involvement with schools (Fletcher, 1999, p. 172). For others, poverty, apathy or parents' past negative experiences of their own schooling were contributory factors, with some perceiving involvement as primarily attending to the eco-nomic/financial needs of their families (Carlen et al., 1992, pp. 137-8; Zappone, 2002, p. 34). Changes in society and mothers' participation in the workforce raise serious questions about the need for new links be-tween home and school (Archer and Shortt, 2003, p. 114). Schools, according to Feiler et al. (2006, p. 465), will need a variety of activities that will suit different parents at different times. Such a mix, with fami-lies choosing what they are going to get involved with, carries with it the need for individual decisions to be respected and negative infer-ences avoided.

Decision-Making and Governance

National policy, as outlined in the *Education Act 1998, Educational Wel-fare Act 2000* and the *Primary School Curriculum* (DES, 1999a), pro-motes the involvement of parents in school decision-making and govern-ance. Parents may become active partners by being elected to the BOM and/or Parents Association or by being a member of a policy-working group (SDPS, 2004). However, opportunities for getting involved in school decision-making are limited. Only two parents can sit on the BOM at any one time. Only 24 per cent of primary schools in Ireland have Parents Associations that are members of the NPCP (Colgan, 2003). Only two out of every five schools in the initial HSCL liaison report had a parents' committee (Ryan, 1994, p. 25). There was no men-tion of whether these committees were affiliated to NPCP. Neither the HSCL (Ryan, 1994) nor the OECD (1997) reports mention parental in-volvement in policy formation. In fact, the OECD (1997) report found that parents had no influence on the approach taken by individual schools or teachers to the teaching of the curriculum. Since the estab-lishment of the SDPS Service, there has been an increase from 8 per cent to 14 per cent in the percentage of parents involved in school planning (DES, 2003a, p. 29). This had mostly been in organisational rather than curricular areas. However, the inspectorate (DES, 2006b, p. 81) suggested that school-based structures to accommodate the systematic and continuous involvement of parents in the planning process have not yet been established in most schools.

There are also question marks over whether parents who join these organisations are typical of parents as a whole and represent their views (OECD, 1997, p. 16). Most parents are more interested in the advancement and activities of their own children than in school or system wide endeavours. Few wish to participate directly in school decisions or be active members of the Parents Association or BOM (OECD, 1997, p. 41; Murphy, 2002, p. 85). In Coleman's Canadian study (1998, p. 148), parents dismissed parent governance as necessary or useful. They saw little connection between it and teaching and learning activities, which they believed were entirely controlled by the teachers. Parents in the evaluation done by the Inspectorate (DES, 2006b, p. 51) held similar beliefs and felt that they were not qualified to comment or make a contribution to the schools' curriculum planning.

Similarly, a major feature of the school boards and governing bodies in England and Scotland was their strong trust in the head teachers' professional expertise and judgement (Munn, 1998). Supporting the school and teachers was seen as their main role and they accepted the policies put forward by the head teachers. Only those schools that had head teachers who were committed to open and consultative management styles had parent representatives in their school development planning groups. Even those parents tended to be guided by the head teacher's interpretation of the salience of the policy initiative for the school.

Parental participation in school decision-making and governance is regulated by the use of power within the school (Foucault, 2000, p. 18). Collaboration between parents and teachers can focus on those areas of school life that are largely peripheral and uncontested in order to minimize conflict and maintain existing power relationships (Blenkin et al., 1992, p. 52). While complying with the national policy of parental involvement, the school can involve only their 'good' parents who comply with school norms and can 'be trusted not to rock the boat' (Simpson and Cieslik, 2002, p. 125). In addition, teachers can insist on their right to be the final arbiters of professional decisions in the school (INTO, 1993, pp.

112-3) with most studies finding that parents were usually informed about changes after the decisions had been made (Oakes et al., 2000, p. 84; Eden, 2001, p. 103; DES, 2006b, p. 62; 2006c, p. 31).

Home-School Communication

Under the *Education Act 1998* schools are obliged to communicate with parents about their children's progress and the operation and performance of the school. This was echoed in the other documentation. Research (Bastiani, 2000, p. 25; Gewirtz et al., 1995, p. 9; NCCA, 2006b, p. 13) shows that parents share the following common expectations about school. They want:

- Regular, reliable and accessible information about what the school is doing and how it affects their children

- Information about their children's progress and achievements; about problems in learning, behaviour and socialisation; and especially about identifying ways in which they can support their children's learning.

Personal contact between home and school tends to be selective and infrequent (Vulliamy and Webb, 2003, p. 281). It focuses on identifying and solving problems rather than continuous, positive interactions with families. While parents can make an appointment to discuss their children's work or problems with the class teacher, there is normally only one report card and one formal parent-teacher meeting per year (Ryan, 1994, p. 25; OECD, 1997, p. 149). There may also be group meetings. These usually take place prior to enrolment and on other occasions such as parent information on school procedures, RSE, the sacraments and talks by experts.

General communication, using newsletters, and notes home, is normally of a fairly limited nature (Hughes et al., 1994, p. 169). It concentrates on the practical side of school life – requests for help or other types of contributions, information about meetings or discussing lost clothing. Only rarely do schools and parents communicate about matters of central educational importance. Communication also tends to be very much one-way and under the control of the school (OECD, 1997, p. 148). Parents are rarely consulted or involved in decisions about the form and content of school-to-home communication (Hughes and Greenhough, 2006, p. 472).

Children appear to play a central role in communication between home and school. Many educational decisions, Smedley found (1995), were made on the basis of children's hopes and fears, fuelled by anecdotes and gossip carried on the playground grapevine. While parents may regularly discuss school, class work and future education choices with their children, both Hughes et al. (1994, p. 168) and Epstein and Seyong (1995) questioned how useful this information was to parents. As much of it was fragmented and incomplete, parents had little insight into why children were learning these skills or how they fitted into the overall curriculum. In addition, they were very much dependent on their children being 'reliable messengers' (Bridgemohan et al., 2005, p. 7).

Parents' views about the value of home-school communication appear to be influenced by their relationship with the school. Most of the parents in Hughes et al. (1994, pp. 164-5) study did not want to have any more contact with the school than they already did. Beside other commitments and the attitude 'It is there if you want it', there was also a pervasive feeling of intimation about approaching the school, either to obtain information or to discuss a particular problem. The parents, who were interviewed in the NCCA's study (2005, p. 208), identified the class teacher as the first and main point of contact when they wanted information or help with their children's learning. However, all these parents were involved with the school and so may be the more 'conscientious' (Ibid., p. 226) or 'good' parents. While the participants in Hanafin and Lynch's study (2002, p. 41) sometimes described the class teacher as being helpful, open and easy to talk to, home-school communication was more commonly spoken about as being inadequate, difficult, off-putting, excluding and frightening. They felt that the large class-sizes adversely affected the parent-teacher relationship. While these parents were described as being the 'interested' ones by the teachers, the researchers felt that they also represented some peripheral voices as they saw the research as a rare opportunity to express their feelings about the school.

The 'more marginalised' (Conaty, 2002), 'unreachable' (Eivers et al., 2004, p. 174) or 'uninvolved' (Ryan, 1994) parents may be more like those described by Epstein and Seyong (1995, p. 122). In their analysis of the data obtained from the National Educational Longitudinal Study of 1988 and the Hopkins Enhancement Survey, they found that one-third to two-thirds of parents, depending on the measure, were isolated or unconnected with their children's schools and uninformed about their children's class work, homework and curriculum content. Not only did they not attend parent-teacher meetings, they often did not understand report cards and other home-school written communication.

Under the HSCL Scheme, priority is given to activities which enhance communication between home and school (Archer and Shortt, 2003). Almost all of the principals and coordinators felt that the HSCL scheme had a positive impact on the way the school related with parents. In addition, the NCCA (2005, p. 208) found that parents in disadvantaged schools were more likely to be involved in activities that allowed them regular contact with the class teacher. However, the parents who were interviewed by Mulkerrins (2005, p. 66) felt that they needed the support of the HSCL coordinator to communicate effectively with the school.

Parental nostalgia (Hargreaves, 2000, p. 227) and their stereotypical images of the 'good' school and teacher (Eden, 2001, p. 106 [apostrophes in the original], may impact on their communication with the school. Most parents operate their own surveillance system. They check their children's homework (Is it signed/corrected/ given?) along with their books and copies (Do they have them? Are they used or unused? How do they compare to my friend's/sister's children?). Notes to and from school all convey messages about what is expected. Direct communication is not always necessary. Conversations at the school gate, comments made to children, remarks at meetings along with reports to the principal and/or outside agencies can be just as, if not more, effective.

The effectiveness of the school, and the teacher in supporting learning, is most often questioned when parents become aware of their child's inability to cope with the task set by the teacher and his or her frustration or confidence in the support received (MacBeath, 1999, p. 44). Parents' expressions of strong feelings on the subject of bullying and racial harassment touch on one of the more sensitive areas of home, school and community relations, and conflict of values (Wyness, 1994, p. 204). Uninformed of the school's policy, while yet aware of what was happening through the child/parent/community network, regular home-school communication is necessary to maintain positive relationships.

Questions

Using the research indicators (Table 2.4), this section explored parental involvement in their children's education. As relationships are a key element in the partnership process, this study will examine the home-school relationships in these schools. How do they influence home-school involvement? What impact does the school's ethos and the parents' values have? How are parents involved in the home curriculum? To what extent are they involved in their children's schools as audiences, volunteers and decision-makers? As communication underpins home-school partnership, how does it support and encourage parental involvement in their children's education?

Conclusion

This chapter examined the development of the national policy of parental involvement. The complexity of the educational system with its vast array of vested interests makes both the development and implementation of change a very slow process (Coolahan, 1989, p. 61). The *Education Act 1998*, the *Education Welfare Act 2000*, the *Primary School Curriculum* (DES, 1999a) and related documentation were analysed with particular reference to the overall policy objectives and the rights and responsibilities of parents. Four indicators of parental involvement were chosen to evaluate the national policy of parental involvement. These were

- Open, caring, respectful relationships

- Home-school communication

- Parental involvement at home

- Parental involvement in schools.

The relationship between the participants in this research and the schools to which they send their children will be examined. The emphasis on partnership in both the consultative process and the subsequent documentation would suggest that parents and schools should be working together to support children's learning. Communication systems are important in establishing and maintaining this relationship. However, apart from ensuring that children attend school regularly, neither laws nor policies can force parents to be involved in their children's education. Parental involvement in schools can be seen as a continuum. It starts with the totally uninvolved parents who never go near the school to the parents who are active partners in both curriculum and organisational decision-making processes within the school.

This study will examine how the national policy as expressed in the official documentation is being implemented at local level. What aspects of the policy are working well? What changes or improvements are needed? What supports or impedes the full implementation of the policy? How could the policy be more effective in promoting partnership between home and school? The research methodology is outlined in Chapter Three.

Chapter Three

METHODS AND METHODOLOGY

Research Questions

Home-school partnership is one of the core principles underlying national education policy. 'A range of measures aimed at fostering active parental partnership with schools' (Department of Education, 1995, p. 139) are outlined in the *Education Act 1998*, the *Education Welfare Act 2000* and the *Primary School Curriculum* (Department of Education and Science [DES], 1999a) and the supplementary information booklets, which informed parents of the legislative and curricular changes. These documents were developed through the partnership process at national level between representatives of the DES, parents, teachers and managerial bodies.

There are four elements to partnership between home and school at local level. The first is parental involvement in home learning, which Macbeth and Ravn (1994, p. 8) argue is one of the most neglected aspects of educational systems throughout Europe. Parents get very little credit for this work. The second is parental involvement in the school, which is normally initiated and controlled by the school. It can range from sending one's child to school to being involved in decision-making and governance. The relationship and communication between parents and the school are the last two elements.

Implementing any policy is a complex process and predicted outcomes are never guaranteed. Policies like partnership, which are deeply symbolic, and lack the necessary resource commitment and implementation strategies, pose particular difficulties. Implementation has been delegated to schools (see Table 2.3) who differ in their motivation to involve parents. Moreover, even when schools are highly dedicated and have been given the resources to implement the policy, parents are not passive recipients. Neither the State nor the schools can compel them to be interested and involved in their children's education and schooling. As outlined in Chapter One, parental roles and identities will shape their interactions with the education system.

From the State and schools' perspectives, parents are seen as providers of the raw materials, namely the children, to help the State and school achieve their aims of educating the workers and citizens of the future. 'Partnership' on these terms means supporting the work of the school. 'Involvement' means meeting the shortfall in resources, whether they are financial or personnel.

Parents, for the most part, are far more interested in their own children's welfare and education than in school or national issues. In this they are encouraged by the market-driven consumer society. Most parents are aware of the factors which support their children's learning and will use their 'cultural capital' (Bourdieu, 1997, p. 47) to ensure their children's success in school and life. Involvement in the school is on their terms and in the interests of their children. Partnership is a misnomer to them. They want the teachers to do their job and leave them alone to do theirs. The result is often a mismatch between national policy and the reality at local level.

This research will examine, from the perspectives of parents, the degree of parental involvement in five Catholic primary schools in North Dublin. The rhetoric of national policy as outlined in the *Education Act 1998*, the *Education Welfare Act 2000* and the *Primary School Curriculum* (DES, 1999a) and other documentation will be compared with the perceptions and experience of these parents.

Research Methods

Evaluation research is a complex field where the benefits of multiple methods are particularly clear (Rossi et al., 1999). For this reason the case study method was used. It allowed the use of multiple sources of evidence ranging from the loose and unstructured to tight and heavily prestructured (Robson, 1993, p. 157). The mixture of qualitative and quantitative methods allowed the exploration the diverse phenomena surrounding parental involvement and provided insights into the complex relationship, which exists between home and school (Cohen et al., 2000). This, it was hoped, would increase the credibility and validity of the research.

Researchers need to be explicit about the values and theories that inform their work (Ali et al., 2004, p. 24). I am a forty plus Irish middle class Catholic parent of four children who attend their local primary and secondary schools. I am also a primary school teacher, having worked in a north Dublin disadvantaged school for twenty years before being seconded to the School Development Planning Support (SDPS) service. As a teacher, I had a lot of contact with parents through mainstream class teaching, HCSL and Early Start. As an SDPS facilitator, I support schools in developing and implementing their school plan. Partnership between home and school is one of our core messages. At planning meetings, with principals, staff and occasionally parents, we discuss how parents will be involved in the planning process. These experiences influence my values, which are embedded in my research process and theories (Silverman, 2004, p. 64).

Practitioner research (Anderson et al., 1994) and a qualitative-ethnographic research method (McKernan, 1996) were used to collect data that was difficult to obtain through other methods. Through observing parents in my local community, the schools I worked with as a SDPS facilitator and my own experience as a parent, I explored the research questions. A research diary and field notes were used to record the development of the literature review, data collection and analysis. These helped me to reflect on the multidimensional nature of the policy of parental involvement. They were also useful in identifying and addressing bias (Ruane, 2005, p. 71) in both the design of the research instruments and the interpretation and analysis of the data.

Indicators were needed to measure the impact of the policy. Therefore, it was important to identify and develop standards that were appropriate, credible and measurable (Fink, 1995, p. 2). As outlined in Chapter Two, the following indicators, which correspond with the overall policy goals as defined in the legislation and other official documentation, were used:

- Open, caring, respectful relationships

- Home-school communication

- Parental involvement in the home curriculum

- Parental involvement in the school.

The categories, as identified by the literature (Epstein, 1992, p. 1145; Esptein and Seyong, 1995, p. 122; OECD, 1997, p. 19), were incorporated as subsections of these groupings. These indicators, which were explored in greater detail in the previous chapter, will be used to assess both the implementation and impact of the policy in the five schools.

While one of the principal characteristics of policy evaluation is, according to Rossi et al. (1999), that its methods cover the gamut of prevailing social research paradigms, information from parents must necessarily be obtained by a survey. It was chosen because of its appeal to generalisability within the given parameters of the research (Cohen et al., 2000, p. 171). As statements are supported by large-scale data from a representative sample population, it creates a degree of confidence in the findings. Interviews and focus groups were used to illustrate and probe deeper in to the findings from the questionnaires. Much of the routine communication by the school to parents is through notes given to the children to bring home (Gaire and Mahon, 2005, p. 188). Documentation from the schools involved in the research was analysed. These included information booklets, newsletters along with notes sent home by the school. They gave an insight in to the relationship and communication between home and school. The data from these research methods was supplemented by the observations in my field diary.

Exclusions and Limitations

The focus of this research is on the extent of the involvement by individual parents in their children's education at local level. The role of the NPCP in the development of education policy at national level and its promotion of partnership with parents at local level is not explored. While the rights of Parents associations are included in the *Education Act 1998,* these rights are separate to the rights of individual parents (Gaire and Mahon, 2005, p. 31). With only approximately 1,000 of the 3,200 primary schools in the country having parents associations affiliated to the NPCP (Kilfeather, 2005, p. 91) and the NPCP modernising to become more flexible and responsive to the needs of individual parents as well as those of Parents Associations, the operation of the parents association will not be a primary concern of this study.

The diffuse nature of the policy, the extended time frame, the application differences between schools along with the lack of a specific implementation plan makes it difficult to evaluate the national policy of parental involvement (Rossi et al., 1999, pp. 51-2). In particular, the lack of base line data (O'Leary, 2004, pp. 136-7) makes it hard to evaluate the degree in which parental involvement has changed since the introduction of the policy. In addition, these changes may have happened anyway without the policy or even with a different policy. They may be as a result of changes in society, the organisation of schools and parental values rather than national policy (Greenberg and Walberg, 1998, p. 174).

Schools are usually founded by powerful or autonomous status groups to provide an exclusive education for their own children, or to propagate respect for their cultural values (Collins, 1977, p. 127). The bulk of parents, at the time when the national policy of parental involvement was being developed, were Catholics, had Irish citizenship and sent their children to the local national school (Redmond and Heanue, 2000). As being part of a distinct status group (Collins, 1977, p. 125) gives people a sense of identity and belonging, I decided to confine my sample to parents who send their children to Catholic national schools. Parents who home school their children were excluded.

Since 1990, there have been major changes in the provision of schools and the diversity of the parent population. Educate Together schools, Gaelscoileanna and other non-Catholic schools have been developed to provide an alternative to the mainstream denominational schools (Gaire and Mahon, 2005). Parental involvement is a major feature in both the establishment and development of these schools. These statements from the three representatives of the governing bodies highlight the differences in attitude towards parental involvement in these schools. Parents are welcome in Catholic schools (O'Connor, 2005, p. 91). In Church of Ireland schools, parents are perceived as having a key role, both individually and collectively, in terms of the development and support of the school and in drawing particular issues and concerns to the attention of the principal and Board of Management (BOM) (McCullagh,

2005, p. 93). Apart from establishing and developing Educate Together schools, parents are encouraged to get actively involved at every level of the organisation, from organising extra-curricular school events, to serving on the BOM, to being elected as a director of Educate Together (Mangaoang, 2005, p. 99). As this may have resulted in a different status and power differential in these schools, they were excluded from the research.

Over the last five years, the number of international parents with children attending Catholic schools has increased. Due to language, racial, culture and religious differences, these parents have to cope with issues of assimilation and integration in Irish society. Consequently, the interactions between these parents and the school may be substantially different to those of the mainstream culture. The schools chosen did not have a large number of international children. Special schools were also excluded as they cater for children with special needs. They also use a different curriculum and have more State intervention and parental involvement than the norm.

Time and resource constraints confined the research sample to five schools. The context of the schools and the personalities of the stakeholders will have an impact the implementation of the policy. In addition, I was the SDPS facilitator for these schools. This was an important factor in gaining access and ensuring the support and co-operation of both the school and the individual class teachers. It was also important in persuading parents to participate in the study. Therefore, the results may not be generalisable to other schools.

Relying on parents to evaluate the impact of a national policy was problematic. In many cases, they may not be aware of the policy, the school's implementation of it or the impact it has had on them as individuals. In addition, parents may be reluctant to appear critical of their children's schools and may be unaware of the extent of their involvement with their children's education. The lack of school records on parental involvement makes it difficult to verify their accounts. Therefore, while social relations and group norms will be explored, caution will be exercised in attributing the opinion of the participants to the whole-school population (May, 2001, pp. 125-6).

As highlighted in the literature review, gender and social class are two important variables in this study. Therefore, I tried to avoid gender and social class bias in both the design of the research instruments and the collection and interpretation of the data. The schools' status, as determined by the DES, will be taken as an indicator of social class. The research instruments were piloted with a school with disadvantaged status in order to minimise the class bias. However, it should be noted that while schools are designated by the DES as either disadvantaged or non-disadvantaged, the boundaries are not as clear in reality. Many parents from disadvantaged areas choose to send their children to non-disadvantaged or middle class schools. Other variables, such as the age of the respondent, their education level, employment and family type will be also be taken in to consideration.

Selecting the Sample

As time and resources did not allow a full-scale representative sample to be used, it was decided to confine the sample to five single sex Catholic primary schools in North Dublin. These were on the database of schools, with which I was working as a SDPS facilitator. These schools were within a three mile radius of each other. Three schools, a boys' and two of the girls', were in a middle class area, while the other two, a boys' and girls', were in a designated disadvantaged area. Both the disadvantaged schools were designated as DEIS Band 1 Urban, which identifies them as two of the 150 primary schools with the highest concentration of disadvantage (DES, 2005d, p. 78). It should be noted that individual parents within these schools are not easily categorised. From working in disadvantaged schools, I was aware of the tendency of a lot of parents in disadvantaged areas to send their children to a school in a middle class area rather than the local school. However, these parents tend to value education more than those to choose to send their children to the local school.

It was decided to take Hughes's (1994, p. 194) advice on letting each family decide who would respond to the request to participate in this research. However, as gender and home education were important elements in this research, attempts would be made to interview a representative number of fathers.

Permission was sought from the SDPS internal management committee and the principals, Parents Associations and the BOMs of the schools in question to use these selected schools as a research sample. Two BOMs only agreed on the condition that the privacy of the parents was protected. Most principals reassured the BOM that I was somebody they knew and trusted. In addition, the informed consent of each individual participant was sought (Sin, 2005, p. 278). Participants were assured that the information that they gave would be confidential and that care would be taken to ensure that they would not be identified in the final report (Ali and Kelly, 2004, p. 120). In addition, as the data from my observation diaries and documentation from my children's school was used to validate and reinforce the findings from the other schools, the principal and BOM of the school my children attended were informed of the research.

My role was one of researcher, active participant and author (Coffey, 1999, p. 116). Participant observation, using my own experience of being a parent of primary school children, was an integral part of this research. Initially I had decided to write in the third person, but as the literature review developed, I began to reflect on my own parenting and my involvement in my children's education and their school. When developing the research instruments, I realised that my own personal experience and knowledge of parenting was underpinning and adding authenticity to the study (Ellis and Bochner, 2003, p. 212). Therefore it was important that I admitted my own subjectivity in insights and feelings (Neuman, 2004, p. 274), contributed and shared my personal experience as appropriate (Daly, 2000, p. 66) and used my own voice (Coffey, 1999, p. 132) by writing in the first person. With fieldwork having a strong impact on my identity as a parent, it was important to engage in a high level of reflexivity or self-reflection (Darlington and Scott, 2002, p. 18) about my part in the research in order not to bias the findings (Greenberg and Walberg, 1998, p. 171). This meant continually checking that the findings were consistent and reliable by frequently referring back to the data, the research questions and the literature review. While I may be an atypical case in that being a teacher and an SDPS facilitator gave me a degree of educational capital which most parents would not have, I was also typical in that I was not overly involved in my children's schools.

Research Instruments

Multiple research methods were used to ensure triangulation (Flick, 1998, p. 230) and enhance the consistency and validity of the research findings. Questionnaires were used to collect quantitative data from a large sample of parents. They provided an overview of the extent in which parents are involved in their children's education and schools along with their awareness of the changes in the education system due to national legislation and curriculum. This helped to identify overall trends and themes and to avoid the 'interviewer effect' (Alder and Clarke, 2003, p. 248), which adds another factor in to the data collection process.

Focus groups and interviews were devised to obtain more specific, in-depth, qualitative data from a smaller sample. This data included the participants' relationship with the school and the education system, their perceptions of their roles as parents and their views on national policy. The factors, which support and/constrain parental involvement in their schools were also examined.

Content or documentary analysis (Robson, 1993) of the notes, news-letters and information booklets, which are used by the school communicate with parents, were analysed. These documents represented a reflection of reality and a method by which power is expressed and social order accomplished (May, 2001, pp. 182-3).

Participant observation was used to support and inform the other research instruments. My anecdotal records (McKernan, 1996, p. 68) and personal action logs (Anderson et al., 1994, p. 136) were used to record and study the dominant educational events and activities that I engaged in as a parent of primary school children over a period of time.

Observation

Participant observation, also called field research or ethnography, was used to explore the research question (Robson, 1993, p. 192) and learn about, understand and describe the interaction between home and school (Neuman, 2004, p. 267). It enabled me to grasp multiple perspectives in a natural social setting (Ibid., p. 268) and was useful in identifying trends, patterns and styles of behaviour in both myself and others (Alder and Alder, 1998, p. 81; Simpson and Tuson, 2003, pp. 30-33). Its flexibility (May, 2001, p. 159) was a major advantage as I could alter my focus in accordance with my theoretical interests and analytic developments. The data was then classified and analysed using the predefined categories identified from literature review.

As description, which is a selective and partial process, is determined by the researcher's theoretical and conceptual assumptions (Darlington and Scott, 2002, p. 75), particular attention was paid to the reliability, validity and objectivity (Creswell, 2003, p. 184) of the observations. This meant basing my observations on the literature review and recording facts, statements and events, rather than opinions and/or feelings.

Data Collection

I used my pre-existing role as a mother to observe and record data on my involvement in my primary school children's education and school. Periods of observation were decided on, with rough notes recorded daily. These were typed up and analysed on a regular basis. Initial observations were general and focused mainly on my contact with the school and networking with other parents. After the literature review was completed, I decided to focus on the home curriculum (Macbeth and Ravn, 1994) and home-school involvement (Epstein and Seyong, 1995, p. 122; OECD, 1997, p. 19). This involved systematic recording using a fixed schedule, which noted the activity and the personnel involved. These observations were categorised under parental roles and types of parental involvement as identified in the literature review. These were central themes in the other research instruments. As the observation continued, the curriculum subjects were identified and recorded.

In addition to my own observations, other parents would be asked to keep a diary describing their involvement in their children's education, including their contact with the school, over a week. A diary, similar to the one I used to record my own involvement in my primary school children's education, was devised. However, the pilot with an inner city disadvantaged school was not successful for two reasons. Time constraints and delays meant that it was not completed in time to send out with the main questionnaires and interview invitations. In addition, the parents, selected by the HSCL teacher as being her 'better' parents, had difficulty completing the diary. Differences between the parents' perceptions as what could be considered educational and my own meant that the full range of activities would not be recorded. According to the HSCL teacher (IHSCL, 22-02-06), the parents did not consider things like getting the uniform ready as being involved in their children's education. To them school-related items were visiting the school, attending courses, meeting the teacher. The examples given in the sample diary confused them as they were 'amazed' that items such as going to the cinema and taking your child for a walk actually contributed to their children's education. The HSCL teacher explained that the school did 'talk to them about it but they do not get it'. Literacy was also an issue and assistance was required from the HSCL teacher to fill in the diaries. This created a bias as the HSCL teacher, feeling that the diaries were 'illegible', not filled in 'properly' and that the replies were 'not fair' to the school, rewrote the diaries in conjunction with the parents. As a result it was decided not to proceed with the parents' diaries.

Data Analysis

Through observation and systematically recording the data in my diary, I realised the variety and intensity of the parental role. As a mother who works full time and is a part-time PhD student and involved in local community activities, I would have felt guilty that I was neglecting my children and their school. Parental 'guilt' (McKeown et al., 1998, p. 208), the feeling that you could do more for your children, appears to be common and may influence the findings of this research. However, through observing the mundane, trivial, every day minutia (Neuman, 2004, p. 278), I discovered a vibrant, informal home curriculum, supported by both home and school, and a dynamic home-school communication system with the children at the centre. These findings are identified by their code, i.e. the abbreviation for field notes [FN] followed by the date on which they were observed.

Questionnaires

Questionnaires were chosen for their versatility, time efficiency (Ruane, 2005, p. 143) and ability to provide quantitative data for triangulation purposes. As respondents answer the questions privately, there is less social pressure and interviewer bias (Gorard, 2001, p. 83). However, while the confidential and anonymous responses are assumed to lead to more truthful answers, there is no way of checking the identity of the respondent or if the questions were understood and the responses are accurate (Robson, 1993, p. 243).

An initial questionnaire was devised using the research questions and the literature review. Being aware that some parents may not have high literacy levels, the questionnaire was designed to be easy to read and complete. Closed questions (De Vaus, 2002b, pp. 99-100) were used as they are quick and easy to answer and do not discriminate against the less literate respondents. It was hoped that they would encourage a high response rate with the choices acting as prompts and clarifying the meaning of the questions for the respondents. However, closed questions may obscure true differences or similarities in answers and responses may be ticked even when they do not really ring true (Ruane, 2005, pp. 131-2). Two open questions were included. One on the changes in education was left open so as not to bias the participants' responses. The final question allowed the respondents to write a free response to the research question in their own terms, enabling them to explain and qualify their responses to the closed questions (Cohen et al., 2000) if they so wished.

Questions were designed to be non-threatening and within the capabilities of the respondents (Peterson, 2000, p. 10) but yet specific enough to answer the research questions. Simple language was used as far as possible and specialised language such as technical terms, jargon and abbreviations was avoided (May, 2001, p. 106). A variety of question formats, including Likert scales, checklists, binary and multiple-choice formats were used to make the questionnaire interesting (De Vaus, 2002b). Clear, simple instructions in different fonts from the questions were used.

Both the cover letter (Robson, 1993, p. 271) and the front page of the questionnaire provided a context for the research. It emphasised the importance of the study and gave assurances of confidentiality and anonymity (Peterson, 2000, p. 105). My name, address and phone number were included so that respondents could contact me if they had any queries about the questionnaires or the study. As the questionnaires would be returned to the school there was a fear of participants over reporting socially desirable, respectable behaviour and conforming to social norms rather than true responses (Gorard, 2001). Questions were therefore structured in such as way as to make respondents feel that all answers were equally legitimate (Ruane, 2005, p. 129)

Pre-test

My husband critiqued and pre-tested the initial draft of the questionnaire and his comments were used to amend it. One question, which involved ranking items in order of their importance, was omitted completely as he found it very confusing and frustrating (Gorard, 2001, p. 102). On reading his replies, I noticed several discrepancies and instances of under reporting. For example, he strongly agreed that women were primarily responsible for childcare. Yet he job shares and works evenings so that he can mind the children during the day, while I work full time. On question 6, he does at least three of the four tasks, which he said were done only by me.

The amended version of the questionnaire was e-mailed to the author's supervisor, regional co-ordinator and eight of the author's SDPS colleagues who were parents. Being aware of the above gender discrepancies, this SDPS group were asked that both they and their partners complete and critique the questionnaire separately. This delayed the replies with only two of the questionnaires returned by the due date. In two cases, only one member of the couple completed the questionnaire. As a result, it was decided that only one questionnaire would be given to each household.

To ensure that the data could be analysed (Babbie, 1990, p. 225), it was coded and entered into Microsoft Excel. Excel was used because it could be used to process small data sets simply and quickly (Black, 2002, p. 252). Following analysis of the data, the questionnaire was amended using the results and suggestions made by the respondents. The questions were rearranged in a more logical sequence with vague, ambiguous and meaningless statements omitted (De Vaus, 2002b, p. 96). Questions on the additional variables of employment, religion, educational attainment and citizenship were added.

Two ethical issues arose during the pre-test. My husband questioned the impact of the questionnaire on participating schools and their parents, particularly its focus on roles and responsibilities. The impact of the questionnaire on parent identity was reflected in some of the comments and replies. One respondent wondered if she should be doing all these things, while others used question eighteen to comment how parents can be interested in their children's education and not be involved in their schools. One of the respondents mentioned that question five sent her on a 'guilt trip' because she had a lot of negatives in the middle of the question. Therefore, this and other questions were rearranged to try to ensure that the expected 'no' answers were interspersed within the questions. Also, while the literature (De Vaus, 2002b, p. 96) recommends discrimination within questions to ensure variation in replies, questions that would yield low variance were included in order to lessen parental anxieties and guilt feelings, avoid over reporting and ensure that the questionnaires were completed.

Due to inaccuracies and gender bias, question six, which asked respondents to allocate responsibility for school-related tasks in their household, was amended. The respondents were now asked to report on how often they themselves completed the tasks. Interviews and focus groups would be used to explore gender issues in parental involvement in schools and children's education. An attempt was also made to shorten the questionnaire, as suggested by one respondent. However, as all sections were important to the research questions, none could be excluded. The font and layout of questions were altered to make it more user-friendly. As it took my husband approximately eleven minutes to complete the revised questionnaire, it was piloted with a group of disadvantaged parents.

Pilot

The questionnaire was piloted in a suburban two-teacher disadvantaged school in order to determine its social class bias and readability. Fourteen families received the questionnaires, the cover letter and a return envelope addressed to the researcher at the school address. Twelve questionnaires were returned within the timeframe, which is a response rate of 86 per cent. There was no follow-up on the non-respondents. A Special Needs Assistant working in the school also filled out the questionnaire. All except one who replied were mothers. The data was coded and entered into Microsoft Excel.

Most appeared to have no problems answering the questions though the response rate to the two open questions was limited. Analysis of the data was used to make minor adjustments to the questionnaire. These included omitting 'making the school lunches' and 'taking your child to after-school activities' in question seven and strengthening the statements in two other questions.

One of the participants, a member of staff in a residential children's home, suggested that schools should use the term 'guardian' instead of 'parent' as not all children have parents. This would help children realise that their parents are their guardians. As this might be confusing for the majority of parents who did not see themselves as guardians, the wording of the questionnaire was not altered. One of the teachers mentioned the difficulty of completing negative questions, but these were retained to check that respondents were actually reading the statements and not just agreeing for the sake of it (Ruane, 2005, p. 140). A copy of the results was forwarded to the school.

The final questionnaire consisted of nineteen questions. Questions one to four, along with questions thirteen to seventeen, were seeking information in order to develop a profile of the respondents and to be able to check if there was a difference between the replies of the respondents based on the variables of gender, age, citizenship, family status, religion, employment and education levels. The ages and life stages of their children were also asked. The relationship between the respondents and the school was explored in question six. Questions five and seven were used to examine how involved the parents were in their children's education and schooling. Respondents were asked to detail the extra-curricular activities of their children in question eight. Participants' views on their responsibilities and involvement in their children's education were explored in questions nine and ten. Question eleven sought information on where parents got support and advice on educating their children. Participants' knowledge of the changes in education policy was explored in questions twelve and eighteen. The final question asked the respondents if there were any comments they wished to make on parental involvement in children's education and schools.

Data Collection

The questionnaire was delivered to the secretaries of the four schools in North Dublin on the same day. Each school received four bundles of envelopes containing the questionnaire along with a cover letter, instructions on how to fill out the questionnaire and a return envelope addressed to me. They were to be given out to the children in Senior Infants, Second, Fourth and Sixth Classes. The child would bring them home, ask their parents to fill them out and return them to their class teacher. The schools were given approximately three weeks to distribute and collect the questionnaires.

The response rate was dependent on the support and efforts of the principal, school secretary and the respective class teachers in each school. It also reflected to a certain extent the degree of parental co-operation with and support of the school. While two phone calls were received from parents expressing concerns as to what use would be made of the data, none of the schools experienced any issues with the questionnaires. All were highly supportive and expressed their regret that the returns were not higher. In middle class girls' school, the principal had explained the research at the Parents Association and there had been no objections. In the middle class and the disadvantaged boys' schools, some parents had asked if they had to fill them in and were informed that it was entirely up to them. The principal in the disadvantaged boys' school suggested that literacy may be issue. In addition, there may be survey fatigue as parents had already been asked to fill in another survey on their children's reading habits. In the middle class boys' school, additional questionnaires were found during the clean up for the summer holidays and these were included in the survey.

Two hundred and sixty-four parent questionnaires, which is a return rate of approximately 62 per cent, were returned from the four schools (Table 3.1). This is considered a good response rate for analysing and reporting (Babbie, 1990, p. 182). As the class sizes were larger, more returns were received from the middle class schools than the disadvantaged schools (Table 3.5). The difference in the levels of attendance between disadvantaged and middle class schools (National Educational Welfare Board [NEWB], 2005, p. 27) may also have impacted on the survey returns.

Table 3.1: Questionnaire Returns

		Disadvantaged Boys' School	Disadvantaged Girls' School	Middle Class Boys' School	Middle Class Girls' School
6th class	Number of questionnaires returned	13	10	25	27
	Number of children in the class	24	22	31	34
4th class	Number of questionnaires returned	10	7	16	24
	Number of children in the class	14	22	33	33
2nd class	Number of questionnaires returned	23	13	22	24
	Number of children in the class	37	21	34	34
Senior Infants	Number of questionnaires returned	10	10	17	13
	Number of children in the class	18	22	23	25
Total	Number of questionnaires returned	56	40	80	88
	Number of children in the classes	93	77	121	126
	% returned	60	52	66	70

It was difficult to assess the number of non-respondents for several reasons. While the percentage of questionnaires returned varied, these figures are based on the number of children in each class. However, as some children were absent when the questionnaires were being given out and did not receive one, there was in several cases a discrepancy between the number of questionnaire given out and the number of children in the class. For example, in the sixth class in the middle class boys' school, there were 31 boys in the class but only 25 were given out. As all teachers did not return the unused questionnaires, it is difficult to gauge exactly how many were given out. In addition, parents, who had children in the other classes or schools and received more than one questionnaire, would have only filled in one form.

A unique identification code (Bourque and Fielder 1995 pp. 80-91) was written on the back of each page of the questionnaire to ensure that the schools, classes and participants would not be confused during the data collection and analysis. Each respondent was given a unique number that corresponded to the code on their questionnaire. After several unsuccessful attempts were made to collate the data using a machine, it was decided to enter the data manually into SPSS. A handwritten note was made of both the identification number and comment of the thirty-nine respondents who had written comments and explanations beside various questions.

Data Analysis

While not every respondent answered every question, all are included in the findings. As the size of the various groupings differed, both the percentage and number of respondents are included. There was not enough variation to make valid comparisons between the vast majority of respondents who were Irish Roman Catholics and other social groupings. Some variables were combined as the number of responses was too low to give a valid result (De Vaus, 2002a, p. 33). These included children under pre-school age, parents over forty, children who had left school. While comparisons were made between the different types of school rather than individual schools, significant differences between individual schools are reported. As percentages were rounded off to whole numbers to simplify the results (Booth, 1992, p. 112), some of the tables show totals of 101 per cent or 99 per cent.

The results were tested for significance using chi-square and it was decided to report all differences if they had a 5 per cent (0.05) or less probability. However, some results that were not significant were reported, particularly when they were part of an underlying trend. With 2x2 tables, the results from the Fisher Exact Test were used rather than chi-square (Foster, 2001, p. 157). The expected number of cases in each cell was five or more. All the results, significant and insignificant, were analysed carefully and interpreted comprehensively (Eichelberger, 1989, p. 235).

The findings from the parents' questionnaires are outlined in the following chapters. Quotes from the respondents can be identified by their code, i.e. abbreviation for questionnaire [Q], the number on the questionnaire followed by the abbreviations for the school's status [Disadvantaged (D) or Middle Class (M)]; gender [Boys (B) or Girls (G)]; and the class their respondents' children attended [Senior Infants (SI); Second (2); Fourth (4); Sixth (6)].

Interviews and Focus Groups

Semi-structured interviews and focus groups, which provide rich insights into people's experiences, opinions, values, attitudes and feelings (May, 2001, p. 120), were designed to follow up on issues from the questionnaires. However, while they allowed for the concentrated and uninterrupted focus on the perceptions of the participants (Darlington and Scott, 2002, p. 62), the results may be a product of the social dynamic (Fontana and Frey, 2003, p. 64). Accuracy may be sacrificed in favour of the respondents trying to impress, please or manipulate the interviewer and each other.

Open questions were designed using the themes outlined in the literature review and the analysis of the pilot questionnaires. Prompts were written in italics. Open questions were used so that the data would supplement the more quantitative closed format of questionnaire. 'What?' and 'How?' questions were used instead of 'Why?' questions for their unobtrusiveness and their ability to encourage people to describe their experiences (Darlington and Scott, 2002, p. 57). While the questions were specific, there was freedom, if explanations were not forthcoming to probe beyond the answers (Robson, 1993, p. 231; May, 2001, p. 123) and look for clarification and elaboration on what was said.

The introduction contained an explanation of the purpose of the interviews, the importance of each person's views, and the rights of the participants to withdraw or remain silent (Sin, 2005, p. 287). The rules of the focus group (Ruane, 2005, p. 158) were explained. Permission was sought to tape the interview and to take notes. A closing statement, which asked for any further comments and allowed the participants to ask questions, was included.

Interviews

While the questions and format of the semi-structured interviews were similar to those of the focus groups, the interviews were intended to be more personalised and specific to participants' own experience of parental involvement in their children's education and schools. More flexibility would be allowed, both in terms of the areas explored and the direction of the discussion (Darlington and Scott, 2002, p. 49).

In the interviews, parents were asked about their hopes and fears for their children in question one. The factors, which influenced the decisions they made on behalf of their children, were also explored. The roles of parents, teachers, the State and the Catholic Church in children's education were studied in question two. Questions three and four examined the involvement of parents in children's socialisation and learning, both at home and at school. Question five probed the respondents' relationship with the school. Particular attention was paid to the home-school communication systems and how involved these parents were in the school. Participants were asked to outline the changes they had noticed in the education system in question six. Question seven was used to develop a profile of the respondents.

Focus Groups

It was hoped that the social interaction of the focus groups would produce a dynamic and insightful exchange of information, which would spark ideas, aid recall and produce rich data (Darlington and Scott, 2002, p. 62). While group interviews take the pressure off individuals to respond to every question and reduce the influence of the interviewer, they may, through peer pressure, innate reserve and fear of potential embarrassment, interfere with individual expression (Fontana and Frey, 2003, p. 73). As some participants, lower socio-economic status women in particular (Madriz, 2003, p. 381), may be less likely to participate in discussions than others, it was important to establish rapport and trust (May, 2001, p. 130) between myself and members of the groups and let it be known that it is acceptable for them to disagree on issues. Therefore, the rules of the focus group were outlined at the beginning of each session.

Question one in the focus group asked the participants to describe the qualities of a good school. In question two, the factors which influenced parents were explored. The roles of parents, teachers, the State and the Catholic Church were discussed in question three. Questions four to seven were used to explore the home-school relationship and the involvement of parents in their children's schools. Participants were asked to outline the changes they had noticed in Irish education in question nine.

Pilot

There were two pilot interviews and one focus group. One interview was with my husband and the other was with the Special Needs assistant in the pilot school. Both, while being involved in their children's education, found the questions quite difficult to answer as neither of them had considered these issues before. The pilot focus group was also held in the pilot school. The principal arranged for the parents to be at the school an hour earlier than they normally would to collect their children. Seven parents/guardians turned up which is about half the parent population in that school. The pilot focus group was interesting in that the group, while very happy with the school and the education their children were receiving, appeared to have very little educational capital. They felt that the role of parents was to send their children to school and it was up to the school to educate them. They found many of the questions difficult and somewhat abstract.

These pilots highlighted the need to be more flexible during the interviews, more reflective about the participants' replies and not to be discouraged by people's inability or unwillingness to answer questions (Michael, 2004, p. 438). There was also a need to concentrate on the overall presentations as well as the answers to individual questions. The possible value in the attitudes, comments, gestures as well as the recorded answers needed to be recognised.

As the interviews were held after the questionnaires were returned, the existing questions were reviewed and altered some to include real-life examples that participants could relate to and perhaps answer more easily. I realised that I had to take into consideration that I had reflected on these issues more than most parents.

Data Collection

One of the principals, to make it easier for the school, suggested that parents would receive a letter requesting an interview. This seemed to be ideal in that the school would not be mediating which parents would be interviewed. A letter was drawn up explaining the purpose and format of the interview and distributed to all parents in first and third classes. There was a very low response rate. The reasons given by some of the parents were that they had already filled in the questionnaire for another child, they were apprehensive about doing an interview or that they were simply too busy doing other things.

There were four replies from the middle class girls' school – three mothers and a father. All four, when contacted, agreed to be interviewed. Two were interviewed in their homes, one in the school and one at work. While two parents from the middle class boys' school agreed to be interviewed, one was unavailable as she had just had a baby. The other, who was on the parents association, had agreed to represent them on the focus group. While no parents from the disadvantaged boys' school agreed to be interviewed, two parents from the disadvantaged girls' school agreed to be interviewed in the school. One never showed up and the other was a grandfather, who had reared his own family and was now guardian to his granddaughter. In order to ensure a balance between the views of middle class and disadvantaged parents, the HSCL teacher arranged for me to interview three other parents in the school.

Arranging focus groups was also difficult. The HSCL teacher for the disadvantaged schools arranged one focus group for me. The seven parents who took part were, according to the principal, a mixed group. The principals in the middle class schools raised the issue with their parents associations. In the middle class boys' school, two parents volunteered to be interviewed. While the principal said that he'd try to get a few more, it did not work out. At the parents association meeting one of the parents agreed to phone me and arrange the time for the interview. Her child was in hospital and she forgot. When I turned up in the morning there was no one there. The principal phoned both parents and set a time for after school that day. In the middle class girls' school, the principal gave me the phone number of the chairperson of the parents association. However, she warned me that the parents had done tremendous work fundraising for the school and that they were a little burnt out. When I rang the chairperson she felt that people had had enough and we agreed not to go ahead with the focus group.

Data Analysis

The tape of each interview and focus group was transcribed. The content was analysed under the various themes. These included educational values and decision-making; influences and supports; roles of parents, teachers, State and Church; home-school relationships and communication; involvement in their children's learning and schools; and finally changes in education. These were integrated with the results from the questionnaires. A unique identification was given to each interview and focus group. This code described the research method [Interview (I) or Focus Group (FG)]; the order in which the data was collected [7 or the seventh person interviewed]; school status [Disadvantaged (D) or Middle Class (M)] and the participants' relationship to the child [Mother (M); Father (F); Grandfather (GF)].

As it was more authentic hearing from the interviewees themselves, sections of the interviews were extracted to illustrate their views. All names of people and places were taken out to preserve anonymity. An alternative wording was typed in square brackets in order to fill the gaps and ensure that the meaning of the extract was preserved. What I said is written in italics, while '…' was inserted to indicate that part of their speech was left out. Individuals are not identified in the focus group, though a new separate line was used to show that someone different was talking.

That school has a really good record now

That young one now she was the lucky one

A lot of her neighbours and friends now didn't get their children in (FG1D)

When analysing the data, it became obvious that some participants had difficulty understanding the questions and had not previously thought too deeply about the topic.

> *What or who influences your decisions around your child's education and schooling?*
>
> Really, can you break it down a bit? I do not really understand what you mean by that? (I2DM)

Even when asked about the role or job of the teacher, there was an acceptance that teachers teach but what that involved they were not too sure.

> *How would you describe the teacher's job in children's education?*
>
> God bless us, I do not know how they do it
>
> *Yeah, but what do you think they should be doing? What is their role? How is it different from yourself and your husband?*
>
> I know what you mean, yes, the role, you know what, the role, I do not know – give them the facts, you know. (3MM)

There were also gaps in knowledge particularly around the curriculum and school governance.

There also appeared to be a social class difference in the linguistic and cultural competence (Bourdieu, 1977a, p. 494) of the interviewees with some of the disadvantaged parents reluctant to elaborate on or explain their views. Several questions were required to get the same amount of information middle class parents gave in one question. Middle class parents appeared to be more at ease in discussing their views with others and often considered several aspects of an issue when replying. These two discussions around the ethos of the school are good examples.

> *How important is the Catholic ethos of the school to you?*
>
> [Pause] It'd be important, you know what I mean but they do not go to Mass. They do not but if there is anything going on in the school they could participate in it
>
> *Would you send your child to a school that was non-Catholic?*

No

Why not?

I just wouldn't [Laughter] (I7DM)

How important is the Catholic ethos of the school to you?

In the school – I wouldn't say it is – it is a Catholic school and we did consider sending [our child] to [the Church of Ireland school] and the main reason we didn't was from, it wasn't from the religion perspective. It was more from a facilities perspective and from a size perspective. It is a very good and a very happy little school but they do not have a huge amount of resources for the kids – in terms of facilities and so on. So having said that I would still – but I still wouldn't have any problem sending any of ours to [the Church of Ireland school] from that perspective but they do look after the religious education of the kids. I consider that important and we are Catholics so [the local Catholic school] – well I am not sure how they do it but they do look after the first communion angle even within [the Church of Ireland school] so any Catholic kids in [the Church of Ireland school] are still looked after from the Holy Communion perspective. So I do think that it is important that they get religion education and as Catholics we would be keen that they would be brought along from that perspective but the fact that the school itself, whether the school itself is a Catholic school wouldn't be a very big factor. (I4MF)

It could also be that the middle class parents had volunteered of their own accord to do the interview. They had been contacted in advance by phone. Three of the disadvantaged parents, who had been recruited by the HSCL teacher, may have had very little advance notice. Therefore, they may have had less information and little time to reflect on the topic before the interview. Some were quite anxious about doing the interviews.

Documentary Analysis

Notes, newsletters and information booklets, which are designed to communicate with parents were analysed. These documents represent a reflection of reality and a method by which power is expressed and social order accomplished (May, 2001, pp. 182-3). The rationale behind the documentation, as well as its language and content was analysed

(Creswell, 2003, p. 186). What is excluded may be as important as what is included.

Pilot

While doing the literature review, I collected the notes sent home by my daughter's school for that year. This amounted to fifty notes. They were then categorised and analysed. This data was given to the school in preparation for their Whole School Evaluation (WSE).

Data Collection

As it would be difficult and time consuming for a school to keep track of all the notes sent home during the school year, four of the case study schools were asked for their parent information booklets as well as a sample of the general notes sent home to parents during the year. However, as the principal of one of the boys' school was seriously ill and the other was involved in a Whole School Evaluation, no documentation was obtained from the boys' school. In the middle class girls' school, the principal gave copies of their monthly newsletters for the last two years as well as their Junior Infant information booklet and a general information booklet for parents. The disadvantaged girls' school gave me their information pack for Junior Infant parents, which was developed and used by all the schools in their HSCL cluster. I also received their own information booklet for Junior Infant parents, their pack for all parents, copies of their newsletters for a year as well as a sample of notes and policies. These were analysed and compared with the notes, information booklets and policies sent home by my daughter's school.

Data Analysis

After analysing the content of fifty of the notes sent home by the local girls' school, preliminary categories were devised for interpreting the data. These included requests for parental involvement and finance, support for parents in their role as educators along with information about policies, events and closures/dates. The involvement of other agencies in the school was noted. Having analysed the content of the documentation from the three schools, it was difficult to compare them accurately as each of them had very different styles. Two schools sent out four newsletters a year, which was supplemented by formal notes from the principal. In the local girls' school, the parents association wrote the newsletter, while in the disadvantaged girls' school, it was the responsibility of the HSCL teacher. In the middle class girls' school, a monthly newsletter, which was more formal than the ones in the other schools, replaced the individual notes sent home by the school. However, notes were still sent out for particular issues, which concerned individual classes or were of immediate importance.

In the end, it was decided to compare the newsletters, the information books for Junior Infants and the general information packs for parents. There were a lot of similarities between the documentation and the activities engaged in by the schools. However, when analysing the infant parent information booklets, a possible bias was identified. As I had facilitated staff planning days on the development of these booklets in the two middle class schools, I would have had a certain amount of influence on the content. This is particularly evident in the infant school my daughters attended, where I would have insisted that certain items such as the complaints procedures should be included. I, therefore, decided to exclude the information books from the study.

While, all the newsletters informed parents of school closures/events, events, extra-curricular activities, fundraising and policies, some schools emphasised particular items more than others. The efforts of the children, parents and teachers were acknowledged in all schools and parents were encouraged to get involved in various activities. In the middle class schools, the choices offered were joining the parents association, helping out with fundraising and some school activities. In the disadvantaged girls' school, parental participation in the HSCL classes, learning programmes for children and other school activities was promoted. Parental input in to decision-making or governance was rarely mentioned. All of the newsletters concentrated on local school-related issues. There was no mention of national issues, which impact on parents and education. The parents associations in the middle class schools were affiliated to the NPCP and so their parents should also receive the NPCP newsletter. This contains information about national issues.

Eventually, after some consideration and another attempt to get documentation from the boys' schools, the analysis of the documentation from four of the case study schools was excluded. Each time a piece of documentation is referred to, a code was written beside it. It consisted of the research method [SD], the school [Disadvantaged Girls (DG); Middle Class Girls (MG); Local School (LS)] followed by the year. The analysis of the notes sent home by the local girls' school was included to illustrate the frequency and content of correspondence from school to home.

Conclusion

The purpose of this research is to evaluate the impact of the national policy of parental involvement in their children's education and schooling. The development of the research methodology is outlined in this chapter. The case study method was chosen as it allowed me to use of a variety of approaches (Gray, 2004), both qualitative and quantitative.

Five single sex Catholic primary schools in north Dublin, which were part of my database as an SDPS facilitator, were chosen to be part of the case study. Three of the schools were in middle class areas. The other two were designated as DEIS Band 1 Urban (DES, 2005d, p. 78) and receive additional resources from the DES, which include the services of a HSCL teacher. Questionnaires, interviews and focus groups were used to explore the involvement of the parents in four of these schools in their children's education. Participant observation was used in the fifth school. Specific observations of various aspects of my own involvement with my children's education and school were used to support and further develop the data from the other schools. Documentary analysis was used to investigate how these schools communicated with parents. The findings are reported in the following chapters. As explained in this chapter, each participant was given a unique code to illustrate the research method used to obtain the information along with their social status and gender.

Realising that this research had limitations, I tried to be as reflexive as possible at each stage of the study (Coffey, 1999, p. 126; Darlington and Scott, 2002, p. 18). This meant frequently checking the research questions and the analysis of the data with the literature review and the findings from the various research methods.

Chapter Four

RESEARCH FINDINGS: HOME EDUCATION

Introduction

The findings from the various research methodologies are presented in the next two chapters. As the quantitative data from the questionnaires and qualitative data from the interviews, focus groups and field diaries are used to support and inform each other (Miles and Huberman, 1994, p. 310), the findings are integrated under themes relevant to the research questions, the evaluation criteria and the literature review. As outlined in Chapter Three, a unique code was given to each respondent to ensure that the contributions from particular individuals can be recognised. In addition, the abbreviation of the research methodology used to obtain this particular information is written beside the data and/or quote.

Much of a child's learning takes place outside the school (Macbeth and Ravn, 1994) and parents who may be 'missing' (Edwards and Alldred, 2000, p. 452) from the school's perspective may be very active in the home setting. This chapter focuses on the role of parents as 'the primary educators' (Ireland, 1937) of their children. As the values, norms and identities of the respondents influence their parenting practices, the following section deals with the background information of the respondents in this research. It describes how the various variables, like gender, age, family status, education and employment levels, are both represented and connected with each other in this research. The particular variables, which are most influential on parental practices, are highlighted in all sections of this and subsequent chapters. Section three examines the respondents' perception of their roles and responsibilities in rearing and educating their children. This is followed by the decision-making processes, which the respondents used to guide their children through the education process and to choose both primary and secondary schools for their children. Section five describes the support and network systems, which help parents to educate and rear their children, while the section six looks at parental involvement in the home curriculum. The final section describes how parents support the school at home.

Background Information

This research was a case study based on five single sex Catholic schools within a three mile radius in North Dublin. Two of the schools, a boys' and a girls', were designated as DEIS Band 1 Urban by the Department of Education and Science (DES), which meant that they were two of the 150 Irish primary schools with the highest concentration of disadvantaged pupils (DES, 2005d, p. 78). They were on the one campus and shared a Home School Community Liaison (HSCL) coordinator. A large number of their parents were involved with children's learning programmes and adult education classes. While having no official parents association, they had a parents' fundraising committee. The other two, a boys' and a girls', were in a nearby middle class area. They were about a half a mile apart in the same parish. Both had very active parents associations. Some of their children may have been from disadvantaged areas as there is a trend for parents from disadvantaged areas to send their children to nearby middle class schools. The principal of the girls' school suggested that her school had less of these children than the boys' school.

The fifth school, which is the local school that my children attended, was an all-girls senior school in a middle class area. It had a very active parents association, which was affiliated to the National Parents Council – Primary (NPCP). Like the other middle class schools some of its children came from disadvantaged areas. This school was in the same second level catchment area as the other four schools.

This section examines the profile of the schools as well as the respondents to the questionnaire, interviews and focus groups. It investigates the sample population along with the data on variables such as gender, age, citizenship, religion, employment, education levels of the respondents and their children, along with family type and size. The influence of these variables on the profiles of the respondents is also explored.

The Researcher as a Participant Observer

Initially when I started this research, my theories on parental involve-ment in their children's education were implicit. As the literature review progressed the multidimensional nature of the policy of parental in-volvement became apparent. As an integral part of the State's family policy, it was not only linked to many other national policies, but to de-mocracy, globalisation and the substance of the welfare state itself. The relationship between parents, society, schools, the Church and the State is discussed almost daily in the media. The tensions between the tradi-tional patriarchal familism policy paradigm and the more recent para-digm of egalitarian individualism (Fahey, 1998) are apparent as the country tries to come to terms with and plan for changes in society. The changing roles of the bishops and the laity were central to discussions on the future of the Catholic Church in Ireland, not just in education, but also in the community. As a practising Catholic, these issues were im-portant concerns in my life.

At a local and personal level, I became aware of the 'cultural capital' available, not only to me as an educated professional parent, but to other parents. It was interesting to observe how parents networked to get in-formation on parenting strategies, their children's developmental and educational needs along with information on their schools and individual teachers. They used this information along with their cultural and eco-nomic capital to influence the schools' agendas and to supplement the education being provided by the school. I also became aware of how my children used my 'cultural capital' (Bourdieu, 1997, p. 47) to their ad-vantage in their interactions with their teachers. The gender aspect of parenting was obvious, not only in my relationship with my husband, but also in the relationships of other couples. There seems to be a continuous negotiation of parenting responsibilities and individual interests, with couples weighing up their choices in terms of their commitments to their work, partners and children. I also became more aware of my parenting style and skills, the tactics I used to 'display responsibility' (Silverman, 2004, p. 66) as a parent and the often subtle ways I supported my chil-dren's education and school. These issues influenced my values, which are embedded in the research process and theories (Ozga and Gewirtz, 1994, p. 122).

Questionnaires

Two hundred and sixty-four questionnaires were returned from four of the schools (Table 3.1). The majority of respondents described themselves as Irish (93 per cent, N=230) citizens. The remaining 7 per cent (N=18) were equally divided between citizens from the European Union (EU) (excluding Ireland) and non-EU countries. All four schools were Catholic schools under the patronage of the Catholic Archbishop of Dublin and the majority of respondents described themselves as Catholics (94 per cent, N=240). The remainder either had no religion (2 per cent, N=6) or belonged to other Christian religions (3 per cent, N=8) or to a non-Christian religion (1 per cent, N=2).

More questionnaires were returned from the middle class schools (Table 3.1). As outlined in Chapter Three, lower pupil-teacher ratios, parental literacy and poorer attendance levels in the disadvantaged schools may have accounted for the variations in the returns. As can be seen from Table 4.1, respondents from the middle class and disadvantaged schools differed from each other on variables such as gender, family status and employment and education levels.

Table 4.1: Differences between Respondents from Middle Class and Disadvantaged Schools

Variable	Middle Class Schools		Disadvantaged Schools		Total	
	N	*%*	*N*	*%*	*N*	*%*
Fathers	21	88	3	13	24	101*
Third level qualifications	50	82	11	18	61	100
Two-parent families	132	75	45	25	177	100
Paid employment (both full and part-time)	115	74	40	26	155	100
Total number of respondents across school type	168	64	96	36	264	100

* Result of rounding to whole numbers

Gender had a major influence on who returned the questionnaires. Most were completed by mothers (85 per cent, N=224). Only 9 per cent (N=24) were completed by fathers. They tended to be over forty (63 per cent, N=15) and have children in the senior classes of the middle class schools (71 per cent, N=17). In fact, 54 per cent (N=13) were from the middle class boys' school. They were also more likely to be in two-parent families (92 per cent, N=22) and in full-time paid employment (78 per cent, N=18). The remaining 6 per cent (N=15) of respondents were either guardians (3 per cent, N=8) or couples (3 per cent, N=7). As there were very few responses from guardians or couples, these variables will not be analysed and the term parent will be used to describe the respondents to the questionnaires.

Fifty-two per cent (N=136) of respondents were from the boys' schools and 49 per cent (N=128) were from the girls' schools. While the number of questionnaires returned by parents in the senior (N=132) and junior classes (N=132) was exactly the same, there were differences between classes. Twenty-eight per cent (N=75) of the respondents had children in sixth class, 22 per cent (N=57) had children in fourth, 31 per cent (N=82) had children in second and finally 19 per cent (N=50) had children in senior infants. Lower class sizes accounted for the low number of returns in senior infants, while the disadvantaged boys' school had two second classes. As can be seen from Table 4.2, the profile of the respondents who had children in junior and senior classes differed. Respondents with children in junior classes tended to be younger and have preschool children. They were less likely to have older children who had either left school and/or were attending secondary school. More fathers replied from the senior classes. Children's stage of development also seemed to impact on employment levels.

Family size varied from one to six children. Fifteen per cent of respondents (N=38) had only one child, 33 per cent (N=85) had two children, 30 per cent (N=78) had three children and 22 per cent (N=58) had between four and six children. No family had over six children. While middle class respondents tended to have smaller families, the percentage of respondents in one-child families was similar in the middle class and disadvantaged schools. As can be seen from Table 4.3, parents with smaller families tended to be younger.

Table 4.2: Differences between Respondents Who Had Children in the Senior and Junior Classes

Variable	Senior Classes		Junior Classes		Total	
	N	*%*	*N*	*%*	*N*	*%*
Fathers	18	75	6	25	24	100
Older children who have left school	18	69	8	31	26	100
Full-time paid employment	40	66	21	34	61	100
Children attending second level schools	56	65	30	35	86	100
Pre-school children	20	28	51	72	71	100
Aged under thirty	11	26	31	74	42	100
Total number of respondents across class levels	132	50	132	50	264	100

Table 4.3: The Link between the Age of the Respondent and Family Size

Variable	Under 30		30–39		40 and over		Total	
	N	*%*	*N*	*%*	*N*	*%*	*N*	*%*
One child	19	50	12	32	7	18	38	100
Two children	14	17	38	45	33	39	85	101*
Three children	4	5	37	48	36	47	77	100
Four or more children	4	7	24	42	29	51	57	100
Total	41	16	111	43	105	41	257	100

X^2=.000, p<.05

* Result of rounding to whole numbers

Parents from the disadvantaged schools also tended to be younger with only a quarter of them over 40 (27 per cent N=26). In contrast, nearly half (47 per cent N=79) of the respondents from middle class schools were over 40.

While 28 per cent (N=71) of respondents had children under the school-going age, 34 per cent (N=86) had children attending secondary school. Ten per cent (N=26) of respondents had children who had left school. Of these, two were under sixteen and had left school, four were unemployed, nine were in third level education and nineteen were working. Seven of the nine who said that they had children who were attending third level education were from the middle class schools. In addition, the two respondents who had children under sixteen years of age who were not attending school were from the disadvantaged schools as were three of the four respondents whose children who were unemployed. Apart from the respondents with children in second level, these variables are not analysed as the numbers involved are too small.

The family status, employment and education levels of the respondents were also important variables. Most (71 per cent, N=177) were in two-parent families, with little over a quarter (30 per cent, N=74) in one-parent families. While there was an equal number of respondents in either part-time (38 per cent, N=94) or not in (38 per cent, N=94) paid employment, only 25 per cent (N=61) were in full-time paid employment. Most respondents (67 per cent N=169) had a second level education. While 24 per cent (N=61) had gone to third level, 9 per cent (N=22) had attended only primary school. As stated previously, the schools the respondents' children attended and these variables were linked.

Interviews

I interviewed eight parents, four from the disadvantaged schools and four from the girls' middle class schools. While the participants from the disadvantaged area had children in various classes within the school, all the middle class interviewees had a child in first class in the girls' school. There were four mothers, a father (I4MF) and a grandparent (I1DGF). All except one (I5MM) was Irish. She was English and had attended Catholic schools in England. Two of the mothers (I5MM, I6MM) had children with special needs, who were attending learning support.

All of the middle class interviewees were in two-parent families with at least one parent in paid employment. In the case of the two families, where only one parent worked, one had a wife (I4MF) on career break because the children were so small. The other (I6MM) was heavily involved in a children's charity along with supporting her husband's business. All had some form of third level qualification and some (I3MM; I5MM) told me that they were still involved in further education. Most had two or three children. None of their children were in second level education yet. They were all between 35 and 45 years of age. None were members of the parents association. Of these parents, only one was committed to a Catholic education for their children (I5MM).

Three mothers and a grandfather were interviewed in the disadvantaged schools. Two of the mothers were aged between 30 and 39, while one of them was in her twenties. The grandfather was the guardian of the child. His eldest child was 29 and he looked as if he was in his 40s. Two (I1DGF; I2DM) worked outside the home. The three mothers were not living with the children's fathers, though in two cases (I2DM; I7DM) the fathers were still involved with the children. The third case (I8DM) had a partner who was very involved in rearing the children. These women were very active in the school and they were all doing various courses through the HSCL scheme. Two were committed to a Catholic education for their children (I2DM, I7DM).

Focus Group

For the focus group in the disadvantaged schools, I interviewed seven women. Two were very quiet and said little. According to the principal they represented most parents in the school. Most had done courses through the HSCL scheme and helped out with various activities in the school. One woman, the HSCL teacher told me, was very shy. She was one of her success stories as she had got her to do a course after seven years of persuasion. Another was very talkative and acted almost like the spokeswoman for the group. One of her children had ADHD. Having worked in a crèche for several years, she compared the accountability there to the accountability in schools.

In the middle class schools, the focus group consisted of two parents, who were members of the Parents Association in the boys' school. They were both 'stay-at-home' mothers and were heavily involved in both their children's education and the school.

Participants' Profile

The research population reflect the dominant status group in Irish Society. The majority of respondents were Irish Catholics. While both social classes were equally represented in the qualitative data, more questionnaires were returned from the middle class schools. While respondents were equally divided on the age and gender of their children, the majority who participated were mothers.

The profiles of the respondents differed depending on the status of their school and the size of their family. The respondents from the middle class schools tended to be older, living in two-parent families and have third level qualifications. They were also more likely to be employed either full-time or part-time. Younger respondents were more likely to have only one child. The respondents who were interviewed reflected these variables.

Parental Roles and Responsibilities

Parents are described as the primary educators of their child in the Irish Constitution (Ireland, 1937). In this section, the perceptions of respondents as to the roles and responsibilities of parents in their children's education are explored. Traditionally, gender defined the parents' role. Fathers were responsible for providing financial security and mothers were responsible for child rearing (Fahey, 1998). However, these distinctions have blurred in recent times.

Roles and Responsibilities of Parents

All the parents who were interviewed saw their role as nurturing, supporting and encouraging their children. They felt that parents had a crucial role to play in the education of their children.

> You're the nurturer and if you haven't nurtured your child, the child isn't going to do anything really. No matter what they're learning in school if they are not being nurtured and cared for and brought on at home, it just isn't going to click with them, nothing is going to work. (FG2M)

Interviewees also felt that it was important to monitor their children's development, behaviour and social networks both at home and at school.

> Well, not to be funny but to me it is to keep on top of everything like whether it is school or outside school, it is to know where they are, what they are doing, who their friends are, who their friends' families are. (I8DM)

The majority of the respondents to the questionnaire agreed that parents were the most important teachers of their children (88 per cent, N=229) and should always put their children's needs before their own (78 per cent, N=200). It is interesting that the parents in the disadvantaged boys' school had the strongest views on this (Table 4.4).

Table 4.4: Respondents' Perceptions on Whether Parents Are the Most Important Teachers of Their Children

Variable	Strongly Agree		Agree		Did Not Agree		Total	
	N	*%*	*N*	*%*	*N*	*%*	*N*	*%*
Disadvantaged boys' school	40	71	9	16	7	13	56	100
Disadvantaged girls' school	21	55	14	37	3	8	38	100
Middle class boys' school	33	42	31	40	14	18	78	100
Middle class girls' school	41	47	40	46	7	8	88	101*
Total	135	52	94	36	31	12	260	100

X^2=.005 p<.05

* Result of rounding to whole numbers.

While participants acknowledged the valuable work of teachers, very few felt that teachers had sole responsibility for any area of children's learning (Figure 4.1). A small minority thought that teachers were re-sponsible for Maths (16 per cent, N=42), literacy (10 per cent, N=27), socialisation (5 per cent, N=14) and behaviour (5 per cent, N=14).

Parent-teacher co-operation was seen as crucial in the development of children's socialisation, Maths and literacy skills. However, getting the children to school and ensuring that they had their books, pencils, copies and uniform was seen as the sole responsibility of parents. One mother described her role, 'My role is to send them here to school every day and to get them the best education that they can get. Get them to school on time' (I7DM). While a majority of respondents (68 per cent

N=178) took sole responsibility for homework, 32 per cent (N=83) saw it as a joint responsibility.

Figure 4.1: Respondents' Views on Where the Responsibility Lies for Children Having or Doing the Following

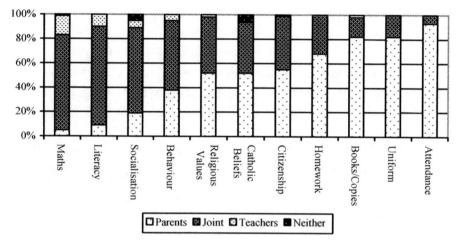

There was less agreement in the area of values and behaviour. While a majority (57 per cent N=146) felt that children behaving well in school was a joint responsibility, a sizeable minority (38 per cent N=98) saw it as being the sole responsibility of the parent and agreed with the interviewee who said, 'If the child is bold in school that is my fault – I'm wrong and the teacher is quite entitled to bring me up' (I1DGF). Similarly, respondents were divided between those who felt that parents were responsible for their children having religious values (52 per cent N=146), being good citizens and good Catholics and those who perceived these tasks as the joint responsibility of both teachers and parents.

Respondents from the disadvantaged schools appeared to feel more responsibility for their children's homework and citizenship. A total of 79 per cent (N=74) felt that parents were responsible for their children's homework as compared with 62 per cent (N=104) from the middle class schools. Similarly, 68 per cent (N=63) of the parents in the disadvantaged schools felt that parents were responsible for their children being good citizens as compared to 49 per cent (N=79) of middle class parents.

Lone-parents also appeared to assume more responsibility for their children than those in two-parent families. Seventy-seven per cent (N=57) of parents in one-parent families felt that parents were responsible for homework in comparison with 64 per cent (N=111) of those in two-parent families. Likewise 69 per cent (N=50) of those in one parent-families felt that parents were responsible for children being good citizens as opposed to 51 per cent (N=86) of those in two-parent families.

The education levels of the respondents influenced their perceptions on who had responsibility for children's education. The higher the respondents' level of education the more they perceived education as a joint responsibility between home and school (Table 4.5).

Table 4.5: Influence of the Respondents' Education Level on Their Perceptions that Education is the Joint Responsibility of Both Parents and Teachers

Variable	Primary School		Second Level		Third Level		Total Who Perceived Joint Responsibility	
	N	*%*	*N*	*%*	*N*	*%*	*N*	*%*
Maths*	13	65	129	77	50	82	192	77
Reading and writing	9	45	133	80	56	92	198	80
Mixing well	8	40	119	71	46	75	173	70
Good citizens*	7	35	65	39	32	54	104	43
Religious values*	5	24	72	45	33	54	110	45
Good Catholics	4	22	68	43	30	55	44	102
Homework*	4	19	51	31	24	39	79	32
Total number of respondents across education levels	22	8	167	67	61	23	252	100

* Not significant p<.05

Respondents with lower educational qualifications were also more likely to consider the teacher responsible for their children's literacy, numeracy and socialisation skills (Table 4.6).

Table 4.6: Influence of the Respondents' Education Level on Their Perceptions that Literacy, Numeracy and Socialisation Were the Responsibility of the Teacher

Variable	Primary School		Second Level		Third Level		Total Who Perceived Responsibility of Teacher	
	N	%	N	%	N	%	N	%*
Reading and writing	7	35	17	10	3	5	27	11
Mixing well	5	25	8	5	0	0	13	5
Maths*	6	30	24	14	10	16	40	16
Total number of respondents within education levels	22	8	167	67	61	23	252	100

* Not significant p<.05

Mothers

Social class influenced the views of the respondents on the role of the mother. In the interviews, disadvantaged parents described the mother's role mainly in relation to their children's behaviour.

> God, they do everything for them. It is how you teach them to look after themselves and how to respect other people and respect themselves, their manners and, you know everything. (I2DM)

Middle class parents talked about the work involved with being a mother. They explained how mothers supported and guided their children and introduced them to positive new experiences.

> By nature, they have the ability to be doing so many different things at the one time – they are able to listen to their children, they are able to do their homework and at the same time they have the shopping done and the meal planned and dinner ready and bag packed for the next day. (I6MM)

> I think try to expose them to as many new positive influences as possible, you know, to go places, take them to the theatre,

anything that you think will be new and novel, that they'd learn from, it is a positive thing and a learning experience. (I5MM)

Some mentioned the inherent conflict and demands of being a mother in today's world.

Tired [laughter], tired with two jobs and two kids

You'd be knackered

Yeah, knackered after all that and then I've got my course on a Friday morning as well, I'm wacked. Ah it a good job though, you get the rewards at the end. (I2DM)

In my case I had no option but to stop working ... All of the things that you'd think were a great loss to you, your career and everything ... but ... when you come to terms with being a stay-at-home mum for whatever reason and come to terms, you know, with being treated like only a mere 'mother' or whatever, ... it is good ... to be at home with the children and ... when children get older it is nearly more important for parents to be around. (I6MM)

It was interesting how many of the respondents felt that mothers were primarily responsible for their children's education (Figure 4.2).

Figure 4.2: Mothers Are Primarily Responsible for Their Children's Education (N=257)

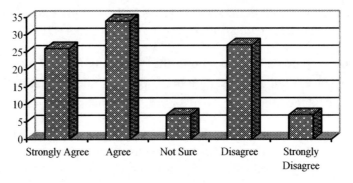

Views varied a great deal among participants. Only a quarter of fathers (26 per cent, N=6) as compared to almost two-thirds of mothers (64 per cent, N=139) agreed that mothers were primarily responsible for their children's education. As can be seen from Table 4.7, respondents from one-parent family felt strongly that mothers were primarily responsible for the education of their children.

Table 4.7: Differences between the View of Respondents from One-Parent and Two-Parent Families on Whether Mothers Were Primarily Responsible for Their Children's Education

Variable	Strongly Agree		Agree		Did Not Agree		Total	
	N	*%*	*N*	*%*	*N*	*%*	*N*	*%*
Two-parent families	31	18	66	38	76	44	173	100
One-parent families	32	44	19	26	21	29	72	99*
Total	63	26	85	35	97	40	245	101*

X^2=.000 p<.05

* Result of rounding to whole numbers.

Parents with children in the disadvantaged schools were also more likely to consider the mother responsible for their children's education. Almost three-quarters (73 per cent, N=69) agreed with this statement as compared with half (52 per cent, N=84) of middle class parents. Naturally enough employment levels had an impact on the perceptions of parents. Those in full-time paid employment were less likely to feel that mothers were primarily responsible for their children's education (Table 4.8). Only three of these were in one-parent families and they did not agree that mothers were primarily responsible for their children's education.

Fathers

Most respondents to the questionnaire agreed that fathers were responsible for their children's education (Figure 4.3).

Table 4.8: Influence of Employment Levels on Respondents' Views on Whether Mothers Were Primarily Responsible for Their Children's Education

Variable	Strongly Agree		Agree		Did Not Agree		Total	
	N	%	N	%	N	%	N	%
Employed full-time	5	9	20	34	34	58	59	101*
Employed part-time	24	26	30	33	38	41	92	100
Not in paid employment	31	34	34	37	27	29	92	100
Total	60	25	84	35	99	41	243	101*

$X^2 = .002$ p<.05

* Result of rounding to whole numbers.

Figure 4.3: Fathers Are Responsible for Their Children's Education (N=261)

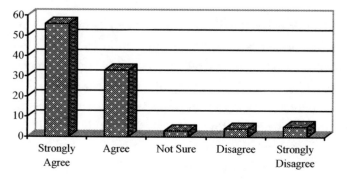

There were only a few differences between the respondents. For obvious reasons, those in one-parent families were less likely to agree with this statement. Only 80 per cent (N=59) agreed that fathers were responsible for their children's education as compared to 93 per cent (N=161) of those in two-parent families. It is interesting that respondents with higher levels of education were more likely to agree that fathers were responsible for their children's education (Table 4.9).

Table 4.9: The Impact of the Respondents' Education Levels on Their Views on Whether Fathers Are Responsible for Their Children's Education

Variable	Strongly Agree		Agree		Did Not Agree		Total	
	N	%	N	%	N	%	N	%
Primary level qualification	9	43	4	19	8	38	21	100
Second level qualification	92	55	58	35	17	10	167	100
Third level qualification	38	62	20	33	3	5	61	100
Total	139	56	82	33	28	11	249	100

X^2=.001 p<.05

Most of those who were interviewed, felt that there was no difference between the mother's and father's role. The two men were very definite about this.

> What we do at the minute as two guardians and grandparents, we both work, she cooks, I clean up, I wash, I iron, anything, she does the same. I think a mother's role right now is the same as a father's ... the mother is the one who bears the child and all that but once the child is out and running about a parent is a parent - in any form, a foster parent, a real parent. I think it is that association you have with the child in the early years that bonds with it, you know. (I1DGF)

> I think no different to the mother's job. I would see it more as a question of the parents' job rather than the father's job in terms of, at one stage both myself and my wife worked – my wife is on a career break – so at various times I would have taken a day's leave to look after the kids. I would have no issues in terms of looking after them. My wife was away for ten days over Easter so I looked after them and in terms of the kids and all the household stuff, my wife would be doing more because she is at home ... I wouldn't see any issue in terms of or distinction between what a father does and what a mother does. (I4MF)

The mothers, however, suggested that it depended on the personality of the father and the circumstances of the family. While fathers could be very supportive and interested in their children, the final decisions and a lot of the work was often left to mothers. This was particularly noticeably in one-parent families.

> *What, do you feel, is the father's job in child rearing and education?*
>
> Basically the same as mine but my role I probably have that bit more say.
>
> *Why would you have more say?*
>
> O, I'm on my own. I do not have a partner. Anything I decide - I make all the decisions.
>
> *Do they see their Dad?*
>
> Yeah, well the littlest one does, the other two do not and he's great like that, he'd come over if there are meetings or anything, he'd come over for the parent-teacher meeting and all that and if there are any problems he'd go up to the school, but at the end of the day the decision would be left to me. (I7DM)

Others suggested that roles were worked out to meet the needs of the family and that fathers had a different, but just as important, role as mothers. Some perceived that fathers were important role models. One mother said that children 'knocked great fun' (I6MM) out of doing physical activities such as sports with their fathers. They could also confide in their father, or in this case the male partner, in a way that they could not confide in their mother.

> Now we have a system in our house where they do not talk to me they talk to him, you know and then like for a long time they'd say to him, 'Do not tell me ma'. He'd say 'right ok', now he did tell me but I wouldn't act on it. He'd deal with it so we had that kind of thing going, you know, so it was handy enough that way. (I8DM)

Some suggested that 'old fashioned' views and women's attitudes prevent fathers from taking more of a role in their children's education and lives.

> I think we stigmafy (sic) fathers, maybe it is old fashioned views that they do not commit. It might be that we do not let them, it is not their fault. It is our fault that they do not come in to it. (FG1D)

'Stay-at-home' mums, through networking, build up their knowledge of the education system. This gives them an advantage over fathers when making educational decisions.

> If you have a stay-at-home mum, whose been at home for maybe five, six, seven years prior to the child starting school, obviously she's going to have been networking and she is going to know things that the Dad is not going to know: 'Who so and so is? What school? Who? What happened? There's drugs where?' This is what you get. (FG2M)

For a lot of parents it was 'the practicalities of the whole thing' (I5MM) with mothers' employment schedules often allowing them spend more time with the children. Lacking confidence in their own abilities, fathers may rely on the expertise of the mother and perceive their role as one of supporting her or 'backing her up'.

> Well I definitely think that the problem is that my husband is not academic. He will always say 'What do you think?' but he's actually very good with them. He will sit with them, do the reading, but sometimes I think it is more me that tends to do it but I am here more as well. I only work three days a week and I think that has something to do with it. (I3MM)

Educational Choices

This section looks at the attitudes of the participants in this research towards their children's education. It examines their hopes and fears for their children along with the strategies they use to ensure their educational future. Participants in this research had a variety of primary and secondary schools to which they could choose to send their children. Their access to and use of information about these schools along with the factors which influenced their decision-making processes are explored. As Bourdieu (1974, p. 33) suggested that parental attitudes towards school are influenced by social class, the differences between the middle class and disadvantaged parents are outlined.

Attitudes and Motivation

Interviewees were asked what their hopes and fears for their children were. The middle class parents wanted their children to be happy, confident, well-rounded individuals who would go on to third level. One (I3MM) was studying herself for a nursing degree and hoped that her daughter would follow her example:

> I feel that it is the norm because she sees me going to college, she sees me studying and it is not normal to see a Mammy doing that … I have to laugh. Sometimes you feel like the big sister because I am talking about being a student in college and doing exams – O my God – and she's only seven. (I3MM)

The disadvantaged parents hoped that their children would stay on at school and get a good job. When asked how long they wanted their children to stay on in education, they said, 'Hopefully on to college' (I7DM, I8DM). Their fears for their children were very specific and centred on their immediate environment or 'street'. Their greatest fear was that their children would meet up the wrong crowd who 'are in trouble with the police or drugs or drink'. (I8DM).

In contrast, many of the middle class parents had vague fears for their children.

> Ah, sure I wouldn't say we have any – what are our fears? Ahem that they are not happy. That they would get into danger in some way or other – that they have accidents. Ahem, ahem, but I wouldn't say – it is not something that we – at the moment. Our focus is on keeping them safe. We try not to worry about global warming or nuclear fall out or what ever. I wouldn't say that there are any dominating fears, you know anything in particular. (I4MF)

They also had fears that their children would not be academically able for school or have a teacher that would let them down. They were very aware of the points systems and tried not to let it duly influence their decisions.

> I do not want my children to be under appalling pressure to get the right amount of points and it is amazing because [the 11-year-old] is extra-ordinarily bright, … and she is already determined what she wants to be and she had already found out and talked to baby minders and older cousins – she knows exactly currently how many points she needs to get – she feels she is not very good at Irish and she asked me recently to organised private classes because she is so determined. (I6MM)

There was also the worry that as teenagers their children would do something that would limit their educational opportunities.

> You never know, you know children's personalities come in to it. When she is sixteen she might be a total bloody nightmare and rebel, some one you can't control. I would hope that from being very young up that she'd have that idea [of going to college]. (I3MM)

When parents were asked what they were doing to make their hopes come through, the middle class parents talked about the importance of proving a happy stable environment, spending time with their children doing different activities and the different methods they used to influence their children. Disadvantaged parents, on the other hand, had a variety of strategies to ensure that their hopes came true. These included bringing their children up properly, keeping an eye on them, having a strict routine especially around homework and helping out in the school. Despite these strategies, there was also the feeling that how their children turned out was out of their control.

> Well I can't really stop them. The only thing I can do is I tell the kids the rights and wrongs and teach them everything there is that I can teach them At the end of the day I have to say to my young fella (sic), you have the information, what you do with it now is your call. It will be down to him. (I8DM)

Choosing Schools

Parents in this study had a good selection of primary and secondary schools to which they could send their children. There was a range of schools in the area including various Catholic schools, Gaelscoileanna, Church of Ireland and Educate Together schools. For two of the middle class parents (I3MM, I6MM) the school their children were attending was not their first preference. One (I3MM) had tried to enrol her child in the Gaelscoil but there were no places. The other (I6MM) had originally sent her children to a small inner city Church of Ireland school but moved them because the children could not socialise.

> There were lots of children coming from, I suppose, disadvantaged areas certainly and a lot of the children there were from one-parent families, which sort of really wasn't a problem but culturally, there was such a huge cultural difference between totally inner city children and I suppose children from a middle class background and what made me move in the end was that the children literally couldn't socialise ... some of the children were so rough and though a few of them were individually lovely children, their parents were – *[short laugh]* – I mean I would be there at the school like a duck out of water. (I6MM)

Likewise, one of the disadvantaged parents (I7DM) had originally sent her children to a Gaelscoil but removed them because 'it did not work out' and she felt that her children's English had suffered. Another of the disadvantaged parents (I8DM), though still involved with school, had moved her child from the disadvantaged school to a more middle class school because she felt that these schools had a better support system.

All the parents were very much aware of the different secondary schools in the area and the reputations. All of the middle class parents had their children's names down in at least one secondary school. These were mainly local schools though two did have their names down for a city centre fee-paying school.

> Yeah. I put her down when she was in Senior Infants and was told that 'Oh, you left it a bit late'. I nearly died. I thought, 'O my God' and they said 'She'll probably get in – not to worry'. Now I did go, it was from other parents I found out who was putting them in, that's where most of the kids were going – word of mouth in the school yard. (I3MM)

In contrast, only one of the disadvantaged parents (I1DGF) was even considering sending their children to the local secondary school. He felt that his granddaughter had had a good education so far and would continue on to the local secondary school with her friends. He had not sent his own children to the local schools but felt in retrospect that they were better resourced because they were in disadvantaged areas. The others were reluctant to send their children to the local school because they felt that they would meet 'nicer kids' (I2DM) in the middle class schools. They also thought that behaviour problems in the local schools would either interfere with their children's education or lead them astray.

> I do not know about the [local secondary school] because I think the [local secondary school] has changed ... They get an awful lot of time off. I suppose there is trouble in every school, beatings and that so I will just have to wait and see ...

> There's stabbings over there

> ... the staff are under unbelievable pressure. Now I am not putting it all down to the school because I am not going to badmouth the school, but they do not have the time for individual students and there is an awful lot of students over there as well. (FG1D)

However, none of them, unlike the middle class parents, stated that they had put their children's names down in the secondary schools of their choice. One woman suggested, '... if you are sending them somewhere, find out a month in advance about the school' (FG1D). The reason may have been as one person suggested in the focus group:

> If I had of lived in a different area I would have been more aware of looking in to schools and had a bit more money, I'd be more aware of looking in to primary schools and going through the system and saying that has a good record for this and ... But ... when you are living here and unemployed when the kids started, the nearest school or whatever was there you took it. While if I had to do it all again ... (FG1D)

There was no awareness that their choice of secondary school was limited if their children's names were not on the waiting list. Many disadvantaged parents had a fatalistic attitude believing that it did not really matter which school you send your children to. At the end of the day if the children were not willing to learn the school could do little about it.

> There is not much difference between schools. If a child is not
> going to learn it doesn't matter what school they go to, you know
> what I mean. (FG1D)

Factors which Influenced Their Choice of School

While many factors influenced their choice of school, the 'good name'
and academic reputation of the school was a primary consideration.
While respondents were influenced by the reputation of the school, its
location to either their home or child care was also important. Many felt
that the 'the logistics of getting them there' (I5MM) was also important.

> The only thing I suppose is maybe if it was your parish school
> and it was a good school I'd say that an awful lot of the children
> would just automatically fall in. I found that now with [the
> Middle Class Girls' School]. Like there was never a question of
> going anywhere else to school because it had a fantastic name
> and it was a parish school. (FG2M)

For some, either they or a member of their family had attended the
school and were happy with it.

> My father went there … All his brothers and sisters were there,
> we were all there so it was a family thing. (I3MM)

Feedback from family, work colleagues and friends, particularly if they
were teachers, was important in helping parents decide on schools.

> My friend – my friend has her boy down there. Now he's doing
> his Junior Cert. She actually recommended [secondary school]
> for me and his teacher as well, his teacher does [coaching for the
> local GAA club] and he recommends the [secondary school] as
> well. (I7DM)

Those not from the locality can find it difficult to access this inside information.

> It is sort of quite hard – it is quite hard to make those decisions
> about school and I am not from Dublin and … I just did not know
> this area and … I didn't know a single person who had children
> in this area either. Most of my friends didn't – or do not have
> children … and it is amazing, once you get it to it, your children

then go to school and you start circulating with other parents, within a few years you have the whole school system. (I6MM)

To ensure that their children attended a school with 'nice kids' (I2DM), they monitored the behaviour of the pupils, both past and present, of the various local schools.

The other thing would be and it is probably myself (sic) – I went to [the local secondary school] and I see the girls coming out. Isn't that awful? I feel an awful snob, but they have that look about them and I say 'Noooo'. I do not want her to go there … Now it could be me really getting old and that. I see them all with the make-up and the hair and all that. (I3MM)

The size and amount of resources available to the school were important features with the middle class father defining resources in the following terms:

All sort of resources – in terms of physical building, in terms of playground, in terms of teaching resources, obviously, good teachers, good ethos in the school, happy atmosphere in the school, good proactive parents committee who have a say in the running of the school. (I4MF)

The 'approachability' of the school, along with its support system and handling of misbehaviour was also an important quality to all parents.

For me it is an approachable school. People in it have to be approachable. A school with a lot of rules and regulations, I have to honest with you and to me a support system is a big plus. (I8DM)

Social Capital

According to Putnam (2000, p. 296), a child's development is powerfully shaped by the social capital of their parents. This section examines the variety of supports that parents find useful in helping them to educate and rear their children. It also looks at parents' networks and how they are used to inform their decisions about their children's education and schooling.

Sources of Support and Advice

Participants got support and advice on educating and rearing their children from various places. They were most likely to get support and advice on bringing up and educating their children from their immediate family members, in particular their parents and their partner (Table 4.10). Quite a few found their own children a useful source of support and advice. Outside the family circle, their child's teacher, their friends and other parents were important supports. Fewer participants got advice and support from parenting courses, the school principal, the Church and neighbours.

Table 4.10: Sources of Support and Advice for Respondents on Bringing Up and Educating Their Children

Sources of Support and Advice	N	%
Family	198	78
Grandparents	170	67
Partner	162	64
Child's teacher	159	63
Friends	136	54
Their children	107	42
Other parents	107	42
Books	95	37
Parenting courses	65	26
School principal	58	23
Newspapers and magazines	51	20
Television	46	18
The Church	43	17
Neighbours	36	14
Public health nurse	34	13
Their doctor	31	12
Internet	23	9
Home school teachers	13	5
Social workers	11	4
Gardaí	7	3
Therapist	7	3

Very few considered the professional services, apart from teachers, supportive. While a few found the public health nurse and their doctor helpful, other professionals such as the HSCL teachers, social workers, Gardaí or therapists were not perceived to be a useful source of advice and support in rearing their children. Apart from books, the media like newspapers or magazines, television or even the Internet was not considered helpful. However, one interviewee did mention using the 'Super Nanny' techniques from a television programme when disciplining her child but did not appear to find them very effective.

> He's [the three-year-old] a devil. He throws tantrums. He throws things … I have been trying Super Nanny, positive reinforcement and all that kind of stuff with him and I used to put him out in the hall but now he just walks out himself now and closes the door. It is totally wasted on him. (I3MM)

Most interviewees felt that you needed to go to someone whose opinion you respected. 'Teacher friends' or teachers who taught in a school other than the one you sent your children were a very useful sounding board to middle class parents.

> Or someone that you know and respect and valued their opinion who already had …

> I think I would ring another teacher from another school. I have a teacher friend so. They would be a lot of support because they would be dealing with the situation and would know.

> Somebody with experience. (FG2M)

Parental Networks

It was interesting to observe how parents networked locally to get information on parenting issues, schools and individual teachers. They used this information along with their cultural and economic capital to influence the schools' agendas and to supplement the education being provided by the school.

Parents can network with other parents outside the school in three ways. They can talk with other parents informally at the school, shops or other venues, join a group outside the school and/or attend talks and

classes organised for parents. The majority (81 per cent N=212) of respondents to the questionnaire talked to other parents about the school
(Figure 4.4). Most, like the women in this middle class focus group, felt
that they were a most useful source of information.

In the school yard listening to

Exactly

Or in the supermarket every morning

'Cause that's where you hear it all

That's exactly where you hear it all

Talking to others

Ear to the ground really. (FG2M)

Figure 4.4: Parental Networking Outside the School

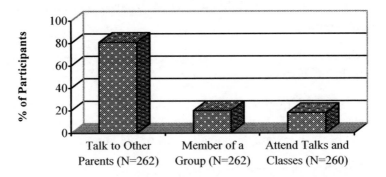

From my observations, these conversations happened informally and
were unplanned. Particularly around times of transitions, parents made a
concerted effort to gather information about the school they were hoping
that their child would attend.

One Saturday morning at a local shop, I stood discussing a local
mixed second level school with a friend. We were asked by a
mother, who was passing by, if we were talking about the
transition year in the local boys' secondary school. A discussion
on our children and their study habits followed. She mentioned
that she had two girls and I asked her what school they were

attending. When she said the local girls' secondary school that my daughter was hoping to go to, I asked her how they were getting on. Then another mother joined in and said that her three girls had gone there and that it was a great school. (FN03-06-06)

Support networks can also be used to establish standards and check if the teacher is doing her or his job.

One of [my child's] friends would be on the other half – there are two classes in the year … you always try not to compare like but the other girl was reading more and quicker than [my child] and was that down to the two girls or down to the teachers and then another friend of ours moved down the country last year and sort of by the end of the year, she was flying along in terms of reading and what not, you know, you say to yourself –well so be it let the teacher do what the teacher does at the teacher's own pace as long as you are happy that the teacher is sort of competent and up to the job. (I4MF)

Few respondents used other methods to network with other parents. Only 18 per cent (N=46) went to talks and classes organised for parents outside the school. Less than a quarter (20 per cent, N=51) of respondents to the questionnaire were involved with other organisations outside the school. These ranged from sporting, community and Church groups. 8 per cent (N=21) were involved in various sporting and leisure organisations. These included the local Gaelic Athletic Association, soccer, swimming and athletic clubs along with dancing and drama. The same amount (8 per cent, N=21) were involved in community groups such as the residents' associations, community games and neighbourhood watch. Three (1 per cent) were doing a course, while only five (2 per cent) were involved in Church activities.

Social Capital

A wide range of variables influenced the social capital of the respondents in this research. These included gender, religious belief, social class including education and lone parenting. Family size and the age of the respondents' children also influenced their perceptions of their support network. As highlighted previously in section one, many of these variables are interrelated.

Regular attendees at church appeared to be better networkers. Seventy-one per cent (N=153) of those who spoke to other parents about the school attended church monthly. Similarly, 85 per cent (N=41) of those who were member of a group outside the school attended church at least once a month. As can be seen from Table 4.11, the majority (96 per cent, N=43) of those who attended talks and classes outside the school attended church at least once a month.

Table 4.11: Influence of Attendance at Church on Attendance at Talks and Classes Organised for Parents Outside the School

Variable	Attended Talks and Classes Organised for Parents Outside School		Did Not Attend Talks and Classes Organised for Parents Outside School		Total	
	N	*%*	*N*	*%*	*N*	*%*
Attended church weekly	28	27	76	73	104	100
Attended church once a month	15	20	59	80	74	100
Attended church less frequently	2	3	64	97	66	100
Total	45	18	199	82	244	100

X^2=.000 p<.05

Middle class parents received more support from their partners, friends and the print media such as books, newspapers and magazines (Figure 4.5). This may reflect the respondents' higher education levels and the number of two-parent families in the middle class schools. It may also be an indication of the educational capital of their friends. 'Teacher' friends featured prominently in the interviews in the middle class schools.

Respondents from the middle class girls' school were more likely to attend talks and classes outside the school (Table 4.12). These were more likely to be older and in two-parent families.

Figure 4.5: Difference in the Support Received by Respondents from the Middle Class and Disadvantaged Schools

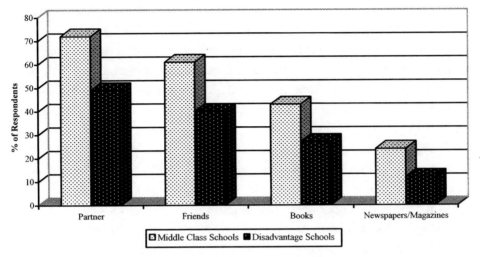

Table 4.12: Influence of School Type on Attendance at Talks and Classes Organised for Parents Outside the School

Variable	Attended talks and classes organised for parents outside the school		Did not attend talks and classes organised for parents outside the school		Total	
	N	*%*	*N*	*%*	*N*	*%*
Middle class girls' school	26	30	61	70	87	100
Middle class boys' school	14	18	64	82	78	100
Disadvantaged girls' school	5	13	35	88	40	101
Disadvantaged boys' school	1	2	54	98	55	100
Total	46	18	214	82	260	100

X^2=.000 p<.05

* Result of rounding to whole numbers

The principal brought all such talks and classes to the parents' notice through the newsletter. I attended a NPCP talk *Transition from Primary to Post Primary* (FN 08-05-06). Not only was there a large group of parents from the middle class girls' school present but the principal was also present. In the small groups, some parents commented on her presence and wondered was she 'spying' on them. At that particular talk, all the parents present were from the middle class schools around the area, though a few had travelled further. There were no disadvantaged parents present.

The educational capital of the respondents also appeared to influence the amount of support respondents got (Table 4.13). While some of the results are similar to above, those with primary education appeared to receive the least support even from their immediate family. Surprisingly, they were also less likely to find their child's class teacher, other parents and their neighbours supportive. Though not significant, only 67 per cent (N=14) of those with a primary education discussed the school with other parents. Twelve of these attended church monthly. In contrast, 82 per cent (N=189) of the more educated parents networked with others. Three-quarters (75 per cent, N= 135) of these attended church monthly.

Obviously respondents from two-parent family were more likely than those in one-parent families to find their partner supportive (Table 4.14). They could also rely more on their neighbours and the Church to support them in their parenting. Interestingly enough they were also more likely to consider books and the television a useful source of advice and support than those from one-parent families. While not significant, those in one-parent families were less likely to find other parents and parenting courses helpful. While there was no difference in whether they talked to other parents about the school, respondents in two-parent families (23 per cent, N=41) were more likely to attend a parenting course outside the school than those in one-parent families (7 per cent, N=5). They (26 per cent, N=46) were also more likely to be a member of a group outside the school than lone parents (5 per cent, N=4).

Table 4.13: Difference in Support Received Based on the Respondents'
Level of Education

Variable	Primary Level		Second Level		Third Level		Total Who Received Support	
	N	%	N	%	N	%	N	%
Family	9	53	129	78	51	84	189	78
Child's Teachers*	7	41	110	67	34	56	151	62
Partner	6	35	105	64	43	71	154	63
Friends	6	35	83	50	42	69	131	54
Their children*	5	29	65	39	32	53	102	42
Grandparents	4	24	116	70	47	77	167	69
Books	4	24	55	33	32	53	91	37
Other Parents*	3	18	72	44	28	46	103	42
Newspapers or magazines	2	12	28	17	20	33	50	21
Parenting Course*	2	12	41	25	19	31	62	26
Church*	1	6	28	17	13	21	42	17
Neighbours*	0	0	22	13	13	21	35	14
Total number of respondents across education levels	22	9	169	67	61	24	252	100

* Not significant at $p<.05$

Gender had an influence on parents' social capital. Mothers (58 per cent, N=125) got more support from their friends than fathers (35 per cent, N=8). They also (84 per cent, N=188) tended to talk to other parents more than fathers (52 per cent, N=12). In contrast, 87 per cent (N=20) of fathers found their partners supportive compared with 63 per cent (N=136) of mothers. This was influenced by the fact that more mothers were single parents. While 82 per cent (N=116) of mothers in two-parent families found their partners supportive, only 25 per cent (N=17) of single parent mothers did.

There were also differences in relation to the gender of the respondents' children. Respondents in the girls' schools were more likely to find their own children a useful source of support and advice. Fifty per cent (N=63) from the girls' schools found their own children supportive as compared to 34 per cent (N=44) from the boys' school.

Table 4.14: Difference in Support Received by One-parent and Two-parent Families

Variable	One-parent Families		Two-parent Families		Total Who Received Support	
	N	%	N	%	N	%
Other Parents**	24	33	81	47	105	43
Partner	18	25	141	82	159	65
Books	18	25	74	43	92	38
Newspapers or magazines**	11	15	38	22	49	20
Parenting Course**	12	17	50	29	62	25
Church	7	10	36	21	43	18
Television	7	10	36	21	43	18
Neighbours	5	7	30	17	35	14
Total number of respondents across family type	74	30	177	71	251	101*

* Result of rounding to whole numbers

** Not significant at p<.05

Family size also had an impact on the support respondents received (Table 4.15). Those with two children, who were more likely to be in two-parent families and middle class schools, appeared to have the best support network, though they were less likely to receive support from their own parents. They were also more likely to talk to other parents about the school. Eighty-six per cent (N=140) of parents with two or three children talked to other parents about the school in comparison with 76 per cent (N=29) of those with only one child and 68 per cent (N=39) of those with four or more children.

Children's level of education influenced parental networking. Sixth class parents (68 per cent, N=50) networked less than other parents (86 per cent, N=162). Interestingly, while 81 per cent (N=128) of the second, fourth and sixth class respondents who networked with other parents attended church monthly, only 60 per cent (N=25) of senior infant parents did. It may be that as one interviewee (I5MM) stated that second class is when the Church begins to play a more influential part in their children's school life and parents have to decide whether they are going to conform to the norms of the ethos of the school.

Table 4.15: Impact of Family Size on the Support Received by Respondents

Variable	One Child		Two Children		Three Children		Four Children		Total Who Received Support	
	N	%	N	%	N	%	N	%	N	%
Grandparents	24	65	48	57	61	78	36	71	169	68
Friends	18	49	56	67	42	54	18	35	134	54
Other Parents*	16	43	40	48	36	46	14	28	106	42
Partner	15	41	67	80	50	64	29	57	161	64
Books*	13	35	41	49	25	32	15	29	94	38
Newspapers or magazines*	12	32	18	21	15	19	5	10	50	20
Their children	9	24	45	54	36	46	16	31	106	42
Parenting Course*	6	16	26	31	17	22	14	28	25	63
Neighbours	3	8	19	23	11	14	3	6	36	14
Total number of respondents across family size	38	15	85	33	78	30	58	22	259	100

* Not significant at p<.05

Parental Involvement as Home Educators

School is only one dimension of children's education. Parents complement the work of the school by engaging in a variety of educational activities with their children at home (Reay, 1998, p. 68). These include teaching values and beliefs as much literacy and numeracy skills. In addition, parents compensate for any gaps they perceive in their children's education by paying for extra-curricular activities and private tutors. This section examines the home curriculum provided by the participants. The variables which influence this curriculum are highlighted.

Parents as Educators

Teaching children how to behave was an important part of the home curriculum. Though some of the middle class parents were reluctant to admit that they had rules, all the parents interviewed had certain behaviours that they actively encouraged. These varied from encouraging children to be polite to others, tidy up after themselves, help with chores, eat good food, do their homework, go to bed on time to warning them against watching too much television, using bad language and fighting.

> Well I suppose certainly – and we do not have a top – there are no top two rules in this house but one of the main things is that I do not allow my children to sit and watch TV unless I know what they are watching and I really object to a lot of this rubbish that is on television so it would be what comes up most. The other rule is that … certain times they need to go to bed and that's it. They might see that as sort of a rule but there aren't rules as such. (I6MM)

Parents used sanctions like reprimanding their children, sending them to their rooms, not allowing them out to play along with depriving them of things like television and sweets when they misbehaved. Two parents with younger children used the 'bold step'. However strategies like modelling good behaviour were seen as more effective in encouraging children to behave.

> Try to set good examples and I do not expect them to tidy up if I leave a mess all over the place. I wouldn't expect them to try and help if I do not help so it is very much a question of we would, as parents, we would try and set the example … (14MF)

In fact, most parents felt that, having taught their children how to behave from early childhood, they had very few behavioural problems.

> Basically if she doesn't, like she knows because I taught her that way from the time she was born, she knows bad language is a no go definitely whether here or in school or out on the street and anyway it doesn't work. Her room – she's a great kid. She has it

done every morning when she gets up, before she goes to school, so there is no giving out to her if you get me. The odd time she will have a falling down and say, 'I'm not doing it' and I say, 'That's fine you are not watching telly' and then she says, 'All right, Okay'. (I2DM)

Finding time to engage in educational activities with children was difficult for some parents, especially if they were in paid employment.

When I can. Oh God, between two jobs it is hard. She's home from school, it is like spend an hour with her, clean up, get the dinner on and then I'm back out to work. Really I do not spend enough time with her as much as I'd like to. 'Cause if I do not work we do not have anything so I have to work *[laughs]*. (I2DM)

As a parent, one of the most surprising aspects of my observations on how I supported my children's learning was the frequency and variety of the activities that we engaged in (Figure 4.6). Most of this was done informally. The items recorded were major discrete incidents. Routine activities like the use of the computer, playing games and looking after animals were not recorded. Normal everyday conversation was not included. Visual Arts included formal lessons as well as informal activities done at home.

Figure 4.6: Subjects Observed as Part of the Home Curriculum

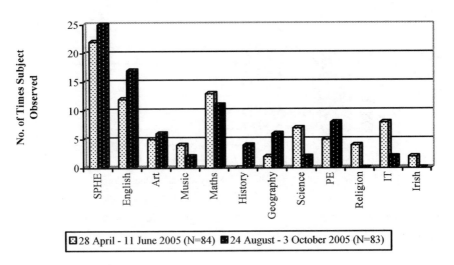

The following observations as taken from my field diary give some idea of the kind of activities involved in the home curriculum.

> D2 helped me make flat pack bookcases. She measured out where nails should go. (FN 24-05-05)

> D2 was reading a book. She wanted to read ½ of it and asked me, 'What is ½ of 132?' I asked her, 'What was ½ of 13?' and then, 'What was half of 12?' (FN 08-06-05)

As outlined in Chapter Three, it was not possible to include parents' diaries in this research. However, respondents to the questionnaire were asked how frequently they engaged in educational activities at home. Most (69 per cent, N=175) respondents read a story to their child at least once a week (Figure 4.7). Many of those who never read to their child wrote on the questionnaires that it was unnecessary as their children were able to read for themselves. This was evident when one analysed the results. Only 40 per cent (N=29) of the sixth class parents read to their children at least once a week in comparison with almost all (94 per cent, N=46) of senior infant parents. In fact, 31 per cent (N=22) of sixth class parents never read stories to their children.

Figure 4.7: How Frequently Parents Read Stories to Their Children (N=255)

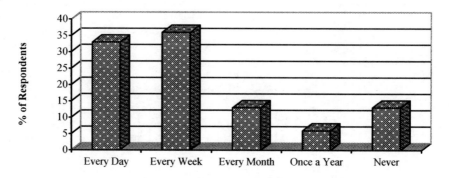

Those who were interviewed also encouraged their children to read. One parent described the culture of reading for pleasure in her home as follows:

They have loads [of books]. They read a lot. They'd all read in bed. The youngest one is just about able to. Although one of the nice kind (sic) of progression is that the middle girl has taken to reading to her. The first child reads of course but she reads on her own now to herself and loves doing that and she likes then reading to her younger sister. It is all a positive reinforcement of her skill and that kind of thing. Yes they all read in bed. Well they read outside it as well. (I5MM)

Eight-seven per cent (N=220) of parents played with their children at least once a week (Figure 4.8).

Figure 4.8: How Frequently Parents Play Games with Their Children (N=254)

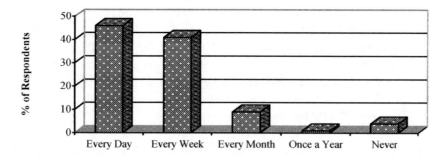

Respondents with only one child were more likely to play with their children. Forty-two per cent (N=89) of those with two or more children played with their children daily as compared to 71 per cent (N=27) of parents with one child. Parents were also more likely to play with their children if they were younger. Over half (56 per cent, N=72) the parents in the junior classes played with their children on a daily basis as compared to 36 per cent (N=45) of parents with children in the senior classes.

Practically 100 per cent (N=260) of parents brought their children on an outing at least once a month, while 74 per cent (N=192) went once a week (Figure 4.9).

Figure 4.9: How Frequently Parents Bring Their Children on Outings,
e.g. Cinema, Park (N=261)

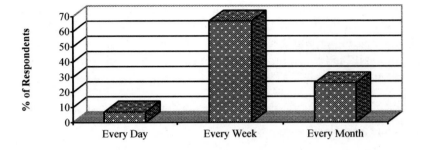

Frequently these outings are used by parents to teach children skills.

> My daughter and I were in the local park. I was teaching her how
> to use the swings on her own and go down the fireman's pole. A
> couple in their late twenties arrived in the park. They had a baby
> in a buggy and a young boy of about three or four. They had
> brought a basket ball and between them were teaching the boy
> how to play basket ball. Even though he could not throw high
> enough to get a basket, they showed him how to dribble and pass
> the ball. (FN 05-03-06)

Middle class interviewees, in particular, described the educational opportunities the outings provided.

> I am a horticulturalist and I am passionate about nature and the
> environment and art. My children have gone to art galleries, they
> meet – they do a huge amount of travelling because we are in the
> … business. They are very well socialised and they're – what I
> notice if I go to the Botanic Gardens … my children have their
> noses stuck in to flowers, they're smelling them, they're talking
> about them, looking at them … they're aware, hugely aware of
> their environment and I think that type of education is absolutely
> invaluable. I suppose we would spend an awful lot of time doing
> things together as a family. That would have been always - sure if
> you are up the mountains or if you down the country visiting
> grandparents or whatever, I think that children can be taught to be
> aware of the birds, be aware of everything. It is a fantastic
> education. (I6MM)

Respondents from one-child families brought their children on outings more frequently. The larger the family the less likely they were to take their children on outings (Table 4.16). Younger children tended to be brought on more outings than older children. Eighty-two per cent (N=107) of parents in the junior classes brought their children on outings once a week in comparison to 65 per cent (N=85) of those in the senior classes.

While only 14 per cent (N=35) of respondents brought their children to the library once a week, 52 per cent (N=134) brought their children at least once a month (Figure 4.10). However, 33 per cent (N=85) never brought their children to the library.

Table 4.16: Influence of Family Size on the Number of Times Parents Brought Their Children on Outings

Variable	Weekly		Monthly		Total	
	N	*%*	*N*	*%*	*N*	*%*
One child	34	90	4	11	38	101*
Two children	66	79	18	21	84	100
Three children	56	73	21	27	77	100
Four or more children	33	59	23	41	56	100
Total	189	74	66	26	255	100

$X^2 = .006$ p<.05

* Result of rounding to whole numbers

Figure 4.10: How Frequently Parents Bring Their Children to the Library (N=256)

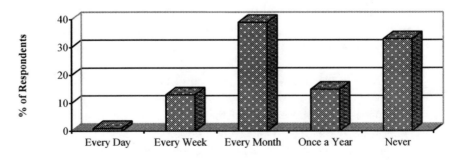

Forty-three per cent (N=106) of respondents brought their children to church once a week, while 73 per cent (N=180) brought them once a month (Figure 4.11). While 13 per cent (N=32) brought them once a year, 15 per cent (N= 36) never brought their children to church.

The ethos of school had an influence on the interviewees' decision to bring their children to Mass.

> It [the catholic ethos] has become more so. It usen't (sic) be –
> when [my eldest child] was in first class, you know making her
> communion; we use to go to Mass every Sunday. You know the
> way you can tell a child who is making their communion and has
> been in Church three times. They are looking around admiring all
> the art work. When the organ sounds they are saying 'oh where is
> that coming from?' I didn't want her to be one of those. I felt that
> if you were making your communion you should have some
> sense of why you are doing it. So she kept that up and then I've
> gone consistently with each of them ever since. (I5MM)

Figure 4.11: How Frequently Parents Bring Their Children to Church (N=248)

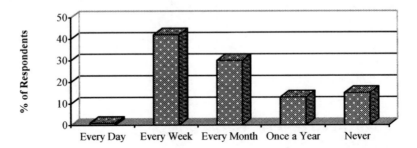

Most felt that they enrolled their children in a Catholic school and had to play by the rules for their children's sakes. They feared that their child would be excluded and bullied if they did not conform to the norm.

> What you do not want for your child is to ostracise her, is that
> what you call it? You know when you make her like. If the school
> runs the Catholic ethos and they go over to the Church to say
> prayers, we'll have Holy Communion, we'll have Confirmation
> then my child goes through that as well because the one thing is
> that you have to be is a team player. Like I am not going to come
> along and say when everyone is going to Church my child will

stay outside. I think she should be with the people and not left out because that's when she gets picked on, that's when she gets the finger pointed. (I1DGF)

Attendance at church was influenced by the school the respondents' children attended. As can be seen from Table 4.17 the respondents from the girls' school, especially the middle class girls' school, attended Church more frequently than those in the other schools. Parents of younger boys, in particular, were reluctant to bring them to church. Only 12 per cent (N=3) brought their children to church in senior infants in comparison with 50 per cent (N=11) of senior infant parents in the girls' schools.

Table 4.17: The Frequency with which Respondents from the Four Schools Attended Church

Variable	Weekly		Once a Month		Less Frequently		Total	
	N	*%*	*N*	*%*	*N*	*%*	*N*	*%*
Disadvantaged boys' school	15	29	18	35	18	35	51	99*
Disadvantaged girls' school	16	44	7	19	13	36	36	99*
Middle class boys' school	28	38	22	30	23	32	73	100
Middle class girls' school	47	53	27	31	14	16	88	100
Total	106	43	74	30	68	27	248	100

X^2=.036 p<.05

* Result of rounding to whole numbers

The age of the respondents had an influence on their attendance at church (Table 4.18) with younger parents less likely to attend.

Table 4.18: Relationship between the Age of the Respondent and the Frequency with which They Brought Their Children to Church

Variable	Weekly		Once a Month		Once a Year or Never		Totals	
	N	%	N	%	N	%	N	%
Aged under thirty	9	23	9	23	22	55	40	101*
Aged between thirty and thirty-nine	47	44	29	27	31	29	107	100
Aged over forty	50	51	35	35	14	14	99	100
Total	106	43	73	30	67	27	246	100

$X^2 = .000$ p<.05

* Result of rounding to whole numbers

Those with only one child were less likely to take their children to church than those with two or more children (Table 4.19).

Table 4.19: Relationship between Family Size and the Frequency with which Respondents Brought Their Children to Church

Variable	Weekly		Once a Month		Once a Year or Never		Total	
	N	%	N	%	N	%	N	%
One child	11	29	8	21	19	50	38	100
Two or more children	95	46	64	31	47	23	206	100
Total	106	43	72	30	66	27	244	100

$X^2 = .002$ p<.05

Extra-curricular Activities

Ninety-two per cent (N=243) of children were involved in some form of extra-curricular activity with sport being the most popular. Three-quarters (76 per cent, N=189) of respondents' children were involved in sport (Figure 4.12). While swimming and football, either soccer or Gaelic, were the most popular forms of sport mentioned, children were also involved in basketball, tennis, boxing, karate, gymnastics, hurling and rugby. One even played golf once a month (Q162MBSI). As can be seen from the following timetable, many children had a full schedule.

Running club	Tues
Karate	Tues
Water polo	Wed
Scouts	Thurs
Basketball	Fri
Swimming lessons	Sat
Lifesaving	Sun (Q148MB2)

Other extra-curricular activities included computers, art, music, dancing, youth clubs, drama and scouts or guides. Piano, choir, singing, drums and guitar were mentioned as the musical activities that children engaged in. Irish dancing was the most popular form of dancing.

Figure 4.12: Involvement in Extra-curricular Activities (N=250)

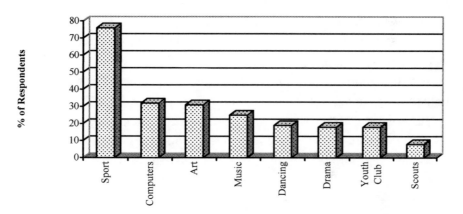

Those who were interviewed were very enthusiastic about their children's involvement in extra-curricular activities. They felt that not only were the activities beneficial to their children's well-being and development but that 'the more they're occupied outside school, the less time they have to get involved with trouble and everything' (I2DM).

> Oh mine are involved in every sport there is. So *[laughter]* between drama and dancing, football and basketball and hurling,

> there is always something going on in my house. They got in to
> them when they were younger. The young fella [sic] was playing
> football since he could walk, I think. The girl always had a love
> of singing, dancing, so she found drama classes so she does that.
> She loves hurling so she does that, but it was camogie in school,
> that's how that started -in school. [My son] does football in
> school and basket ball in school and wall climbing and all them
> [sic] things. (I8DM)

As can be seen from the quote, many of the extra-curricular activities
were school-related in that school either organised them or provided a
venue.

The gender of the respondent made little difference to the extra-
curricular activities their children were involved with. From my observations of parents collecting their children from swimming classes on Saturday mornings (FN 01-04-06 to 24-06-06), fathers and mothers were
just as involved. Mothers were in the majority on only two occasions.
One was on the day of an important football match when 17 mothers and
only three fathers collected their children (FN 20-06-06). The other was
the day of the swimming gala when 26 mothers and 10 fathers attended
the event (FN 10-04-06). However, on the way home we passed a local
park, where a GAA match was taking place and there were more fathers
present than mothers. My husband tells me that fathers far outnumber
mothers at the under-sixteen Gaelic football matches.

However, gender stereotyping influenced attendance at extra-
curricular activities, with many respondents appearing to hold traditional
views on 'appropriate' activities for boys and girls. Girls were more
likely to do dancing, drama and music, whereas boys were more likely to
do computers. Forty per cent (N=51) of boys did computers as compared
to 23 per cent (N=28) of girls.

Dancing was obviously considered a 'girly' thing with 37 per cent
(N=45) of children in the girls' schools being involved in some form of
dance. Only two boys did dancing. Music and drama appeared to be
similar. While 31 per cent (N=38) from the girls' school did music, only
20 per cent (N=25) from the boys' school did. Similarly, while 28 per
cent (N=34) from the girls' schools did drama, 9 per cent (N=11) from
the boys' schools did. It was also remarkable that children in the disad-

vantaged girls' school appeared to play less sport than the children attending any of the other schools (Table 4.20).

Table 4.20: Differences between the Schools in Their Pupils'
Involvement in Sport

Variable	Involved in Sport		Not involved in Sport		Total	
	N	%	N	%	N	%
Disadvantaged Boys' School	39	78	11	22	50	100
Disadvantaged Girls' School	16	43	21	57	37	100
Middle Class Boys' School	68	87	10	13	78	100
Middle Class Girls' School	66	78	19	22	85	100
Total	189	76	61	24	250	100

$X^2 = .000$ $p < .05$

Just as the children's gender influenced their choice of extra-curricular activities, social class was also influential. Thirty-seven per cent (N=32) of children in the disadvantaged schools were members of a youth club as compared to only 7 per cent (N=12) of children from the middle class schools. In contrast, while 12 per cent (N=19) of children from the middle class schools were involved in the scouts/guides, only 2 per cent (N=2) of the children from the disadvantaged schools were.

There were also differences in their response to the open question about their children's extra-curricular activities. Children in disadvantaged schools appeared to be involved in a more limited set of activities. While football, basketball, pool, boxing and swimming were listed for both sets of schools, children in the middle class schools were also involved in karate, running, hurling, horse riding, water polo, chess, tennis and gymnastics. A few middle class parents mentioned that their children went to the gym. Similarly, a variety of dance forms such as hip-hop, majorettes, ballet, ballroom, tap and disco were mentioned for the middle class children. Several were involved with various stage schools. In contrast, only Irish dancing was listed for the children in the disadvantaged schools.

Social class also influenced children's leisure activities. While middle class parents said that their children read, 'played with friends'

(Q201MG4), did 'sewing, knitting' (Q174MG6) and French, they also described their children as doing

> Writing, film making, reading, photography, cinema, plays (theatre). (Q118MB6)

> Cycles, walks, poems & song writing. (Q190MG6)

Parents in the disadvantaged schools, on the other hand, mentioned things like reading, going to the playground, 'plays games with his brother/sister' (Q55DBSI), 'skipping rope, playing chasing' (Q71DG4) along with 'Dancing, singing, playing games, writing, reading' (Q87DGSI)

The class the children were in had an impact on their participation in extra-curricular activities. Apart from computers, drama and music, participation decreased as the child grew older. While 38 per cent (N=48) of children in the junior classes did art, only 24 per cent (N=30) in the senior classes did art. Similarly, while 26 per cent (N=33) of those in the junior classes were involved with dancing, only 11 per cent (N=14) of children from the senior classes were. Sport was interesting in that children in fourth class were most likely to be involved with sports (Table 4.21). Participation declined in sixth class.

Table 4.21: Impact of Class on Children's Involvement in Sport

Variable	Involved in Sport		Not Involved in Sport		Total	
	N	*%*	*N*	*%*	*N*	*%*
6th class	54	76	17	24	71	100
4th class	49	91	5	9	54	100
2nd class	55	71	23	30	78	101*
Senior Infants	31	66	16	34	47	100
Total	189	76	61	24	250	100

$X^2=.017$ $p<.05$

* Result of rounding to whole numbers

Supporting the School at Home

Most mothers in Reay's (1998, p. 66) study described their relationship to schooling as a supportive one in which they responded to teachers' requests to hear reading, learn tables and go over spellings with their children. This section looks at the ways parents supported the school, both informally and formally, at the home. Informal support includes activities such as monitoring how the child is doing at school, reinforcing the curriculum, enforcing the school rules along with providing supplementary resources. Helping with homework and paying for school items are the most typical ways parents support the school formally.

Observations of Supporting the School at Home

In my parents' diary I recorded the ways that I supported the school at home (Figure 4.13). This varied from doing homework, signing notes, attending events and preparing the child for school. The items included providing wood lice for a science lesson and costumes for the school concert.

Figure 4.13: Observations of Supporting the School at Home

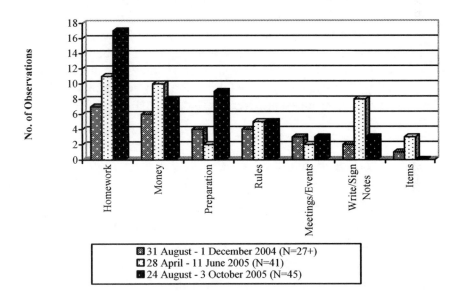

The rules related to the times I reinforced the school rules at home for example by reminding my daughter that her hair was to be tied back or by collecting my daughter from the concert at the time designated by the school. These observations do not include the routine homework such as checking work for mistakes or hearing spellings, tables and reading.

A lot of the support provided is informal and incidental. Having discussed the field diaries with the grandfather from the disadvantaged school, he too began to think about the times he had supported his granddaughter's learning and the school informally at home.

> It would be all out of school, what did you do in school, we done blah, blah, blah, but I'd tell her -like she said to me, 'The teacher was going to do (sic) *The Guns of 1916'*. She was going to read the book. Now I have a hundred books at home … I have all the martyred 1916 executed leaders on the wall so I said, 'Tell your teacher … we have books if she wants books to read'. So that means she comes back to me and says, 'Oh yeah, I was telling my teacher that you have this on the wall'. Now the same with the Irish I'd be telling her I was in the Carra Rua … I enjoyed it and I done a bit of Irish … she'll certainly talk to me about her Irish, which I found very interesting. She'll get words to put into sentences, you know. She had vaccine there the other night for instance. Get the dictionary out and look up vaccine. Now I know vaccine, there's vaccine, vaccination, what does the word vaccine mean? So I am getting educated. Now I know what the word vaccine means but I pretend surprise at this and she has to look up the dictionary … When you sit down and think about it, you find you are involved an awful lot … when you think of all the questions you are asking over a period. (I1DGF)

Supporting the School's Rules

With the introduction of the *Education Welfare Act 2000*, all schools are expected to have a Code of Behaviour that emphasises rewarding positive behaviour as well as the more traditional sanctioning of misbehaviour. Sixteen per cent (N=43) of respondents had noticed changes in the school rules and the behaviour of children. Some felt that the pupil-teacher relationship had improved as a result while others thought that discipline standards had fallen and that there was a lack of respect for teachers from both parents and children.

Respect for teachers and principals has changed with 'some' parents and then of course it moves on to the children. Discipline is slacking. Where are the nuns? (Q194MG6)

The vast majority (90 per cent N=236) of respondents to the question-naire felt that parents should make their children obey their teachers (Figure 4.14). Fifty per cent (N=132) strongly agreed.

Figure 4.14: Parents Should Make Their Children Obey Their Teachers (N=262)

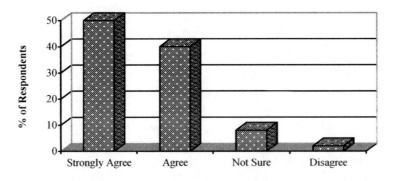

Those who were interviewed appeared to agree that parents should support the school rules.

If I was called in over something that one of my girls did here I would support whatever the school felt was the appropriate punishment. I wouldn't necessarily side with my child just because she is my child. I would be seen to be supporting the school. (I5MM)

There were gender differences in the amount of knowledge interviewees had about the school rules. Mothers were more likely to mention the rules that their children talked or worried about the most.

Being on time is one of the major ones she gets herself in a tizzy over. If we are running a couple of minutes late she's nearly having a heart attack. The food, not, you know, I think they are trying to curb the – the proper diet – I hear that with her. Those seem to be the ones I hear all the time. (I3MM)

The men, while being aware of the school rules, found it difficult to list them.

> *What are the top two school rules?*

> The top two rules [long pause] ah Jesus, I wouldn't have a breeze. Look I could take a stab at it, you know. (I1DGF)

The middle class father, while also being unable to recall the school rules, felt that they permeated all aspects of school life and were reinforced by the teachers in a positive way.

Parents could describe the variety of sanctions schools used to encourage children to obey the rules. These included detentions, punishments, extra homework, being sent to the principal's office. Only one parent (I2DM) mentioned a reward system. Most felt that parents should be held responsible for their children's behaviour.

> They should call their parents up like and talk to them. I know a lot of the parents that have kids in the school are probably half not on this earth, em, They just need to get a little bit tougher, you know what I mean, they really do, they need to get a little bit tougher. I just think parents will sit back. (I2DM)

While parents supported the school in enforcing the rules, they also explained the rules to their children and helped them cope with demands and consequences of the rules.

> I'd back the school up with the rules, because you have to ... but definitely I do try to ease the fear a little bit ... this fear of the principal's office ... I try to allay that fear but at the same time she knows that she has to do as she's told. (I3MM)

Some felt that you had to explicitly teach children how to cope with the school's expectations and their handling of misbehaviour

> There is a lot of things you can teach your child, like if she had a bad experience in school like or she had a – if the principal approached her, not to be cheeky and just talk. Talking to someone is better than shouting in somebody's face ...

> Just how to get on ...

How to deal with confrontation …

Have manners, whether she's getting bit off, her head is getting bitten off just to hold back and have manners …

And respect. (FG1D)

Despite some consultation by the schools on certain issues, most parents felt that they had very little say over the school rules. However, most agreed that they would approach the school if they believed that a rule was unreasonable. While the rule would probably not be changed, they thought that the principal would do some thing about their concerns.

If one of the teachers had a rule that I thought was completely ridiculous or whatever I would be happy enough to go to the teacher and say it.

But let us say it was a school rule and the teacher had no choice in it?

I do not know. I suppose you just have to live with it. (I5MM)

Supporting the School's Curriculum

Most (87 per cent, N=225) respondents to the questionnaires agreed that parents needed help from teachers to educate their children. One respondent suggested that teachers also needed 'the help of parents to make learning and education a positive experience' (Q161MGSI). Similarly those who were interviewed saw the teachers' and parents' role as complementary and felt that there should be continuity between home and school.

I seen them as being complementary rather than being – that there's continuity rather than the strict demarcation line between school and I think it is better for them [children] if they see more of a flow in the whole thing. (I5MM)

Respondents to the questionnaire were almost equally divided on whether 'teaching should be left to the teachers who are the experts' (Figure 4.15). Respondents with a primary education were more likely to agree that they should leave their children's education to the expertise of the teachers. Nearly three-quarters (70 per cent N=14) agreed with this statement as compared with 43 per cent (N=96) of those with higher levels of education.

Figure 4.15: Education Should Be Left to the Teachers Who Are the Experts

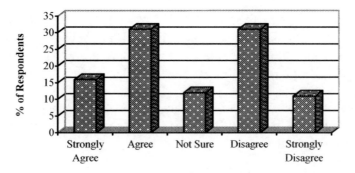

Those who were interviewed also agreed that their children's education was too important to be left to the teachers. If children were to succeed in school, parents needed to play their part.

> I think to keep a good eye on it. I think it is up to you really. The teacher can only do so much. It is up to the parents to do the homework and if there is a problem to go in about it. (FG2M)

Keeping 'a good eye' on their children progress helped them to spot if their child was experiencing difficulties in school and either help the child themselves or seek help from the school. Some parents felt that their knowledge of their children was not acknowledged or recognised by the school. When they identified learning difficulties, their concerns were not addressed and their children's needs went unsupported by the school.

> I felt let down by the school in regards to my middle child. I noticed his reading and spelling was poor compared to his oral ability. I brought it to the attention of his 1st class teacher. I was told he did not qualify for remedial reading or any help. All school year I tried and kept in close contact with the teacher. In second class I was told he now qualifies for help. I met with the remedial reading teacher. He told me he was not going to help my

child read phonetically but through poetry and different methods. I kept in close contact all school year. I sometimes got the impression from the school principal & teachers that I was being a fussy mother but I knew something was wrong. After much pressure from me the school organised tests and we discovered that he is severely dyslexic. Both myself and my husband had to make a hard decision that he needed to go to a reading school. He is now at this school learning to read through phonics. I am very disappointed with the school and the lack of back up I received when given this news (no back up). My fears were not given consideration and I felt very much on my own regards my sons' education. (Q110MB6)

Daily discussions about the school with their children gave parents an insight into how their children were getting on. It also gave their children an opportunity to share any difficulties that they may have with them.

Besides the child will say it themselves when they get in from school how they are getting on, if they find anything hard and when you are doing homework it is fairly obvious if they are having problems. They are going to learning resource and it was obvious with the first one that went there that she was having difficulties with reading. (I5MM)

Parents also got a lot of information from their children's copies and workbooks with the majority (99 per cent, N=258) checking them at least once a month (Figure 4.16).

Figure 4.16: How Often Parents Looked at Their Children's Copies and Workbooks (N=261)

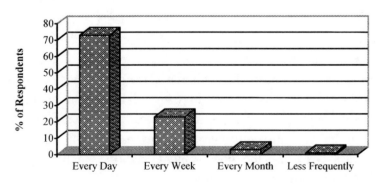

One mother (Q145MB2) complained that her children were not allowed take their books home which made it difficult for her 'to help them out at home or to teach them something they haven't grasped in school on that day'.

Mothers and those with children in the more junior classes were more likely to look at copies and workbooks on a daily basis. While over three-quarters of mothers (79 per cent, N=169) looked at their children's copybooks every day, only half of the fathers (50 per cent, N=11) did. The numbers who examined copies and workbooks decreased steadily as children went up the school (Table 4.22).

Table 4.22: The Difference the Class the Respondents' Children Were in Made on the Frequency with which They Looked at Their Children's Copybooks and Workbooks

Variable	Every Day		Every Week		Total	
	N	%	N	%	N	%
6th class	40	58	29	42	69	100
4th class	39	72	15	28	54	100
2nd class	65	83	13	17	78	100
Senior Infants	46	96	2	4	48	100
Total	190	76	59	24	249	100

$X^2 = .000$ p<.05

Most respondents helped their children with homework daily (Figure 4.17). Several variables influenced the frequency with which respondents helped with homework. Mothers (93 per cent, N=202) were more likely to help with homework on daily basis than fathers (70 per cent, N=16). The class the children were in also influenced whether respondents helped with homework. Children in the higher classes got less help with homework on a daily basis than children in the junior classes. Almost all (96 per cent, N=125) of the parents with children in the junior classes helped with homework daily compared with 84 per cent (N=106) of those with children in senior classes. Many parents with children in a senior class wrote on the questionnaire that they only helped with homework when asked by the child.

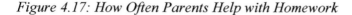

Figure 4.17: How Often Parents Help with Homework

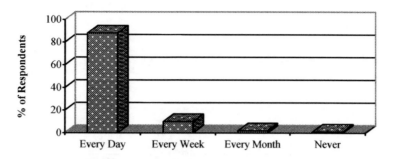

All of those who were interviewed helped with homework and many ex-plained the structures they had put in place to ensure homework was done and that children got the help they needed.

> We always do one-to-one homework. Well the older girl does homework upstairs on her own and I just go up and check it afterwards but the other two, when they are doing it we will use the dining room table so there's no stimulation. It is just one of them and me in that room until they are finished. Then when the older one is finished the next one comes in. I think it is easier for them to concentrate. Then I tell them not to answer the door bell every time it rings and then they do not go out until they've done their homework. (I5MM)

Supporting the School Financially

Despite the 'free education' system, parents are expected to pay for vari-ous school-related items such as uniforms, books and equipment along with contributing to the school's fundraising efforts. There are also other incidental costs like trips and events that occur during the year.

Nearly all the respondents (99 per cent, N=253) paid towards school items, e.g., pencils, copies. However, nearly three-quarters (71 per cent, N=182) paid for school items at least once a month (Figure 4.18).

School books in my local school cost on average €90 to €100 a year per child (SDLS 2004-05; 2005-06). This does not include dictionaries, table books and atlases, which are used from year to year. School equip-ment such as pens, pencils, copy books, Pritt sticks were extra. Along with the book list, there was a bill for approximately €65, which covered elocution and dancing classes, photocopying, arts and crafts, book rental and progress tests. At least another €100, which does not include money contributed towards fundraising, was paid over the school year to cover outings, events and other items (SDLS 2005-06).

Figure 4.18: How Often Parents Pay for School Items e.g. pencils, copies (N=256)

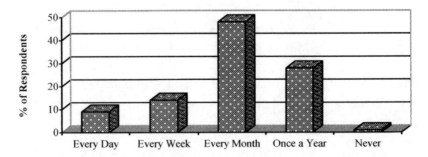

The disadvantaged girls' school operate a book rental scheme, which is subsidized by the DES. Parents paid €30 a year to cover school books, pencils, copies, photocopying, art and craft and kindergarten materials (SDDG 2005-06). They also pay 70c a week for dancing lessons and €10 for ten swimming lessons.

Despite the book rental scheme, respondents in the disadvantaged schools felt that they paid for school items more frequently than those in the middle class schools (Table 4.23). It may be that middle class parents are expected to pay the total amount at the beginning of the year, while disadvantaged parents pay in instalments throughout the year. For example, the disadvantaged girls' school charged Irish dancing classes weekly, while my local school asked parents for this money at the start of the year.

Seven per cent (N=19) of the respondents to the questionnaire commented that uniforms, books and various other school activities had become more expensive over the past six years. It was more difficult to buy second hand books 'because [the] curriculum changed nearly every year' (Q156MB4). Those with children in second level would be particularly aware of this as revised editions are produced every three years. My daughter could only use one of her brothers' Junior Certificate books in first year, even though they had just finished their exams. I tried to sell the other books second hand but could not as they were all out of date

(FN 26-08-06). One mother (Q70DB2) suggested that 'books should be free, whether working or not and given back to the school'.

Table 4.23: Differences between the Perceptions of Respondents from Disadvantaged and Middle Class Schools on how Often They Paid for School Items, e.g., pencils, copies (N=253)

Variable	Weekly		Every month		Once a year		Total	
	N	*%*	*N*	*%*	*N*	*%*	*N*	*%*
Disadvantaged schools	31	33	42	45	20	22	93	100
Middle class schools	27	17	82	51	51	32	160	100
Total	58	23	124	49	71	28	253	100

$X^2=.008$ p<.05

All parents are expected to support the school's fundraising efforts; 95 per cent (N=248) of respondents stated that they gave money towards the school's fundraising events. Interesting, younger respondents and those with only one child were less likely to contribute financially. 83 per cent (N=35) of those under thirty contributed towards fundraising as compared with 97 per cent (N=211) of those over thirty. Similarly, 84 per cent (N=32) of those with only one child helped the school financially in comparison with 97 per cent (N=213) the larger families.

While there was no difference between middle class and disadvantaged schools in the number of respondents who contributed to fundraising, there were differences in their newsletters as to the frequency of their fundraising and the amount of money raised. The Christmas raffle (€4,500) and school walk (€8,500) appeared to be the two main annual fundraising events for the middle class girls' school (SDMG 2004-06). This money was mainly spent on building repairs. In 2006, they had a once-off major fundraiser and raised €28,000 at a parents' night along with another €1,000 from bag packing in Tesco's supermarket and a non-uniform day. Parents were also encouraged to collect Tesco tokens, for which the school had received four computers and software over the last few years. They were also asked to send in used printer cartridges and old mobile phones, which could be used to reduce their printing bills or get additional Tesco tokens. In addition, the sixth class children fund-raise approximately €1,500 to €2,000 annually for various charities. The school also supported Simon (€320), Saint Vincent de Paul society (€320), Operation Christmas Child (over 500 shoe boxes), Dyslexia Association (€428), Trocaire (€3,858) and the MSReadathon.

While some fundraising took place in the disadvantaged girls' school, it was not as frequent and did not raise as much money as in the middle class schools (SDDG 2005-06). They included a coffee morning for the Hospice (€349), a Christmas Fair (€1,000) and collection for the Meath Hospice (€671). They also had a raffle (€400), Halloween fancy dress and a fashion show of confirmation and communion outfits (€481). This money went in to school funds.

Conclusion

This chapter profiled the research participants as well as focusing on the parental involvement in their children's education at home. It examined the roles and responsibilities of parents along with their hope and fears for their children. These perceptions influenced their decision-making processes especially around the area of school choice. The social capital of the parents and the supports they received were also examined. Finally the home curriculum and the support they give to the school were outlined.

The majority of participants were Irish Catholics. There were differences between the respondents from the middle class and disadvantaged schools. Middle class parents were more likely to be older, have higher education qualifications, in paid employment and two-parent families. While only a minority of fathers responded, they tended to come from the middle class schools. Younger respondents tended to have one-child families and children in the junior classes. These variables influenced the respondents' social capital along with their involvement in the home curriculum and the school.

Most parents felt that they were responsible for their children's development and education. Some perceived areas, such as literacy, numeracy, socialisation and values, as a joint responsibility between home and school. Others, particularly those in disadvantaged schools and with lower levels of education, perceived home and school to have separate, though complementary, responsibilities. While most parents, apart from those in one-parent families, agreed that fathers were responsible for their children's education, there were mixed views on the role of the mother. Respondents from one-parent families, the disadvantaged schools and with lower levels of education tended to hold traditional views. Many felt that the parents' personalities and employment levels influenced their views and practices.

Most parents hoped that their children would do well in school and go on to third level education. The reputation of the school, the approachability of the staff and its location in relation to their home were important influences on their choice of school. They got advice from their family, friends and other parents. Middle class parents had vague fears for their children's futures and were proactive in ensuring that their children's names were down in their chosen second level schools. While, disadvantaged parents had specific fears about the influence of the 'street' on their children, they were less proactive about choosing schools.

Respondents appeared to get support and advice from their family, friends, the class teachers and other parents. Professionals, such as the doctor, Garda etc were not perceived as supportive. Very few accessed parenting talks and classes or were members of a group or organisation outside the school. Most, however, networked informally with other parents. Social class, religion and gender had an influence on their social capital. Those with lower levels of education and in one-parent families appeared to be the most 'marginalised' (Conaty, 2002).

The respondents in this research were very active home educators. They read stories, played games and took their children on outings. Most attended church monthly with the Catholic ethos of the school influencing this practice. Family size and the educational stage of their children influenced the frequency of these practices. Most children were involved in a wide range of extra-curricular activities. Social class and their children's gender influenced the frequency and type of activity chosen.

All participants agreed that they needed to support the school at home. They did this by encouraging their children to obey the schools' rules and helping with homework. Participants also monitored their children's progress at school by discussing the school day with them and examining their copies and workbooks. In addition, they bought uniforms and books along with contributing to the schools' fundraising efforts.

Chapter Five

RESEARCH FINDINGS:
THE EDUCATION SYSTEM

Introduction

While Chapter Four focused on the role parents play in their children's education at home, this chapter examines parental involvement in the education system at local level. The variables which affect respondents' participation in their children's school are highlighted.

The first two sections concern partnership and policy at national level. They seek to assess the respondents' 'educational capital', i.e., their knowledge of the education system and the recent legislative and curricular changes. These sections explores parents' views on the roles and responsibilities of the main stakeholders, i.e., the State, the Catholic Church and parents along with their knowledge of the changes in Irish Education, particularly the *Education Act 1998,* the *Education Welfare Act 2000* and the *Primary School Curriculum* (Department of Education and Science [DES], 1999).

The last three sections focus on home-school partnership at local level. Home-school relationships are explored in section four. Participants' perceptions on their welcome in the schools along with their knowledge of and confidence in the complaint procedures are described. The next section investigates home-school communication. The methods both parents and schools use to communicate with each other are outlined, as is the content of notes sent home by the local school. The amount of information respondents have about their children's learning and school events and activities is also investigated. Finally, the involvement of parents as audiences, volunteers and decision-makers within the school is described along with the reasons why parents do not get involved.

Partnership at National Level

This section looks at the respondents' awareness of the roles and responsibilities of the stakeholders at national level. Their understanding of the function of the State and the DES to provide an education for their children, along with the role of the Catholic Church as the patron and owner of the schools concerned, is examined. While the influence of parents at national level is explored, the National Parents Council Primary (NPCP) is omitted as it was not mentioned by any of the participants.

Role and Responsibility of the State

The participants viewed the State as having total responsibility for the education system. In the interviews and focus groups, it was described as having responsibility for inspecting the school, maintaining standards as well as providing funding and 'enough teachers to make sure that the school can be run properly' (I7DM). According to the participants, the State, or perhaps more accurately the DES, also decided the curriculum as taught in the schools and set national policies, which had to be implemented at local level. There was no understanding of the partnership process at national level and the role of the NPCP in representing the views of parents. The middle class father summed up the State's role as follows:

> To provide the infra structure in terms of schools and facilities, to provide the resources in terms of teachers and funding that might be required for any programmes, to provide the curriculum that is appropriate to children and to try and I suppose, particularly at second level, to try and ensure that that curriculum is appropriate to modern Ireland in terms of factoring in technology, environmental issues and issues like that. (I4MF)

Many were dissatisfied with the State and felt that it could be doing more to fulfil its responsibilities.

> I think that the State lets down our children extremely badly. From the moment children are born in this State they are so badly

neglected ... from the maternity units to the way children are treated especially children with long-term special needs like my daughter ... simple things that I need ... imagine the school can not provide them as they do not have the resources they say. (I6MM)

Class size was mentioned by 9 per cent (N=23) of the respondents to the questionnaire as one of the changes they had noticed in schools over the last few years. While parents in disadvantage schools noticed that class sizes had decreased, those in middle class schools, especially the girls' school, complained that class sizes were too large. As one respondent wrote

I strongly feel that classroom sizes are too big and have had to take a very hands (sic) on approach to watching reading and maths levels in my own children. (There is just too many to teach) (Q238MG2)

With expansion of the welfare state, some respondents wished the State to act as a 'good parent' (Pinkney, 2000, p. 116) or provider and subsidise the costs for parents. Suggestions included providing or at least subsidising extra-curricular activities (I3MM), assessments and any additional help required for homework, e.g., computer aided programmes etc. (Q181MG6). Apart from assessments, these were traditionally considered the responsibility of parents.

Role and Responsibility of the Catholic Church

While acknowledging that the Church owned and was responsible for the operation for the schools, most of those who were interviewed were ambiguous about its role in both education and the school.

The Church – I suppose. Traditionally they had a big – like isn't there one in the Board of Management in these schools anyway?

They own the school.

Do they own this one?

Yeah, the [religious order] own this one ...

Well I do not think they have any influence, do they? I do not think they have much of an influence in this school

Well this school maybe not but [the middle class girls'] school now, they probably have more of an influence, because they are near the Church and they are always popping in and out there. (FG2M)

However, most respondents to the questionnaire (73 per cent, N=192) agreed that the Catholic values of the school were very important. For three (I5MM, I2DM, I7DM) of the parents interviewed it was a deter-mining factor when choosing a school. While one emphasised that it was part of the commitment made by the parents at baptism (I2DM), another (I5MM) felt that the Catholic ethos positively influenced the children to 'be involved, look outside themselves, to be a bit more forward looking and less selfish'. Others had mixed views. Once the children received a religious education and access to the sacraments, as one respondent (I4MF) stated, the Catholic ethos of the school did not really matter. Those that brought their children to Church more frequently were more likely to feel strongly that the Catholic values of the school were impor-tant (Table 5.1)

Table 5.1: The Connection between the Frequency of the Respondents'
Attendance at Church and Their Views that the Catholic Values of the
School Were Important

Variable	Strongly Agree		Agree		Do Not Agree		Total	
	N	%	N	%	N	%	N	%
Weekly	43	41	45	43	17	16	105	100
Once a month	13	18	45	61	16	22	74	101*
Less frequently	9	13	28	42	30	45	67	100
Total	65	26	118	48	63	26	246	100

X^2=.000 p<.05

* Result of rounding whole numbers

The involvement of the local clergy in visiting the schools, teaching children about God (I2DM) and preparing them for the sacraments was highlighted and welcomed by many. However, it was acknowledged that the connection between schools and Church had weakened over the years.

> I can give you an example of that in the sense that today the Church seems to operate on a separate basis. There's the family mass on Sunday, the family mass procession, Good Friday, in the Church, you know, all those feast days. There is never anything from the school. That's done separately to a parish group. Like I would never get a note home from [my child] saying that the parish mass is, the family mass is at 10.30 next Sunday, the procession will be - would your child like to go – you never get that. It is up to you to go and join the family mass group so that you can participate. It is not like down the country years ago, or even here years ago where, they would automatically assume, if they were in the Communion class, they'd be in the Holy Communion procession. That doesn't happen anymore. (FG2M)

However, some were unhappy with the Catholic ethos. The recent Church scandals, their own lack of faith along with the changes in society made respondents question the Church's involvement in schools. Two felt strongly that the days of denominational education were over and that there should be clear demarcation lines between Church and State.

> I do not think seriously that the Church has a place in education. I do not think that because of their inability to actually deal with it [child abuse] and confront it they deserve a place is how I would see it … and I think that a lot of – so many parents really do not feel part of the, I think, the sort of current Church, if you want to put it like that.

> I also think that having a totally Catholic ethos is unfortunate especially again in a school like this … where you see … children from lots of different back grounds now and different ethnic origins and they are not all Catholics. (I6MM)

Influence of Parents at National Level

When asked what parents could do to ensure that the State and Church met children's educational needs, most participants felt that they had very little influence. Nobody mentioned the role of the NPCP in negotiating partnership agreements and national educational policy and there was little confidence that parents' views would be listened to and acted on.

> Shout loudly. In some sense, what can you do? I mean, being a civil servant, knowing the way the system works – a lot and probably very little. I know they can sort of agitate, they can try and get together via the parents' councils, or whatever, either at local or national level, you know, in terms of making representations to Departments and local politicians and what not … in terms of whether parents can actually get more resources for schools or what I doubt that very much. Having said that look at the success that the parents in Inchicore had last week with the Christian Brothers and in keeping the school open for a year, you know. I suppose it does show the people power to some extent. In terms of the Church, well I suppose depending again locally, whether there is sort of openness to or whether people having voices. Now there are all these Pastoral Councils and things so there is sort of facility for people sort of to have their voices heard. Now to what extent the Church will act on it or can act on it or have the resources to act on it I do not know … (I4MF)

Another gave an example of how parents had tried to stop the closing of a local swimming pool and failed.

> I suppose if it's things for the children that you would get out and get involved. Like when they were trying to save the swimming pool, the likes of everyone got out and tried to stop them closing the pool … but it didn't work
>
> *Why do you think it didn't work?*
>
> Because I think that the whole place is being taken over by private companies to be honest and they are not leaving anything for kids. (I7DM)

Educational Capital at National Level

Irish education has undergone a period of immense change over the last decade. Sixty-six per cent (N=175) of questionnaire respondents mentioned the various changes that they had noticed over the last six years

(Table 5.2). These included changes to the curriculum, attitudes towards parents and in-service days. Many of these changes are the result of the implementation of the *Education Act 1998, Education Welfare Act 2000* and the *Primary School Curriculum* (DES, 1998). Respondents' educational capital or their knowledge of the national policy decisions, which impact most directly on their children's education, will be examined in this section.

Table 5.2: Changes Noticed by Parents in Schools Over the Last Six Years

	N	%
Changes in the curriculum	62	24
Positive attitude to parents	54	21
In-service days and holidays	43	16
Changes in children's behaviour	43	16
Changes in teachers' attitudes and approaches	34	13
Improvement to the buildings	33	13
Additional activities and programmes	25	10
Size of classes	23	9
More international pupils	22	8
More expensive	19	7
Introduction of healthy lunch policies	17	6
Changes in rules for attendance	16	6
Support or lack of support for children with special needs	11	4
Other e.g. homework	9	3

Education Welfare Act 2000

Parents appeared to be very aware of the implications of the *Education Welfare Act 2000* (Figure 5.1), which obliges them to send their children to school.

Figure 5.1: Respondents' Knowledge of the Education Welfare Act 2000

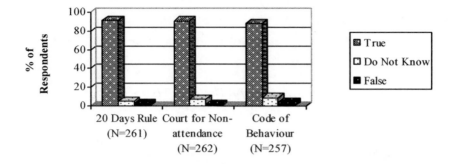

The vast majority (91 per cent, N=238) knew that parents could be taken to court if their child did not attend school. They (92 per cent, N=240) were also informed about the twenty day rule. If their children missed twenty days in a full school year, respondents knew that the school would report them to the Education Welfare Officer (EWO). In addition, 88 per cent (N=226) were aware that they were entitled to a copy of the schools' Code of Behaviour. In the light of this figure, it is interesting that only 61 per cent (N=159) of respondents stated that they had a copy of the school rules and/or Code of Behaviour.

Education Act 1998

Parents were less knowledgeable about their rights under the *Education Act 1998* (Figure 5.2). Only 77 per cent (N=202) of respondents to the questionnaire knew that they were entitled to their children's school re-cords, while even less (65 per cent, N=168) knew that they could take a Section 29 appeal to the DES if a school refuses to enrol their child.

Parents' knowledge of their right to be involved in the schools' deci-sion making and governance under the *Education Act* 1998 was also lim-ited (Figure 5.3). While three-quarters (73 per cent, N=188) of respon-dents to the questionnaire knew that there were parents on the Board of Management (BOM), over a quarter (27 per cent N=71) were unaware of the fact. As one parent who was interviewed said

> As I have said before, they need to communicate an awful lot more, even you know like that, the Board of the school the way it is. Is there a parent on it? (I2DM)

There was a similar pattern with respondents' knowledge of the BOM's obligation to keep parents informed of school matters. Even less knew that they had the right to be consulted on school policies (50 per cent N=130) and to see the school's financial accounts (29 per cent, N=75).

Figure 5.2: Parents' Knowledge of Their Rights in Relations to Their Children's Education under the Education Act 1998

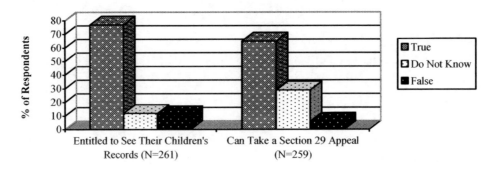

Figure 5.3: Parents' Knowledge of Their Rights in Relation to School Decision-making and Governance under the Education Act 1998

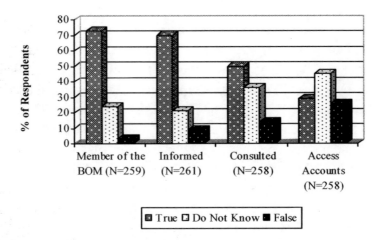

Under the *Education Act 1998,* parents are entitled to a copy of the school plan, which includes both organisational policies and curriculum plans. Over half (65 per cent N=168) the respondents agreed that they needed a copy of the school plan (Figure 5.4).

Figure 5.4: Parents Need a Copy of the School Plan (N=257)

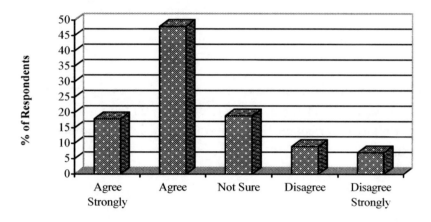

Primary School Curriculum (DES 1999a)

Whatever about their knowledge of the primary school curriculum, parents appeared to be very aware of the number of curriculum in-service days, for which the school is closed. Sixteen per cent (N=43) of respondents mentioned them as one of the changes they had noticed over the past six years. Most agreed with following respondent who wrote:

> Too many half-days, days off, in-service days, they seem to happen just before or after mid-terms, bank holidays weekends etc. Why?? As this week has shown, they are only back after a full week off and they are off again today 24/2/06. After Xmas they returned to school for 2½ days out of 5. Ridiculous. My daughter started school in Sep '00 and there has been in-service days (sic) since then. How many years are they going on for!! (Q201MG4)

Twenty-four per cent (N=62) of respondents mentioned that they had noticed changes to the curriculum over the last six years. There was mixed opinions on the curriculum. Positive comments included

Less concentration on rote learning

More oral work/self expression in classes e.g. drama

> Excellent history, geography/science introduction in 3rd/4th class. (Q129MB4)

Others were not as convinced of the benefits of the revised curriculum.

> Lack of learning times tables → less numerate students
>
> Alternative means of addition inappropriate (has it been tested). (Q169MBSI)

Despite the level of awareness of curricular changes and the in-service days, slightly less than half (48 per cent, N=123) the respondents knew that a revised curriculum had been introduced in Irish primary schools (Figure 5.5).

In the interviews and focus groups most parents had little knowledge of the curriculum.

> I do not really know. Ok from doing her homework it is obvious what she does in terms of reading, writing and maths and Irish but in terms of what else they do. For instance I was surprised last year, when … at the end of the year she came back laden down with all sorts of books. I was surprised at what she was actually doing, you know, it was so sort of advanced and so broad and what not. I hadn't really a sense of what the curriculum was. Now whether that is a good thing or a bad thing. I am quite happy that the curriculum is good and I am quite happy to leave it to the teachers but you know it mightn't be any harm if parents knew that. (I4MF)

Figure 5.5: Respondents' Knowledge of whether a Revised Curriculum Had Been Introduced in Irish Primary Schools (N=254)

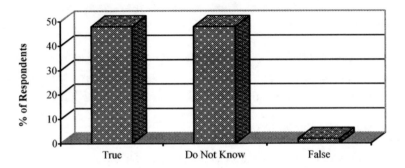

Social, Personal and Health Education (SPHE) is a new subject introduced with the revised curriculum. It is the one subject on which parents
are supposed to be consulted (DES 1999e; 2002a; 2003b) but from this
conversation it is obvious that some of the parents' knowledge of it was
sketchy.

> When the children are being taught like SPHE
>
> SPHE – what's that?
>
> It is sex education or something?
>
> Sex education and drugs education I think S stands for, I do not
> know …
>
> Is it sixth class that they do that in, is it?
>
> No, third class up …
>
> It is going to tell you all about sex …
>
> Is that to do with the leaflet in first and high babies about keeping
> yourself safe? ...
>
> It is all them brochures and things that comes home over the years.
>
> It is very good because it helps you along if she has questions. They
> know a bit already and you know what to give them. (FG1D)

Influences on Educational Capital

Certain variables influenced the educational capital of the respondents.
These include the social class, education and age of the respondent along
with the educational stage their children were at.

Parents with children in the middle class schools were more likely to
know about their rights under the *Education Act 1998*. 81 per cent
(N=136) of middle class respondents knew that there were parents on the
BOM as compared to just over half of the disadvantaged respondents (57
per cent, N=55). Similarly, 36 per cent (N=58) of middle class parents
knew that they were entitled to see the school's financial accounts as
opposed to only 18 per cent (N=17) of the disadvantaged respondents.
They were also more aware of the introduction of the revised curriculum

and the associated in-service days. A fifth of middle class parents (21 per cent N=35) commented on the number of days the children had off as compared to only 8 per cent (N=8) of those in the disadvantaged schools. Parents who had children attending the middle class girls' school were far more aware of the introduction of the revised curriculum than those from other schools (Table 5.3).

Table 5.3: The Differences between the Respondents from the Four Schools on Their Knowledge of the Introduction of the Revised Curriculum

Variable	True		Do Not Know		Total	
	N	%	N	%	N	%
Middle class girls' school	60	72	23	28	83	100
Middle class boys' school	37	47	42	53	79	100
Disadvantaged boys' school	18	33	36	67	54	100
Disadvantaged girls' school	8	21	30	79	38	100
Total	123	48	131	52	254	101*

X^2=.000 p<.05

* Result of rounding to whole numbers

As would be expected, those with higher qualifications appeared to have more knowledge of the system. Forty-three per cent (N=26) of those with third level qualifications knew that parents were allowed see the school's financial accounts compared to 24 per cent (N=45) of those without third level qualifications. Similarly 87 per cent (N=53) of respondents with third level qualifications knew that parents were represented on a school's BOM as compared to 68 per cent (N=129) of those without third level qualifications. Moreover, educational qualifications also influenced respondents' knowledge of their right to see their children's records (Table 5.4).

Table 5.4: Influence of the Respondents' Level of Education on Their Knowledge of Their Entitlement to Their Children's School Records

Variable	True		Either Do Not Know or False		Total	
	N	%	N	%	N	%
Primary level qualification	11	50	11	50	22	100
Second level qualification	130	77	39	23	169	100
Third level qualification	52	85	9	15	61	100
Total	193	77	59	23	252	100

$X^2 = .003$ $p < .05$

In contrast, 96 per cent (N=21) of those who had primary education knew that the BOM must keep parents informed of school matters as compared with 67 per cent (N=156) of those with a higher level of education. Interestingly, they were also less likely to agree that they needed a copy of the school plan. Only 35 per cent (N=7) of those with a primary education felt that parents needed a copy of the school plan in contrast with 68 per cent (N=152) of those with higher levels of education.

The educational capital of respondents with older children appeared to be higher. Over three-quarters (83 per cent N=71) of parents with children in secondary school knew that there were parents on the BOM as compared to 68 per cent (N=116) of those with no children at second level. Likewise, 40 per cent (N=34) of those with children attending secondary school knew that they were entitled to see the school's financial accounts in contrast with 24 per cent (N=41) of those without children in secondary school. Parents of older children were also more likely to know that a revised curriculum had been introduced. Approximately three fifths of those with children in the senior classes (61 per cent, N=79) and in second level (60 per cent, N=52) were aware of the changes as compared to over two fifths of those with children in the junior classes (42 per cent, N=56) and not attending second level schools (47 per cent N=79). It appears that the longer parents are in the education system the more educational capital they acquire.

Of course, those with older children were more likely to be older themselves. Three-quarters of those over thirty (77 per cent, N=170) knew that there were parents on the BOM compared with only 48 per cent (N=20) of respondents under thirty. Similarly, 32 per cent (N=69) of those over thirty knew that they were entitled to see the school's financial accounts as opposed to only 12 per cent (N=5) of those under thirty. There was also a noticeable difference between the age of the respondents and their knowledge about the curriculum changes (Table 5.5).

Table 5.5: The Influence of the Age of the Respondent and Their Knowledge that a Revised Curriculum Had Been Introduced in Irish Primary Schools

Variable	True		Do Not Know		Total	
	N	%	N	%	N	%
Aged under 30	6	15	34	85	40	100
Aged between 30 and 39	47	43	63	57	110	100
Aged 40 and over	69	68	33	32	102	100
Total	122	48	130	52	252	100

X^2=.000 p<.05

Home–School Relationships

This section examines the relationship between the research participants and the schools their children were attending. It investigates the welcome they receive and how comfortable they feel about complaining. The variables which influence the relationship between home and school are also explored.

Relationship with the School

The vast majority of questionnaire respondents (96 per cent, N=252) agreed that they felt welcome in their children's schools (Figure 5.6).

As one interviewee said:

> I know that if I needed to see any of the teachers there wouldn't be any difficulty in organising that. That's just a feeling I get from them that they are amenable to it – it is a whole school kind of ethos thing. (I5MM)

Figure 5.6: Respondents' Perceptions of Their Relationship with the School

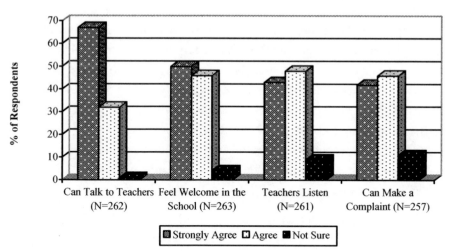

In addition, 21 per cent (N=54) of the respondents to the questionnaires mentioned that they had noticed a change in the home-school relationship over the last six years. Teachers had become easier to talk to (Q37DB2), 'more approachable' (Q172MG6) and there was 'better communication between schools and parents' (Q199MG4). As one respondent to the questionnaire wrote

1. Increased parental involvement in school matters.

2. Parents are actively encouraged by the school ethos to be more involved in their children's education – reading, homework, sport, etc.

3. Greater sharing of information between schools and parents. (Q250MGSI)

The 'approachability' of a school was very important to parents and they felt that

You should be made to feel that you can walk in at any time – ring up to say that you are on your way or you are coming in or even out in the yard ... I know here, at half one, half two, you can just come in to the yard and the head teacher is always there and you can just go up with any problem. I know of some other schools where you have to ring, you have to make an appointment and you might get your appointment. (FG2M)

Most respondents had met the principal (96 per cent, N=252) and their child's teacher (99 per cent, N=260). They felt that they could talk to the teacher (99 per cent, N=260) and that teachers listened to them (91 per cent, N=237). It was interesting that more strongly agreed that they could talk to the teacher (67 per cent, N=177), than strongly agreed that teachers listened to them (43 per cent, N=112).

Most parents were very aware of and sympathetic to the difficulties experienced by teachers and the increasing demands placed on them by the changes in society.

I think teachers do what they have to do extremely well, sometimes under extremely difficult circumstances, with a lot of overcrowding and children with all sorts of problems … but my experience of the teaching, the teachers my children have had, they have all been fantastic. (I4MM)

There are huge demands being made on teachers now to be up-to-date as regards any health issues. ADHD is a huge thing. Whereas years ago children were bold but now-a-days everybody seems to have ADHD and they have special problems and I am sure that there is a huge book that every teacher has to read about an ADHD child …

Oh, I think, I think a teacher has to be just so aware of all social issues now and then like sure every second child at the back of your class probably won't speak English if you've got junior or senior infants, so you have that to contend with as well. (FG2M)

The middle class father suggested that parents added to these pressures as they were much more inclined to question teachers today than they were in the past. He felt that

Between you and me it sort of gone too far, because from friends of mine who are teachers you get parents that, you know, are beating down their door, you know, complaining about everything. (I4MF)

Most respondents (88 per cent, N=228) felt that they could make a complaint in the school. However, prior to approaching the school, the interviewees said that they would discuss the issue with their child and see if there was anything they could do at home to help. One person felt that if a child had problems it was just as frustrating for the teacher as for the parents and that both needed to work together to help the child (I6MM). It appears that parents try to deal with problems diplomatically, starting at the lowest level possible.

> First of all I would ask her about it, you know, say to her what's wrong. If there was a problem, I'd go straight up to her teacher the next morning and speak to her teacher.
>
> *And what happens then, if it didn't solve it?*
>
> I'd talk to the principal and if that didn't work and nothing was done about it I'd go to the Board of Education about it and complain. (I2DM)

However, some parents, particularly if they were unsure of their rights, preferred to contact the DES before the school. They rang the DES

> If they weren't sure about what the school's policy was. If there was something happening at the school that they were not happy about and they needed to find out what is supposed to happen in these particular circumstances. (FG2M)

However, one middle class mother felt very uneasy talking to teachers.

> I have – I am going to tell you now – the idea of walking in to a teacher, in to a principal or anything – I hate parent teacher meetings.
>
> *Really?*
>
> Oh yeah, I am shot back 20 years – Oh Christ I hate them.
>
> *Yeah?*
>
> Oh yeah! Dreadful I think its *[laughing]* past experience coming back on me. I do not know *[laughing]* … You know these parent-

teacher meetings I never feel very comfortable at them. I'm hanging on the edge. (I3MM)

She had approached a teacher about her child and felt that her concerns were not listened to or acted on.

> I had a terrible phobia about [my child] not mixing so well and I went to the teacher in the school yard about it and it was kind of 'ah no I'll keep an eye on her, it is grand' and then I went back again a few months later and it was the same. I actually felt that she hadn't really paid attention to me, to be honest with you – that kind of thing. I know she probably felt that I was getting worked up about nothing but she [her child] was exceptionally shy at the time and I did feel that I was kind of bothering the teacher, she was busy and I felt like a bit of an idiot then. 'Oh my God she thinks I'm stupid'. It was a bit of a missing link. (I3MM)

She felt she would try to help her child at home rather than complaining to the teacher.

> Oh God, I do not know … rather than approach the school, I think I would be more inclined to sit down and help them myself, teach them myself. I'd feel I wasn't qualified nearly to go up and say – because I know a girl, her little one had a huge amount of homework. She challenged the teacher and the teacher told her 'Well, you know, she's in third class now and she has to expect this homework' and she just felt that she's not able for it. It is too much but she got nowhere with it … she was told sorry she had to learn it whether she likes it or not. So I think that is where I am coming from. Even if you did go up you wouldn't get anywhere. (I3MM)

Others felt that their concerns about their children were not taken seriously and that they had to put a lot of pressure on the school before they would act. One parent who was interviewed described her experience as follows:

> My child, for three years I asked for an assessment report to be made out, this is the truth. All my children have gone to the school, I choose the school, it is a school that done them good so it is not a big knock down, I was three years and she couldn't read and I really mean that right. She was going in to third class

at this stage, how many is that four years or whatever, and I said, 'I need an assessment done on her. Can I have the psychologist, you know the educational psychologist?' Because she's passing her sigma and micra tests, ok, she was barely passing them, she couldn't get, she wasn't eligible for these, she wasn't good enough to go on for this, so I was stuck in the middle. It was like you are going to have this child who is like, not great, and below par but not enough below the par to so she is going to go through school left in the class and then goes to secondary school and by second year the child leaves school, because she has no interest. So I had a fight and I asked to pay for the psychologist report myself because the report has to be paid for. The Board of Education pays for two and school board pays for another two and that's it. I'd have paid for it myself but thanks to them I didn't have to pay for it. They got it done a week later. I was told she had ADHD, which I knew she had, right and I'd been telling them three years she had and she'd have got her resource hours, for three years. It was terrible hard, it really was and now she is getting all the support she needs and I mean all the support she needs. She has her resource hours and she has come on like, she's nearly at her age for reading now. That's needn't have been the case. You have to really fight. (FG1D)

Factors which Influence the Home–School Relationship

Some of the factors which influenced the respondents' relationship with the school were unexpected. Apart from gender, the respondents' personal characteristics and/or the school their children attended had no bearing on their relationship with the school. Home-school communication and parental involvement in both the home curriculum and the school were more significant factors.

Mothers appeared to be more actively engaged in establishing and maintaining a relationship with the school. They tended to talk to the teachers more frequently. Over a quarter (27 per cent, N=55) spoke to the teachers at least once a week as compared with 10 per cent (N=2) fathers. They were more likely to have met the principal (Table 5.6). However, there were no significant gender differences in the perceptions of the questionnaire respondents on their relationship with the school. Fathers felt just as welcome as mothers.

Table 5.6: Gender Differences in Having Met the Principal

Variable	Yes		No		Total	
	N	*%*	*N*	*%*	*N*	*%*
Mother	218	97	6	3	224	100
Father	19	79	5	21	24	100
Total	237	96	11	4	248	100

$X^2=.002$ $p<.02$

There were gender differences between interviewees when defining the teachers' role. The mothers were vague as to what the teachers' role was, with one woman going as far to say, 'I do not think I have any role on saying what teachers should do' (I6MM). While emphasising how great the teachers were and the positive part they played in their children's lives, they described teachers as educating, disciplining, teaching and giving children the 'facts'. One mother acknowledged how teachers had supported her and her children emotionally in time of crisis.

> Teachers, one would be discipline, two would be to educate them but to me I find that, over the years, with the teachers my kids had, they were kind of counsellors too. Like my kids had a lot of trouble when their father left, when me (sic) mother died and me father died and I found great support from the teachers through all that. They have a bigger job than just teaching, you know. (I8DM)

The men, on the other hand were very explicit about the teachers' role. They saw it as teaching children to 'read, write, learn' (I1DGF). The middle class father also saw the development of qualities which support children's learning as being important.

> In terms of typical order – right at the very start in terms of playschool try and get the kids used to – giving them a little bit of independence, helping them to develop as little individuals and then moving through sort of primary level and trying to put some structure on the kids' day and on the kids' approach to any activities and then obviously the mechanics of reading and writing and just giving them a general education in terms of nature, the environment, science and whatever else. I think

changing then at second level to trying to get, rather than simply spoon feeding and giving young adults – trying to develop in them a responsibility – their own responsibility and trying to give them a questioning nature and trying to facilitate their learning rather pushing it on them, setting the agenda, trying to trying to facilitate the students so that they are eager to learn and they are setting the agenda to an extent. (I4MF)

Communication was an important element in the development of positive home-school relationships. Not surprisingly, the more the respondents talked to their child's teacher the more they felt that they were listened to (Table 5.7). They also tended to feel more comfortable about making a complaint. Over half (59 per cent, N=37) of those who spoke to the teacher daily strongly agreed that they could make a complaint in comparison with 35 per cent (N=61) of those who spoke to the teacher less frequently.

Table 5.7: Influence of the Frequency with which Respondents Spoke to Their Child's Teacher and Their Perception on whether Teachers Listened to Them

Variable: Spoke to the Teacher	Strongly Agree that Teacher Listened to Them		Agreed that Teacher Listened to Them		Disagreed that Teacher Listened to them		Total	
	N	*%*	*N*	*%*	*N*	*%*	*N*	*%*
Once a week	35	56	27	43	1	2	63	101*
Once a month	42	42	48	48	10	10	100	100
Once a year or never	26	34	40	53	10	13	76	100
Total	103	43	115	48	21	9	239	100

X^2=.042 p<.05

* Result of rounding to whole numbers.

Even written communication has an impact of parents' perceptions of their relationship with their children's teacher (Table 5.8). Over half (53 per cent, N=58) of those who read notes daily strongly agreed that they were listened to by the teachers as opposed to 36 per cent (N=49) of those who read notes weekly or monthly. Similarly respondents who read the notes sent home on daily basis were more likely to strongly agree that they could make a complaint.

Table 5.8: Influence of the Frequency with which Respondents Read Notes Sent Home by the School and Their Perception on whether They Could Make a Complaint

Variable: Read notes	Strongly Agree that Could Make a Complaint		Agree that Could Make a Complaint		Do Not Agree Could Make a Complaint		Total	
	N	%	N	%	N	%	N	%
Once a week	60	55	38	35	11	10	109	100
Once a month	32	34	47	51	14	15	93	100
Once a year or never	12	28	26	61	5	12	43	101*
Total	104	42	111	45	30	12	245	99*

$X^2 = .007$ p<.05

* Result of rounding to whole numbers.

Support for the ethos of the school along with parental involvement in certain aspects of the home curriculum and in the school tended to influence their relationship with the school. Those who strongly agreed that the Catholic values of the school was important also strongly agreed that teachers listened to them (Table 5.9). Similarly, 58 per cent (N=39) of those who strongly agreed with the ethos of the school felt that they could make a complaint as compared with 36 per cent (N=69) of those who did not strongly agree.

Those who attended church weekly were more likely to strongly agree that the teachers listened to them (Table 5.10). Similarly, 51 per cent (N=53) of weekly attendees felt strongly that they could complain as opposed to 36 per cent (N=50) of those who attended less frequently.

Table 5.9: Relationship between Agreement with Catholic Values of the School and Respondents' Perception that Teachers Listened to Them

Variable:	Strongly Agree that Teachers Listen to me		Agree that Teachers Listen to Me		Do Not Agree that Teachers Listen to Me		Total	
	N	*%*	*N*	*%*	*N*	*%*	*N*	*%*
Strongly agree with Catholic values	41	61	22	33	4	6	67	100
Agree with Catholic values	49	40	65	53	9	7	123	100
Do not agree with Catholic values	22	31	36	51	12	17	70	99*
Total	112	43	123	47	25	10	260	100

$X^2 = .002$ p<.05

* Result of rounding to whole numbers.

Table 5.10: Relationship between Attendance at Church and the Respondents' Perception that the Teachers Listened to Them

Variable: Attend Church	Strongly Agree that Teachers Listen to Me		Agree that Teachers Listen to Me		Disagree that Teachers Listen to Me		Total	
	N	*%*	*N*	*%*	*N*	*%*	*N*	*%*
Once a week	56	53	43	41	6	6	105	100
Once a month	30	41	37	51	6	8	73	100
Once a year or never	20	29	37	54	11	16	68	99*
Total	106	43	117	48	23	9	246	100

$X^2 = .015$ p<.05

* Result of rounding to whole numbers.

Respondents who checked their children's copies daily also had a stronger sense that teachers listened to them. Half (50 per cent, N=94) of those who looked at their children's copies and workbooks daily strongly agreed that teachers listened to them in comparison with only a quarter (24 per cent, N=14) of those who looked at them weekly. Likewise 48 per cent (N=90) of those examined their children's copies daily felt strongly that they could make a complaint as compared with a quarter (29 per cent, N=17) of those who examined them weekly.

In addition, 56 per cent (N=40) of those that helped out in the school strongly agreed that the teachers listened to them as opposed to 38 per cent (N=70) of those that did not help out. Similarly, 'helpers' felt more comfortable about making a complaint (Table 5.11).

Table 5.11: The Relationship between Helping Out in the School and Perceptions on Making a Complaint

Variable	Strongly Agreed that They Could Make a Complaint		Agreed that They Could Make a Complaint		Disagreed that They Could Make a Complaint		Total	
	N	*%*	*N*	*%*	*N*	*%*	*N*	*%*
Helped out in the school	43	61	23	32	5	7	71	100
Did not help out in the school	64	34	96	52	26	14	186	100
Total	107	42	119	46	31	12	257	100

X^2=.001 p<.05

Home–School Communication

As seen in the previous section, effective and frequent home-school communication is central for developing positive relationships between home and school. This section explores how parents and schools communicate with each other, the extent to which parents were satisfied with the existing communication systems and the factors which influenced home-school communication. My observations and analysis of the notes sent home by my local school details the extent and variety of home-school communication.

Observations of Home-School Communication

From my observations, I found home-school communication revolved around four main areas (Figure 5.7). These included providing each other with relevant information, upcoming events along with the continuous requests for money. In addition, I had to act as an advocate for my children with the teacher and school.

> D2 was worried about the maths she had done in school. She was not sure whether she was to do number one or the whole page. The teacher will be correcting it tonight. We discussed it and were undecided whether I would write a note or we would just leave it. (FN 09-06-05)

> D2 asked me to write the note to her teacher about the Maths before she left for school. When she came home from school that evening I asked her what happened. She said that they were only supposed to do question one. (FN 10-06-06)

Figure 5.7: Observations of Home–School Communications

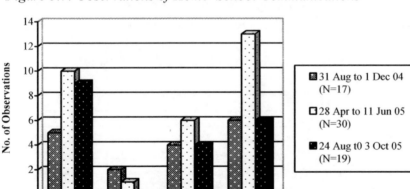

The time of the year and the stage the child is at can make a difference to the amount of communication there is between home and school. In May 2005, one of my daughters was making her first communion and the school concert was also on, so there was a lot of communication between home and school. The following extracts illustrate the types of requests from the school.

D2 brings home a letter from the school regarding the communion. It provides information about the ceremony and a request for €5 for leaflets, flowers etc. (FN 09-05-05)

D2 brings home a note from other parents asking for €5 to buy flowers for the teachers, priest and principal. (FN 10-05-05)

D2 brings home a note about the communion photographs. They are looking for permission to take the photographs and are also asking the children to wear their communion clothes to school on Monday. It will be €75 for full package of photographs. (FN 11-05-05)

D1 and D2 bring notes home regarding tickets for the concerts. We have to decide on date for us all to attend. The tickets cost €8 each. D2 asks me for a black shawl for her play. We search the house but unfortunately we can not find one. D1 asks me for rosary beads for her play. Luckily we have some. (FN 12-05-05)

The local school sent home about fifty to seventy notes in the school year (Figure 5.8). This averages one every third day over the course of the school year. Only half the notes school were from the school.

Figure 5.8: Origin of Notes Received from the Local School

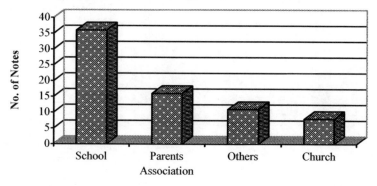

A quarter came from the Parents Association and the rest were from the Church and others like Dublin City Council, Health Board, Summer Camps and the MSReadathon. The Parents Association notes concerned the AGM (Annual General Meeting), an educational talk for parents, Communion, Newsletters and fundraising. Again, apart from the invitation to join at the beginning of the year, there were no requests for input into decision-making or policies of the Parents Association or the NPCP.

Most of the notes home concerned events that were taking place in either the school or community (Figure 5.9).

Figure 5.9: Content of Notes Sent Home from the Local School

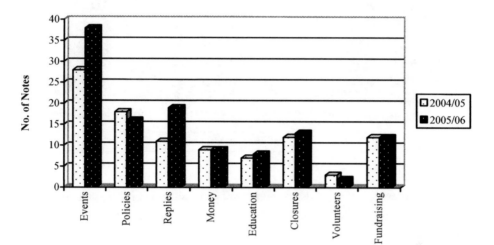

A lot of them outlined various organisational policies. Parents were re-quested to reply to twelve of the notes. Most of the requests for money, which was in addition to fundraising, were for extra-curricular trips and events.

Methods of Communication

From the replies to the questionnaires, it was obvious that written com-munication between home and school tended to be one-way (Figure 5.10).

Ninety-eight per cent (N=247) of respondents to the questionnaire received a note from the school at least once a month. In contrast, less than half (46 per cent, N=115) the respondents wrote a note to the school on a monthly basis. In fact, almost a quarter of the parents (24 per cent, N=61) never wrote to the school. Parents appeared to prefer oral com-munication with most parents meeting the teacher at least once a year.

Figure 5.10: Home–School Communication

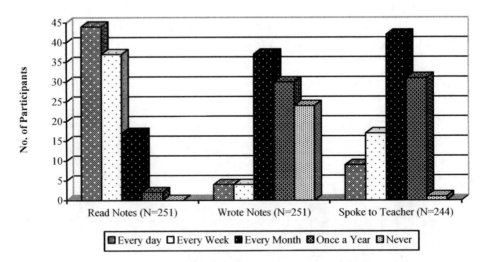

Interviewees mentioned parent-teacher meetings, end-of-year reports and homework as the ways they found out how their children were doing in school.

> If you are doing the homework and you see the teacher has corrected it, and you'll see the sort of comments from the teacher on that. I mean they would have a little spelling test every week or two and again you'd get the feedback from that in the sense that [my child] would come home with the little thing with the teacher's stamp on it – congrats – the subtle sort of informal stuff and then you would have the parent-teacher meetings whatever once or twice a year.

> *And do you feel that you get enough information from that?*

> Oh yeah, … I was surprised at the level of information coming back in terms of the detail. It was clear that I mean the teachers really knew the kids and sort of knew the strengths and, you know, weakness and issues with the kids, you know. I would have thought that if she was standing up in front of thirty seven year olds, that she was almost doing well if she knew their names at the end of year, whereas they really, I was surprised at the very sort of insightful, feedback on the sort of end-of-year report. (I4MF)

Children also seemed to play a major role in keeping parents abreast of what was happening in school.

> [My child] comes home and tells me she passed a test. That's what I find... There is no real information for me. I get a lot of information from the tests or if she has done well in something. It is usually her that tells me. (I3MM)

Some felt that children were unreliable and they had to be involved with the school if they were to keep themselves up-to-date and informed.

> Now my young fella wouldn't tell me too much myself so I find it beneficial for me to go to the Parents', to get involved, because otherwise I know nothing. Then he's involved with sports so I hear it from the other lads on the side line so I have my ear there the whole time. It would really depend because my child would tell you nothing. Other kids will come home and might say more. Do you remember the time they had the dinosaur exhibition here? Sure I knew nothing about it. [My child] never opened his mouth so I never knew, I'd hear nothing unless I ...
>
> *There was a note home about that so he didn't give that to you either.*
>
> There, you go. (FG2M)

Several variables had an influence on the amount and type of communication between home and school. Parents in the disadvantaged schools appeared to have more contact with the teacher with 40 per cent (N=35) of them speaking to the teacher weekly (Table 5.12). In contrast, a similar percentage (42 per cent, N=64) of middle class parents only spoke to the teacher once a year.

In addition, the respondents' age and their children's class had some influence. Forty-one per cent (N=50) of the respondents with children in the junior classes spoke to the teacher at least once a week as compared to 11 per cent (N=13) of respondents in the senior classes. In fact over half the parents in senior infants spoke to their child's teacher at least once a week. Younger respondents tended to have children in the junior classes and this may be why 40 per cent (N=14) of those under thirty spoke to the teacher weekly as compared with 18 per cent (N=17) of those over forty.

Table 5.12: Influence of Social Class on the Frequency with which Respondents Spoke to Their Children's Teacher

Variable	Weekly		Once a Month		Once a Year or Never		Total	
	N	%	N	%	N	%	N	%
Disadvantaged schools	35	40	40	46	12	14	87	100
Middle class schools	28	18	62	40	64	42	154	100
Total	63	26	104	42	76	32	241	100

X^2=.000 p<.05

Respondents with children in the senior classes and in second level education were more likely to use written communication. Just over half of those with children in the senior classes (56 per cent, N=71) and in second level (55 per cent, N=45) wrote notes to the school on a monthly basis as compared with 35 per cent (N=44) of those with children in the junior classes. Obviously, there is no need for parents who are meeting the teacher on a regular basis to write notes. This may be why 33 per cent (N=41) of parents with children in the junior classes and 44 per cent (N=17) of those under thirty never wrote notes to their child's teacher/school.

Quality of Information

Most questionnaire respondents (86 per cent, N=223) felt that the schools told them what is happening (Figure 5.11). As one respondent to the questionnaire wrote

> The school always keeps us informed on what's going on & asks our opinion which is great. We always know about what changes are being made. (Q13DB4)

Not surprisingly, those who helped out in the school were more likely to strongly agree that they were told what was happening. Nearly half (47 per cent N=33) of those who helped strongly agreed that they were kept informed as opposed to 30 per cent (N=56) of those did not help out. In addition, those who examined their children's copies and workbooks on a daily basis were more likely to strongly agree that the school kept informed. Forty-one per cent (N=76) strongly agreed that the school told them what was happening compared with 22 per cent (N=13) who looked at the copies weekly.

Figure 5.11: Respondents' Perceptions on Whether the School Tells Them what is Happening (N=259)

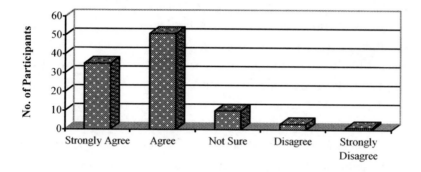

There was mixed responses from those who were interviewed with some feeling that they were kept very well informed and others feeling that they needed more information.

> Very informed because if there is anything going on there'd be a little letter sent home ... There is a little newsletter sent out, I think, at the end of each term and that has everything that has happened. If there was fund raising and how much they made and if somebody's sister had a little brother or what ever. (I7DM)

> Like you'd never hear anything back. It would just stay in the school and that's it. If a problem arises, nobody has a clue what going on or anything. 'I never heard that before'. (I2DM)

As part of my role as an SDPS facilitator I occasionally work with groups of parents on various topics. The following observations were made while helping the Parents Association of a Special School develop an information booklet for parents. It is included as it illustrates some of the difficulties for parents in communicating with schools. While all these parents had children with special needs, they also had children in mainstream and felt that the situation was similar there.

All the parents present agreed that they were getting information from schools. However, they felt, 'They are telling us but yet they are not really telling us.' They felt that schools were managing both the situation and them rather than being open and honest about things.

One mother said that she knew her child's timetable. The others said that they didn't and asked how she knew. She said that she had asked at the IEP (Individual Education Plan) meeting. She kept reiterating during the night: 'You have to know the questions to ask?'

Most had very little knowledge of school's organisational policies and curriculum plans. There were more questions than answers to put in the booklet. Most were in and out of the school so they knew what was going on. They also asked questions but as another mother said to me, 'We'd need you at case conferences. Often we do not know what to say without antagonising people' (FN 13-03-06).

Most respondents to the questionnaire felt that they were informed of both the standard of teaching and learning in the school (85 per cent, N=220) and their children's progress (95 per cent, N=260) (Figure 5.12).

Figure 5.12: Respondents' Knowledge of Children's Learning

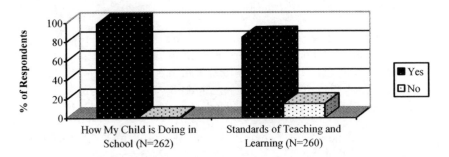

The vast majority of respondents to the questionnaire agreed that schools needed to keep parents up-to-date both on curriculum changes (97 per cent, N=254) and their children' progress (100 per cent, N=260) (Figure5.13). More were inclined to strongly agree that they needed to be kept up-to-date on their children's progress (77 per cent, N=200) than on curriculum changes (59 per cent, N=153).

Figure 5.13: Respondents' Views on Whether Schools Should Keep Parents Up-to-date on These Items (N=261)

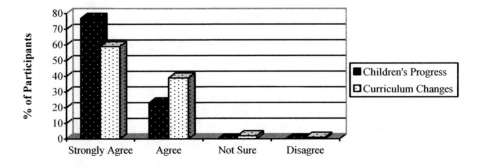

While there were no significant differences between the individual schools, five respondents in the middle class girls' school felt very strongly that parents should be given the standardised test results without having to ask for them. This, they felt, would inform parents of their children's progress and ensure that they knew the level their children were at. It also meant that parents could either help the child themselves at home or get help for them, if needed.

> I feel that all parents should be given the results of the Drumcondra tests so over time you can see if your child is struggling in any area. Also the IQ results should be given without asking for these results. Sorry schools do not give these out unless you ask. (Q243MG2)

Another (Q201MG4) thought that 'parents should be informed a little more about their child's progress, not just once a year at the parent teacher meeting or when there is a problem'. The participants in this focus group would like a monthly report on how the children are doing.

> It would be nice to have a report monthly on their behaviour, their position in the class, meaning how they were getting on … so when your child is coming home with mood swings or really happy or what ever you have a picture of what is going on, because children do not always tell you stuff, you know.

> *I know.*

> Especially when they are reaching puberty and going to secondary school and you are lost, they are telling you one thing and teachers are telling you a different way. (FG1D)

Most felt that the parents should be informed immediately if their child is experiencing difficulties and that the end-of-year report should contain no surprises.

> That happened me, my little one was having killings with the teacher, for a whole year and I didn't know it. Anytime I went up and the teacher was saying she's fine, she's fine, and it wasn't until she was leaving in the summer and I got her report and I opened it when I went home and I thought there's be nothing – and there was nothing but bad in it … It was saying she wasn't doing that and she couldn't do this, and she couldn't speak to her and my little one was too outspoken, she couldn't do. (FG1D)

In the interviews and focus groups, participants expressed mixed views on whether they needed to be up-to-date on curriculum matters, particularly if they felt that the teachers were doing their job properly. However, as the child got older they expected that they would need more information.

> It is, I suppose, trying to keep a balance between having an active and healthy interest and not interfering or trying to go too far. Let the teacher do what the teacher does at the teacher's own pace as long as you are happy that the teacher is sort of competent and up to the job and certainly in terms of the two teachers she has had to date, both have been excellent so we are sort of happy enough to sort of stay back and to what ever extent we need to get involved, we get involved but really apart from doing the homework, we do not really get involved yet but I see that sort of changing as time goes on.
>
> *In what way?*
>
> In the sense that you'd get more involved, I mean, I do not know, but I'd imagine just out of interest if nothing else. I mean I suppose, given physically I do not expect her to be hauling a whole load of books in and out at this stage but as they get older, I presume they will be and just to have a look at what they are doing and try to support them that little bit more. I suppose going in to second level in terms of – ahem – maths or chemistry or

biology or whatever that if they were sort of having difficulties, you'd try and gen back up on it again so that you could sort of support them, if needs be. (I4MF)

Even the most involved parents felt that the Curriculum was handed down from the DES and parents had no business interfering in how it was implemented.

What about if it was something that was being taught to the children?

Sure that's all come down.

No, sure we'd have no say.

We'd have no say in that.

I wouldn't expect it to be honest with you.

Like if it has come through the Department we'd just take it as. (FG2M)

Despite 'taking it as is', the same parents got confused and worried when they perceived that the curriculum was not being covered.

I had a boy who didn't seem to be doing any Irish. I was getting really worried it … but I suddenly found out that they weren't supposed to be doing any. The curriculum had changed. The Irish, it was all the, you know the old buntus and learning how to speak and all that and there was … no book, no writing or no spellings any more but I didn't know that. So I was fretting over nothing. You have to just ask, find out – that's what I found.

I think we were the same because I remember we had bought the Irish books and other books and we were reading them. (FG2M)

They were delighted to receive the DVD from the National Council for Curriculum and Assessment (NCCA). They felt that because it told them what their children should doing in each class for each subject, it would help them monitor the education their children were receiving and help them 'know whether the job was being done or not' (FG2M).

Parental Involvement in Their Children's Schools

There were three levels to parents' involvement in their children's school: audiences, volunteers and decision-makers. This section examines parental involvement in their children's school under these three areas and the factors which influenced their involvement.

Audiences and Volunteers

Most parents' involvement in their children's school was limited to attending the 'set pieces' (I4MF) (Figure 5.14). The vast majority of questionnaire respondents attended parent-teacher meetings (96 per cent, N=253) and other school events, e.g., plays, games, concerts, etc (89 per cent, N=236). However, only half (52 per cent, N=135) the respondents went to classes and talks organised by the school, while 35 per cent (N=92) went to activities (AGM, fundraisers, talks etc.) run by the Parents Association.

Figure 5.14: Involvement of Parents as 'Audiences' in Their Children's Schools

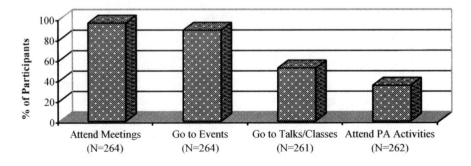

Others were volunteers and were among the batch of 'reliable' parents who volunteered to help the school on a regular basis.

> I am one of a small batch of parents who are at home so anything
> that's happening, some of the teachers are going to contact me
> and ask me would I accompany them or help out, which I always
> do if I can. (I6MM)

The number of volunteers was much lower than that of audiences (Figure 5.15).

Figure 5.15: Involvement of Parents as 'Volunteers' in Their Children's Schools

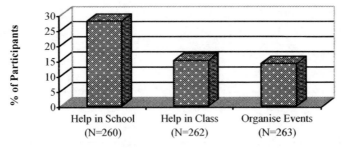

Most respondents who helped out in the school also stated that they helped in their children's classrooms or in organising fundraising and other event. As can be seen from Table 5.13, most volunteers had a pre-ferred activity with very few choosing to be involved in everything.

Table 5.13: The Links between Helping Out in the School, Helping Out in Your Child's Classroom and Organising Fundraising and Other Events

Variable		Help Out in My Child's class		Do Not Help Out in My Child's Class		Total	
		N	%	N	%	N	%
Help out in the school	Help organise fundraising and events	10	32	21	68	31	100
	Do not help organise fund-raising and events	24	60	16	40	40	100
	Total	34	48	37	52	71	100

$X^2=.031$ p<.05

School Decision-Making and Governance

The 'decision-makers', who got involved with the Parents Association and the BOM were in the minority. While they may have got 'fed up every now and then', they felt that if they did 'not go, nobody will' (FG2M). Only 13 per cent (N=34) of questionnaire respondents stated that they either were or had been members of a parents association. Even fewer (3 per cent, N=8) respondents either were or had been members of the BOM.

Not surprisingly, the majority of the respondents to the questionnaire did not feel involved in school governance and decision-making (Figure 5.16).

Figure 5.16: Perceived Involvement in Decision-making

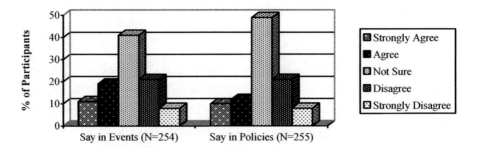

Very few felt that they had a say in school related events (30 per cent, N=77) and policies (22 per cent, N=56). While most of the parents who were interviewed agreed that parents could have more of a say in what was going on, many suggested that it was their own fault because they had not got involved with either the BOM or the parents association.

> We were asked, a good few years ago, our views in a little questionnaire sent out about school uniform. They surveyed all the parents and got the answers to that. The other way you'd have any influence is if you do something like putting your name forward for the Board of Management and because I can't and I haven't, it is the same idea as if you do not vote in the general election you can't really whinge (sic) about it. I could be more involved if I wished. It is not that the school is excluding me it is just that I haven't been involved. (I5MM)

Some were also reluctant to take on the extra responsibilities.

> You should have your say, but I mean who wants all that responsibility anyway but everybody should hear some of it anyway, you know what I mean. (FG1D)

Most were satisfied that if they had an issue they could deal with it on an individual basis with the principal.

> Well I suppose you weren't happy and had something to say that [the principal] would sit down and listen to you. I think you would have a say, yes. (I7DM)

However, even those who were heavily involved in the Parents Association recognised that certain issues were off limits to parents and that their suggestions had to suit the school's agenda.

> On the major issues, it is very limited in terms of which teacher a class will get, the structure of the school year – those kinds of issues, we wouldn't really have any say but the smaller issues, say underneath those, you would get to influence input – if you were right. Then again, you could come up with some thing and be way off. *[Laughter]* (FG2M)

When asked what they would do if the school sent home a policy with which they disagreed, most parents would let the school know how they felt.

> Well I would have no problem about ringing the principal and just talking to her about it. I wouldn't think twice about doing it if I had to do it. (I6MM)

Some however felt that they never got the opportunity to give feedback on policies.

> Ah, I would. If they sent me home deliberately something I would comment ... but you just never get the opportunity really. You are never invited *[laughs] to* give an opinion ... I would love to get more of an invitation from the school as to how they do things. (I3MM)

Some thought that parents had no place in school decisions.

> I think parents should make decisions at home and the school should make decisions at school and the parents should be big enough to stand up and abide by it, you know, if it is a lawful decision... Unfortunately there are people no matter what decision you make, they want to find everything that is wrong

with it. How many of those people are going to see the big picture – very few, very few, you know, so people will grunt and groan and moan about the decision because they do not want it. That's a stupid decision. Why should my child have to wear black shoes? But everybody else has to. That's the decision of the school – abide by it or move on. (I1DGF)

At the end of the day, parents felt that if they were unhappy with the school they would move their children to another school. In a sense this is the parents' ultimate sanction and can cause damage to the schools' reputation through the parents' networking system.

My attitude is that if I'm not happy with my child here and I feel I have to be up here all the time there is something wrong. I just would actually - if I wasn't getting anywhere, I'd just take the child out and get him in somewhere else. (FG2M)

The personal characteristics of the respondents or the schools their children attended made no difference to their views on decision-making. However, home-school communication, involvement in the school and attendance at church influenced whether respondents perceived that they had a say in school policies (Table 5.14) and events.

Table 5.14: The Link between Respondents' Attendance at Church and Their Perception that They Had a Say in School Policies

Variable	Agreed that They Have a Say in School Policies		Not Sure that They Have a Say in School Policies		Disagreed that They Have a Say in School Policies		Total	
	N	*%*	*N*	*%*	*N*	*%*	*N*	*%*
Attended church weekly	34	34	40	40	27	27	101	101*
Attended church monthly	12	17	42	58	18	25	72	100
Attended church once a year or never	6	9	35	53	25	38	66	101*
Total	52	22	117	49	70	29	239	100

$X^2 = .001$ $p < .05$

* Result of rounding to whole numbers.

Similarly, 44 per cent (N=45) of respondents who attended church weekly felt that they had a say in what was happening in the school as opposed to 32 per cent (N=23) of those attended monthly and only 11 per cent (N=7) of those who attended once a year or never.

Volunteers were more likely to feel that they had a say in school decision-making. Forty-seven per cent (N=17) of those who helped organise fundraising and other events felt that they were consulted on school policies compared with 18 per cent (N=39) of 'non-organisers'. Likewise, over half (58 per cent, N=21) the organisers agreed that they had a say in school events as compared with a quarter (26 per cent, N=56) of 'non-organisers'. Similarly, respondents who helped in the classroom were more likely to agree that they had a say in school policies. Thirty-seven per cent (N=14) agreed that they had a say as compared with 19 per cent (N=42) of those who did not help in the classroom. However, there was no difference between classroom 'helpers' and 'non-helpers' in whether they had a say in school activities. 'Helpers' were also more likely to agree that they had a say that they had a say in school policies (40 per cent, N=27) than those who did not help (15 per cent, N=28). They were also more likely to feel that they had a say in what was happening in the school (Table 5.15).

Table 5.15: The Link between Respondents' Helping Out in the School and Their Perception that They Had a Say in What Was Happening in the School

Variable	Agreed They Have a Say in What Was Happening in School		Not Sure They Have a Say in What Was Happening in School		Disagreed They Have a Say in What Was Happening School		Total	
	N	*%*	*N*	*%*	*N*	*%*	*N*	*%*
Help out in the school	36	51	21	30	13	19	70	100
Do not help out in the school	39	22	83	46	59	33	181	101*
Total	75	30	104	41	72	29	251	100

X^2=.000 p<.05

* Result of rounding to whole numbers.

Members of the parents association also felt more involved in the policy formation (Table 5.16) and decision-making processes in the school.

Table 5.16: The Link between Membership of the Parents Association and Respondents' Perception that They Had a Say in School Policies

Variable	Agreed They Have a Say in School Policies		Not Sure They Have a Say in School Policies		Disagreed They Have a Say in School Policies		Total	
	N	*%*	*N*	*%*	*N*	*%*	*N*	*%*
Member of the Parents Association	17	50	13	38	4	12	34	100
Not a member of the Parents Association	39	18	113	51	68	31	220	100
Total	56	22	126	50	72	28	254	100

X^2=.000 p<.05

Fifty-five per cent (N=18) of respondents who were members of the Parents Association felt that they had a say in what was going on as compared with 27 per cent (N=60) of those who were not. While the numbers were small (N=8), only one BOM member agreed that they had a say in school policies and activities, while six were unsure. Similarly, only two BOM members agreed that they had a say in what was going on, while six were unsure.

Respondents who went to activities organised by the parents association and attended talks and classes for parents were also more likely to feel that they had a say in school activities. Forty per cent (N=51) of those who attended parenting talks/classes felt they had a say in what was going on as compared with 21 per cent (N=26) of 'non-attendees'. They (29 per cent, N=37) were also more likely than 'non-attendees' (15 per cent N=19) to feel that they had a say in school policies. Similarly, 46 per cent (N=41) of respondents who attended activities run by the parents association felt that they had a say as opposed to 23 per cent (N=37) of 'non-attendees'. Interestingly, attending parents association activities made no significant difference to respondents' perceptions that they had a say in school policies.

Just as the number of notes sent home appeared to influence the respondents' relationship with the school they also impacted on their perceptions on their involvement in decision-making. Respondents who read notes sent home daily by the school were more likely to feel that they had a say in school decisions (Table 5.17). Similarly, 33 per cent (N=35) of those who read notes daily said that they had a say in school polices as compared with 19 per cent (N=17) of those who read notes weekly and 7 per cent (N=3) of those who read notes monthly.

Table 5.17: The Link between the Frequency with which Respondents' Read Notes Sent Home by the School and Their Perception that They Had a Say in What Was Happening in the School

Variable	Agreed that They Have a Say in What Was Happening in the School		Not Sure that They Have a Say in What Was Happening in the School		Disagreed that They Have a Say in What Was Happening in the School		Total	
	N	*%*	*N*	*%*	*N*	*%*	*N*	*%*
Read notes daily	44	41	40	37	23	22	107	100
Read notes weekly	27	30	29	32	35	39	91	101*
Read notes monthly	5	12	28	65	10	23	43	100
Total	76	32	97	40	68	28	241	100

$X^2=.000$ p<.05

* Result of rounding to whole numbers

Likewise, those who spoke to the teachers at least once a month (38 per cent N=61) felt that they had more of a say in what was going on than those who only spoke to them yearly (19 per cent, N=14). Speaking to the teacher had no influence on their involvement in school policies. It appears that those who engage with the schools are the ones who feel more involved in the schools' decision-making processes.

Factors which Influenced Parental Involvement

Lack of time and energy due to other demands were cited as the reasons why people did not get involved. If people were working, had small children or were involved in other organisations outside school, they may not have the time to give to the school.

> They wouldn't have the time, in this day and age.

> They might have younger kids to be minded.

> If you're coming in after work, you're going to get the dinner, get the homework done, put the kids to bed, it is a lot to be running out the door again …

> *You're probably involved with so many other things anyway.*

> Exactly – you can only commit to one or two things – so if you're involved with the Church on a grand scale or you might be involved with the Girls' school or … (FG2M)

For some it was a matter of timing or having the necessary supports to get involved.

> I'm not personally involved in activities in my children's school at the moment. This is due to me having younger children in our family. But I have been given every opportunity to get involved and will accept this in the near future. (Q24DB2)

Others felt that if the school did not encourage involvement and the principal was not 'approachable' or open to the ideas of others, that people would be put off getting involved.

> If the principal is there, that he's welcoming and he's nice and he's approachable and that you can talk, you know.

> There is nothing worse than going to a meeting and you are afraid to talk up.

> Or you can't open your mouth.

> Or you are made to feel that what you are saying is not valid or …

[The principal] would never do that, no matter how stupid or whatever.

He's very easy going.

He'd always make you feel like there was no problem with whatever you said. (FG2M)

Knowing people in the group encouraged some to become involved.

Do not know, Just other people and other people, they say I'm doing it and you say I'll try it. (I2DM)

However, the fear that the group was a clique and would not be welcoming was off-putting to many.

I think that a lot of things if they think it is the same crowd all the time, like walking in to a clique, like there is always the fear that there's be a clique. (I8DM)

Two parents from the same school (Q141MB2, Q129MB4) commented that the same parents were always involved and that they would like to see some new people involved. Another (Q199MG4) stated that she felt that the parents association were 'very unapproachable and they are usually parents from the wealthy families'.

Lack of interest by some parents was mentioned.

And then well, they just probably do not want to, you know what I mean, you will always get someone that doesn't want to, couldn't be bothered.

Why would you think that they couldn't be bothered?

Maybe because it doesn't affect them and they probably think that it is got nothing to do with me so why should I go out and do it. (I7DM)

Gender also influenced attendance at school events. From my observations of the attendance at meetings and events, I estimated that there is normally a ratio of three to one in favour of women. Several factors appear to influence the attendance of fathers. Men are more likely to attend meetings in second level rather than primary schools. They were less likely to attend meetings, which discussed RSE (Relationships and Sexuality Education). In 2005, my husband attended the RSE meeting because I was working and he was the only man present. Thirdly, men are more likely to attend, when both parents are specifically invited. Children can put enormous pressure on their fathers or other male relatives to attend.

> For a week before the Christmas play, my daughter continuously reminded us of the date and time. One mother told me that her child was insisting that both parents attend as they 'had' to bring two people. Her husband was working so her older brother attended instead of him. Another woman's husband was delayed getting parking and she was fretting that he would be late and the child would be upset. I counted fifteen men and twenty-five women in the audience. Since the play started at 2.00 pm, most people had to get time off work to attend. (FN 21-12-06)

The timing of the activities may affect men more than women. As most of the men were in full-time paid employment it may be more difficult for them to get time off work. The findings from the questionnaire appear to confirm my observations. There were no differences between mothers and fathers in their attendance at parenting talks/classes and/or activities organised by the parents association, which are normally held at night. However, there were differences in their attendance at school events and parent-teacher meetings, which are held during the day. Ninety-eight per cent (N=219) of mothers attended parent-teacher meetings as compared with 88 per cent (N=21) of fathers. Likewise, 91 per cent (N=204) of mothers attend school events, e.g., plays, concerts, etc., as opposed to 75 per cent (N=18) of fathers. While not significant, 16 per cent (N=36) of mothers helped out in their children's classroom as opposed to only one man (4 per cent, N=1). One of the male interviewees suggested that child protection issues put men off getting involved, especially when it was a girls' school.

> [She] is a girl and my participation would be in a school with little girls. It only has to take the child to say something wrong and I'm, I'll never regain my status, no matter what who, right or wrong so I mean, so it is a bit like, you could risk everything,

your whole, you could just destroy yourself for nothing so I would be standbackish (sic) from getting involved because of the, you know. (I2DG)

Social class had an impact on parental involvement in their children's schools. Disadvantaged parents were more likely to help out in the school and the classroom (Table 5.18).

Table 5.18: Impact of Social Class on Respondents' Involvement in Their Children's Schools

Variable	Disadvantaged Schools		Middle Class Schools		Total Involved	
	N	*%*	*N*	*%*	*N*	*%*
Help out in the school	34	36	38	23	72	28
Help out in my child's class	25	26	14	8	39	15
Attend activities run by the Parents Association	15	16	77	46	92	35
Help organise the fund-raising and events in this school	5	5	32	19	37	14
Member of the Board of Management*	8	8	0	0	8	3
Total number of respondents across school type	96	36	168	64	264	100

* Not significant at p<.05

In contrast, middle class parents were more likely to both organise and attend the fundraising and other events in the school. In all four schools, the parents who went to these activities were also more likely to be in two-parent families and attend church more frequently.

The activities described by the interviewees reflected these results. Parents in the disadvantaged schools mentioned 'Maths for Fun', courses and other activities run by the Home School Community Liaison (HCSL) Coordinator. 'Maths for Fun' is where parents are encouraged to come up to the school and play Maths games with their children. The participants from the middle class school spoke about fundraising and helping out on trips. Some parents resented having to fundraise, particularly when they saw it as the only involvement accepted by the school.

> Parents should be involved in day to day decisions and not just allocated fundraising activities. (Q195MG6)

Some participants felt that lack of involvement might be due to a bad school experience.

> May be if as a parent, you had a negative school experience yourself you mightn't be too keen to become overly involved in your child's education. You just see it as somewhere you send them to in the morning and collect them in the afternoon and that's the end of it. (I5MM)

Just as those with lower educational qualification were the least likely to get support and advice from others they were also less likely to attend school events and help out in certain activities (Table 5.19).

Table 5.19: Impact of the Respondents' Education Levels on Their Involvement in Their Children's Schools

Variable	Primary Level		Second Level		Third Level		Total Involved	
	N	*%*	*N*	*%*	*N*	*%*	*N*	*%*
Attend parent-teacher meetings*	18	82	163	96	61	100	242	96
Attend school events e.g. plays, games, concerts etc.	14	64	154	91	58	95	226	90
Go to class and talks organised for parents by the school*	8	36	90	54	34	58	132	53
Attend activities organised by the Parents Association	4	19	54	32	30	49	88	35
Help organise the fundraising and events in this school*	1	5	23	14	11	18	35	14
Help out in my child's class*	0	0	30	18	9	15	39	16
Total number of respondents across education levels	22	9	169	67	61	24	252	100

* Not significant at p<.05

Adherence to the religious values to the school was also an important factor. Regardless of what school their children attended, practising Catholics were more likely to attend and help out with school activities (Table 5.20).

Table 5.20: Impact of Church Attendance on Parental Involvement in Their Children's Schools

Variable	Attend Church Weekly		Attend Church Monthly		Attend Church Once a Year or Never		Total Involved	
	N	%	N	%	N	%	N	%
Go to class and talks organised for parents by the school	63	60	44	60	22	33	129	53
Attend activities organised by the Parents Association	50	48	26	36	11	16	87	35
Help out in the school	47	45	12	17	11	16	70	29
Help organise the fundraising and other events in this school	27	26	3	4	6	9	36	15
Help out in my child's class*	22	21	7	10	8	12	37	15
Member of the Parents Association	21	20	6	8	6	9	33	13
Total number of respondents who attended church	106	43	74	30	68	27	248	100

* Not significant at $p<.05$

Lone parents also found it difficult to attend school activities (Table 5.21). While there was no difference in their attendance at parent-teacher meetings and helping out in the school they were less likely to be involved in all the other school activities.

Table 5.21: Impact of Family Type on Respondents' Involvement in Their Children's Schools

Variable	One-parent Families		Two-parent Families		Total Involved	
	N	*%*	*N*	*%*	*N*	*%*
Attend school events e.g. plays, games, concerts etc.	61	82	164	93	225	90
Go to class and talks organised for parents by the school	29	40	101	57	130	52
Attend activities run by the Parents Association	13	18	76	43	89	36
Help organise the fund-raising and events in this school*	8	11	28	16	36	14
Help out in my child's class*	6	8	28	16	34	14
Member of the Parents Association*	6	8	27	15	33	13
Member of the Board of Management*	0	0	8	5	8	3
Total number of respondents across family type	74	30	177	71	251	101**

* Not significant at p<.05

** Result of rounding to whole numbers.

One mother (I3MM) who was interviewed suggested that the more children one had in the school the more likely you were to get involved. The results from the questionnaire appear to confirm this (Table 5.22).

Those with only one child were less likely to help out in the school and get involved with the activities of the parents association than other parents. Those with three children appeared to be the most active. It is interesting that respondents with four children, while less likely to help out in the classroom, were more likely to a member of the parents association. These results contrast with the involvement of parents in the home curriculum. As outlined in Chapter Four, respondents with only one child spent more time engaged in educational activities with their child at home than those with larger families.

Table 5.22: Impact of Family Size on Parental Involvement in Their Children's Schools

Variable	One Child		Two Children		Three Children		Four or More Children		Total Involved	
	N	%	N	%	N	%	N	%	N	%
Attend class and talks organised for parents by the school*	16	43	40	48	50	64	28	49	134	52
Attend activities run by the Parents Association*	7	18	31	37	33	43	19	33	90	35
Help out in the school*	4	11	25	30	26	33	17	30	72	28
Help out in my child's class	3	8	12	14	19	24	5	9	39	15
Help organise the fundraising and events in this school*	1	3	14	17	14	18	8	14	37	14
Member of the Parents Association	1	3	10	12	10	13	13	22	34	13
Total number of respondents across family size	38	15	85	33	78	30	58	22	259	100

* Not significant at $p < .05$

Younger respondents, who tended to have smaller families, were also less active in school governance and the activities of the parents association (Table 5.23)

Table 5.23: Impact of the Respondents' Age on Their Involvement in Their Children's Schools

Variable	Aged Under 30		Aged 30–39		Aged 40 and Over		Total Involved	
	N	%	N	%	N	%	N	%
Attend activities run by the Parents Association	8	19	33	29	50	48	91	35
Help organise the fundraising and events in this school	1	2	15	13	20	19	38	14
Member of the Parents Association	1	2	10	9	22	21	33	13
Member of the Board of Management*	0	0	1	1	7	7	8	3
Total number of respondents across age levels	42	16	115	44	105	40	262	100

* Not significant at p<.05

The class the respondents' children were in also had a bearing on whether they helped out in the school. Parental involvement appeared to peak in second class with fewer parents helping out as their children progresses through the school (Table 5.24).

Table 5.24: Impact of the Class of the Respondents' Children on Their Involvement in Their Children's Schools

Variable	Sixth Class		Fourth Class		Second Class		Senior Infants		Total Involved	
	N	%	N	%	N	%	N	%	N	%
Attend class and talks organised for parents by the school	33	44	23	40	53	65	26	54	135	52
Help out in the school	9	12	17	31	35	43	11	22	72	28
Help out in my child's class	5	7	8	14	24	30	2	4	39	15
Total number of respondents across class levels	75	28	57	22	82	31	50	19	264	100

Conclusion

This chapter examined the involvement of parents in the education system, both nationally and locally. Participants perceived the State to have
overall control of the education system. Not alone did it determine the
curriculum, but it provided the resources, which enabled schools to implement it. Many felt that the State needed to provide more resources to
meet their children's learning needs. While the majority of respondents
approved of the Catholic ethos of the school, they were ambiguous about
the role of the Church as patron of the schools. The recent scandals and
the increase in cultural and religious diversity made some respondents
question the relevance of Catholic schools in today's society. Most of
those interviewed were unaware of the role of the NPCP and felt that
parents had very little influence at national level.

The educational capital of respondents in relation to the recent curricular and legislative changes varied. While the vast majority were very
aware of their responsibilities under the *Education Welfare Act 2000*,
they had less knowledge about their rights under the *Education Act 1998*.
Similarly, while many parents noticed the in-service days and the
changes to the curriculum at local level, less than half knew that a revised curriculum had been introduced in Irish primary schools. Middle
class parents along with those with children in the education system for a
longer time had the most educational capital. Those with lower educational qualifications were the least knowledgeable about the changes in
Irish education.

Most respondents felt that they had a very good relationship with the
school. However, there were some who felt that their concerns were not
addressed when they complained. Frequent communication, adherence to
the values of the school along with parental involvement in both the
home curriculum and the school had a positive influence on the home-
school relationship.

Home-school communication took three forms: meeting the teacher,
written notes and information from their children. Parents in the middle
class schools and with children in the senior classes tended to use written
communication. In contrast, parents in the disadvantaged school and
those with younger children met the teacher more frequently. All parents
relied on their children to keep them informed about their learning and

daily events. Communication focused mainly on organisational issues such as events, policies and requests for money. While occasionally it involved the parent acting an advocate for their children, curriculum matters were rarely addressed. Despite this most parents felt that they knew how their children were performing in school. However, some would like to have more information about their children's progress and the curriculum.

Most participants took a keen interest in their children's schooling and attended meetings and events organised by the school. However they only got involved with school activities either because they were asked to by the school or they felt that it was of real importance to their children's education. Their involvement in school decision-making and governance was extremely limited. Attendance at church, involvement in school activities and frequent home-school communication had a positive impact on respondents' perceptions that they had a say in school decisions and policies. While interviewees cited lack of time and fears around the 'approachability' of the groups, social class, gender and adherence to the values of the school influenced the questionnaire respondents' involvement in school activities. The respondents' age, family size and the class their children were in also had an impact on their participation levels.

Chapter Six

DISCUSSION OF FINDINGS: HOME EDUCATION

Introduction

This research evaluated, from the perspective of parents, the implementation of the national policy of partnership between parents and teachers in supporting and planning for the best possible education for children both at home and at school. As evaluation involves the systematic collection of data about the characteristics of a programme (Gray, 2004), a case study approach, involving five schools, was used. The research methodology was outlined in Chapter Three. The findings in parental involvement in the home curriculum were outlined in Chapter Four. This chapter discusses those findings.

As parents' identities have a major influence on their parenting practices, the first section explores the profiles of the respondents who took part in this research. The next section explores the roles and responsibilities of parents with particular emphasis on how gender and social class influence their values and norms. In Ireland, parents have the right to send their children to the school of their choice. Section four examines the factors which influence parents when choosing schools. According to Putnam (2000, p. 296) children's development is powerfully shaped by the social capital of their parents. The supports and networks that participants use to help them rear and educate their children are outlined in section five. Section six details the involvement of parents in the home curriculum. This includes the activities, which parents engage in with their children, along with the children's extra-curricular activities. The final section explores the role of the parents as a 'supporter' of both their children's learning and the school.

Background Information

According to Reay (2003, p. 52), identity is relational and marked out by differences and exclusions. The sample population for this case study was five Catholic schools, all single sex, within a three-mile radius in North Dublin. Two schools were designated as DEIS Band 1 Urban by the Department of Education and Science (DES), which meant that they were two of the 150 most disadvantaged Irish primary schools (DES, 2005s, p. 78). The other three were in middle class areas. One school was the local girls' school my children attended. This section profiles the participants in this research. It also attempts to extrapolate from the findings the profiles of the non-respondents.

Limitations and Exclusions

Like the parents in Eivers et al.'s (2004, p. 174) research in disadvantaged schools, not all respondents returned the questionnaires. These parents have been described by the teachers in other research as the 'unreachable' (Eivers et al., 2004, p. 174) or the 'less interested' (Hanafin and Lynch, 2002, p. 38). In addition, only a small number of parents agreed to be interviewed and they were highly involved in their children's education. As a result, this research may only represent the views of the more 'conscientious' (National Council for Curriculum and Assessment [NCCA], 2005, p. 226) or 'interested' (Hanafin and Lynch, 2002, p. 38) parents. In the two disadvantaged schools, the parents with more middle class values and literacy skills may have been the ones who participated and, as David (1993, p. 170) suggested, have gained most from the Home School Community Liaison (HSCL) scheme and other programmes.

However, a lack of participation may not reflect a lack of interest or involvement (Edwards and Alldred, 2000, p. 452). Some parents may simply not have the time or may have prioritised other commitments over contributing to this research. Fathers, particularly those in one-parent families, may not have been given an opportunity to participate. Nevertheless, it should not be assumed that none of the 'less interested' parents participated. Hanafin and Lynch (2002, p. 38) found that, though the participants in their research were described as the 'interested' parents by the teachers, some represented the peripheral voices in the school as they saw the research as a rare opportunity to express their feelings about the school.

While the results of a case study can not be generalised to the population as a whole, Yin (2000) suggested that the generability of case studies lies in comparing their findings with other research in the same area. Unfortunately, parents were not surveyed in some of the evaluations at national level. In addition, the emphasis has been on measuring inputs rather than outcomes (Archer and Shortt, 2003, p. 104; Kilfeather, 2006, p. 3). The final evaluation report of the HSCL scheme (Ryan, 1994) measured the number of schools involved in the various HSCL activities rather than the number of parents. While there are figures available in the evaluation done by Archer and Shortt (2003, p. 104), they are based on the perceptions of the HSCL coordinators and school principals. The more recent research (Conaty, 2006) also tends to give details of the percentage of coordinators engaged in various HSCL activities and the number of programmes organised by them rather than the percentage/number of parents involved in these programmes. Again the views of parents were not sought. This makes it more difficult to validate the data from this research using these evaluations. However, research by the Taskforce on Active Citizenship presents statistical and other evidence on the level of volunteering in Ireland (O'Mahony and Prunty, 2007; Taskforce on Active Citizenship, 2007b). In addition, the results of the 2006 Census are used to compare the sample in this research with the population as a whole (Central Statistics Office (CSO), 2007a, 2007b).

Profile of Respondents

Issues of identity are crucial to the way parents experience policy (Riddell, 2003, p. 184). The majority of respondents described themselves as Irish and Catholic. The five schools appeared to be relatively unaffected by the recent increase in immigration. The percentage of Irish respondents (93 per cent) to the questionnaire was the same as that reported in the 2002 Census (CSO, 2007a, p. 24). A higher percentage of questionnaire respondents described themselves as Catholic (94 per cent) in this research than was reported for either the 2002 (88.4 per cent) or 2006 (86.8 per cent) Census (CSO, 2007a, p. 31). It appears from these figures that the research population reflects the dominant status group in Irish society.

Social class influenced the profiles of the respondents (Table 4.1). Middle class parents were more likely to be in paid employment, two-parent families and have third level qualifications. The percentage of lone-parents (29 per cent) who responded to the questionnaire was slightly higher than the national statistics (25 per cent) (CSO, 2007a, p. 64). As with other research (Lareau, 1997; Graue et al., 2001; David, 2004), it was mainly mothers who participated. Most of the fathers, who replied to the questionnaire, had children in the senior classes in the middle class schools. The percentage of those not in paid employment (38 per cent) was lower than the national average for women (47 per cent) (CSO, 2007b, p. 12). While the percentage of those with a third level education (24 per cent) was similar to the national average (29 per cent), there were fewer questionnaire respondents with only a primary education. Only 9 per cent of questionnaire respondents had only a primary education as compared to 23 per cent nationally (CSO, 2007b, p. 21). This is probably due to the age profile of the respondents in this research.

The research population was almost evenly divided between those with children in the boys' and girls' school as well those with children in the junior and senior classes. The questionnaire respondents' profile, however, differed according to the stage their children were at (Table 4.2). Respondents who had children in the senior classes were more likely to older, in full-time paid employment and have children attending secondary school. Similarly, those with children in the junior classes were more likely to be under thirty and have pre-school children. They either worked part-time or were not in paid employment.

According to the CSO (2007a, p. 20), family size has declined from over four children in the 1960s to less then two in 2006. This was not reflected in this research. The percentage of questionnaire respondents in one-child families (15 per cent) was less than the national figures in both 1986 (27 per cent) and 2006 (40 per cent). It appears that larger families are over represented in this research and it may be that a sizeable proportion of the non-respondents to the questionnaires were in one-child families. Reflecting the national trend, the respondents in this research who had only one child were more likely to be under thirty (Table 4.3).

Parental Roles and Responsibilities

Parents are the primary educators of their children (Ireland, 1937). This section discusses the findings of the research in relation to the roles and responsibilities of parents. It also examines the impact of gender and social class on respondents' perceptions of parental roles.

Parental Roles and Responsibilities

The majority of parents in this research perceived themselves as educators (Table 4.4). While they acknowledged the valuable work of the teacher, they considered that their children's education was too important to be left to the school (Vincent, 2001, p. 349). Parents, it was felt, needed to keep 'a good eye' on things to ensure that their children were learning and to supplement the work of school by engaging in educational activities with their children at home.

Traditionally, parents were seen as being responsible for the socialisation, moral training and leisure activities of children, while teachers were responsible for their education and academic progress (Organisation for Economic Co-operation and Development (OECD), 1997, p. 25). This was not the case with the parents in this research. They felt that parents had a responsibility for all aspects of a child's development. Attendance and providing their children with the essentials for school was seen as the sole responsibility of parents, while areas such as literacy and numeracy were perceived as the joint responsibility of both teachers and parents (Figure 4.1). However, a minority considered children's literacy, numeracy and socialisation the sole responsibility of the teacher. Interestingly there was less agreement around the areas of values, behaviour and citizenship. Some parents felt that it was the sole responsibility of parents, while others felt that it was a joint responsibility.

Gender

As we saw in Chapter One, research suggests that it is mothers who normally engage with their children's school (Lareau, 1997; Graue et al.,

2001; David, 2004). While most of the respondents to the questionnaire were mothers, the tensions between the traditional patriarchal familism policy paradigm and the more recent paradigm of egalitarian individualism (Fahey, 1998) were apparent.

> It should be exactly equal to the mothers. They seem to, tend to have this idea because they work full time they do not need to do anything with the child, you know what I mean. (I2DM)

There seemed to be a continuous negotiation of parenting responsibilities depending on the employment levels of the respondents. While traditional gender practices and attitudes remain, fathers appeared to be playing an increased role in their children's lives and education (Williams et al., 1998, p. 494). This was more apparent in the middle class schools.

Views varied among participants on whether mothers were primarily responsible for their children's education (Figure 4.2). In a sense, it reflects, as Keohane and Kuhling (2004, p. 6) suggested, the reality of living in contemporary Ireland, which is in-between cultures and identities at present. Respondents in one-parent families (Table 4.7) and the disadvantaged schools were more likely to hold traditional views, while those in full-time paid employment had a more egalitarian outlook (Table 4.8).

However, most respondents felt that fathers were responsible for their children's education (Figure 4.3). While the men who were interviewed felt that they were equal partners in their children's education, the women felt that the fathers' personality and interest influenced their involvement in their children's lives. The age of the child may also be important. The majority of the fathers, who replied to the questionnaire, had children in the senior classes. It may be, as Brooks (2004) suggested, that as children grow older fathers play more of a part in the educational decision-making and networking. As in Craig's (2006, p. 563) findings from the Australian Bureau of Statistics Time-use Survey, the education levels of the parent was an important factor in whether fathers took responsibility for their children's education (Table 4.9). Respondents with higher levels of education were more likely to consider fathers as equal partners in their children's education than those with lower levels of education.

'Maternal gatekeeping' (Allen and Hawkins, 1999) may also be a factor in preventing fathers from becoming more actively involved in their children's education. The lone-fathers in Corcoran's (2005, p. 143) study perceived the mother as having all the control in the relationship. The State, by acknowledging and promoting the rights of the mother over the father, undermines fathers in their attempts to co-parent. At present, fathers have no rights under the constitution if they are not married to the mother. When I worked in the Early Start pre-school intervention scheme, over three-quarters of the children had no fathers named on their birth cert, even though their fathers were involved in their lives. In addition, parents lose their one-parent Family Payment if they cohabit. This gives mothers enormous power over fathers in relation to access to their children.

Some of the mothers in this research suggested that their 'old fashioned' views on the appropriate role for a father prevented them from 'letting' fathers get involved in their children's education (FG1D). Others suggested that it depended on whether the mother was a 'stay-at-home mum' (FG2M). Being at home with the children gave them more time to develop their relationship with their children and to network with other parents. When both parents were working they were both 'as ignorant' (FG2M) and so the responsibility was more likely to be shared. The lack of time for networking, housework and childcare may mean that 'working' mothers have a vested interest in ensuring that fathers play an active role. Not only does it reduce their workload, but their children are less likely to lose out on educational support and opportunities, while they are working. In this context, it is interesting that those in paid employment, particularly full-time employment, were less likely to agree that mothers are primarily responsible for their children's education (Table 4.8).

Social Class

While as Thomas (2006, p. 22) suggested, being effective in displaying parental love is not in anyway tied to a person's economic or social standing, social class influenced the respondents' perceptions of their role as parents. Disadvantaged parents appeared to focus on ensuring that their children were 'good' kids and turned out well. They held traditional values on what constituted 'good' parenting, perceiving child rearing and education to be the sole responsibility of the mother. In contrast, middle class parents tended to focus on developing the talents and abilities of their already 'good' kids. They were also more likely to perceive education as being a 'shared enterprise' (Laureau, 1997) between mothers, fathers and teachers.

It may be that the parents in the disadvantaged schools felt pressurised to demonstrate that they were good parents (Carlen et al., 1992, pp. 165-6) or that they had internalised the message that they were solely responsible for their children's problems (Milbourne, 2005, p. 682). Middle class parents, while they may share these feelings, had a wider support network and unlike disadvantaged parents could afford to access support services privately. This gave them the cultural and social capital (Bourdieu, 1997) to locate professional advice and expertise (McNamara Horvat et al., 2003, p. 14) when needed and to share the responsibility of educating and rearing their children with others.

As almost half the respondents from the disadvantaged schools were in one-parent families, it may be reflecting the reality of their lives. As a single parent they have sole responsibility for their children's education with the father's role being 'really non-existent' (I8DM) apart from occasional visits. As one single mother said,

> It is 24/7 with a child, 7 days a week, for life. It is not only an hour's play here and there. I do not know but men seem to back off an awful lot and leave the mothers to do everything. (I2DM)

Educational qualifications are considered one form of cultural capital (Bourdieu, 1997, p. 47) and a proxy for privilege (Putnam, 2000, p. 186). Just as the education levels of the respondents impacted on their views of fathers as the joint educators of their children, they also impacted on who they considered to be responsible for their children's education. Those with higher levels of education were more likely to perceive education as a partnership between parents and teachers (Table 4.5). While those with lower levels of education took more responsibility for most aspects of their children's education, they appeared to depend more on the teachers to develop their children's literacy, numeracy and socialisation skills (Table 4.6). This may be due to either their lack of skills or lack of confidence in their ability to help their children. Their isolation from others means that they do not have a viable network to help them access support for either their children or themselves.

Educational Choices

Parents had a wide range of both primary and secondary schools to choose from. This section examines the hopes and fears that respondents had for their children. It also explores the decision-making processes used by parents in their choice of schools.

Most parents were careerist orientated (Fuller, 2002, p. 171) and hoped that their children would go on to college and get a 'good job' (I7DM). However, the social class of the participants influenced both their goals for their children and choice of school. Middle class parents expected their children to do well in school and go on to college (Bourdieu, 1974, 1977a). They had vague fears for their children, which centred on the education system failing them in some way. Like the middle class students in Reay's (2003, p. 56) study, their children were continually shaped towards an academic disposition 'in which third level education was the logical end product of a host of earlier academic choices'. There were also extensive familial reserves of expertise with parents, older cousins and babysitters being able to provide advice about attending third level. In addition, many of their parenting activities focused on developing the skills needed for further education.

Disadvantaged parents had the same hopes for their children but were not as confident that their children would stay the course. They recognised the 'street' as a dangerous place, where, despite their best efforts, children may fall in with the 'wrong crowd' (I2DM) and lose out on their educational opportunities.

Respondents had a wide range of schools to choose from in the locality. The 'good name' and academic reputation of the school was a primary consideration with all parents. The 'approachability' of the school, along with its support system and handling of misbehaviour was also important. Most had used their social capital to find out from others the standard of education and behaviour in the nearby schools. While feedback from family, work colleagues and friends, particularly if they were teachers, was influential, they also monitored the academic progress and behaviour of the pupils, both past and present, who attended the school. This was similar to the research done using different samples by Hunter (1991, p. 38), Gewirtz et al. (1995, pp. 28-9), West et al. (1995, p. 30) and Bosetti (2004, p. 398).

The difference in 'cultural capital' (Bourdieu 1997 p. 47) between the middle class and disadvantaged parents was most obvious in their approaches to second level education. To ensure a place in a second level school, parents need to apply early to the school of their choice. All of the middle class parents had their children's names down in a variety of second level schools (O'Brien, 2005, p. 232). This was to ensure that they had a choice, when the time came to make a decision. None of the disadvantaged parents had their children's names down for secondary schools. Even, they themselves acknowledged that if 'they had lived in a different area, they would have been more aware of looking in to schools' (FG 1D). Some felt that it did not matter what school you sent your child to. They had little confidence that either they or the schools could force their children to learn if they were not interested.

It appears that while all parents have similar hopes for their children, middle class parents are more active in ensuring that their children will reach third level education. They use their cultural, social and economic capital (Bourdieu, 1997) to choose schools and to get advice on their children's future.

Social Capital

Social capital results from the social interactions and networks within communities (Fleming and Boeck, 2005, p. 226). Just as it can be a useful source of advice and support, it can also be used to exclude others 'not like us' (Healy, 2004, p. 6). This section examines the respondents' support and social networks. It also explores the influence of the various variables on the respondents' social capital.

Supportive Networks

Respondents, like those in Weiss et al. (2003) and Quinton (2004, pp. 183-6) studies, received support and advice on educating and rearing their children from their partners, family and friends (Table 4.10). Like the respondents in the research done by Abrahamson et al. (2005, p. 193), family was ranked first, followed by their partners. Children, particularly girls, were also important. This is similar to other studies, which found that girls were expected to do more housework more than boys (Leonard, 2004, p. 83; Evertsson, 2006, p. 425). According to Evertsson (2006, p. 425), this is influenced by the gendered behaviour of their parents.

The class teacher was ranked fourth. This differs from the responses in the parents' focus groups, which were part of the NCCA's (2005, p. 212) research. They identified the class teacher as the first and main point of contact when parents required information or assistance to support them in helping their child to learn. There were mixed views among those interviewed for this research. While one mother found her children's teachers very supportive during difficult times, another found the class teacher unsupportive and felt that she would not go to her again for support and advice.

> Like she's a very nice teacher but God bless us, you wouldn't approach her really *[laughter]*. (I3MM)

It was remarkable that so few respondents perceived the professional services as being an important source of support. They were more likely to access the media and parenting courses than even the public health nurse or their doctor. This may be a reflection of the welfare regime in Ireland, which prefers to limit its responsibilities to those most in need (Esping-Anderson, 2002a, p. 15) or the difficulties in accessing services at local level (Purcell, 2006, pp. 40-2).

Despite the fact that television and the internet gave parents access to so much information from a variety of sources (Green, 1997, p. 162), only a few respondents found them a useful source of support and advice. The Church had a similar ranking, though some of those interviewed mentioned the clergy as being very supportive.

> We have a great parish priest down there, Fr [name of priest], I think he's wonderful; he gives great advice when you need it and he's there whenever you want him. (I2DM)

Unlike other research (Hennessey, 2005, p. 59; Mulkerrins, 2005, p. 64) very few respondents mentioned the HSCL teacher as being supportive. It may be that the parents, who the HSCL co-ordinator has most contact with, did not return their questionnaires. Alternatively, the parents interviewed as part of the other research were the most 'involved' parents (Ryan, 1994).

The quality of the support was an important factor with most interviewees agreeing that they would only to go to those whose opinions they respected. These people were perceived as having the educational capital to help them negotiate the system and make good choices about their children's education. 'Teacher friends' were highly valued. They were perceived as having 'insider' knowledge and could ensure that parents did not damage their relationships with the school when making a complaint.

Networking consisted mainly of informal chats with other parents (Figure 4.4). Very few respondents were members of a group and/or attended talks and classes outside the school. From my observations, parents use every opportunity to share information about schools, extracurricular activities and their children's progress. The local shops, the school yard and children's extracurricular activities were particularly useful. These conversations provided parents with useful information that helped them make informed decisions about their children's schooling (West, 1992, p. 216; Hughes et al., 1994, p. 164). They were also used to monitor their children's progress and the work of the teachers. Getting involved with the school was perceived as building on this 'social capital' (Putnam, 2000).

> Parents getting involved in activities helps to build a tight knit community, also you get to know the children that your child spends their day with. (Q24DB2)

Social Capital

Like those in Bell and Ribbens's (1994, p. 246) study, participants normally networked with those whose values and lifestyles corresponded to their own. Regular church attendees were particularly good networkers (Table 4.11). These contacts appeared to shape perceptions of what it meant to be a 'good' parent and what a 'good' school looked like (Ball 2003, p. 38; Williams, 2004, p. 7) and ensured compliance with the local norms and values. One middle class parent (I6MM), who originally chose a school in an inner-city disadvantaged area, found herself excluded from its parents' network.

> No matter how friendly I would be I couldn't integrate. Really I wasn't from the same crowd and it is amazing because it worked the other way as well because the other parents really didn't want to know me at all. I suppose I wasn't sucking on a cigarette outside the school door and you know that sort of thing – it was huge difference. (I6MM)

As a result she moved her children to the local middle class school, which was recommended by her neighbours, even though she was not entirely happy with its Catholic ethos. The fact that she felt that her children 'literally couldn't socialise' with the other children was an important factor in her decision to switch schools.

Children's friendships were important to all the participants in this research in terms of their socialisation and choice of school. They perceived knowing 'who their friends are, who their friends' families are' (I8DM) to be an essential element of monitoring their children's behaviour and ensuring that they kept out of trouble. They observed the students, past and present, from the local schools to ensure that they were sending their children to schools with 'nice kids', whose values and norms corresponded to their own. It appears that parents protect both their identities as 'good' parents and their children's cultural capital by interacting with those who hold similar values to them (Lord, 1997, p. 196; Reay, 1998).

There were several interesting patterns in the social capital of the respondents. Middle class parents had a wider educational network, and thus more social capital, than disadvantaged parents (Figure 4.5). This, as Lareau (1997, p. 712) and McNamara Horvat et al. (2003, p. 19) suggested, provided them with a major source of information about their children's schooling. Apart from their partners and friends, middle class parents were also more likely to receive support and advice on educating their children from books, newspapers and magazines. They were also much more likely to attend parenting talks and classes outside the school (Table 4.12). As a result, they were more knowledgeable about the education system. Their 'cultural capital' (Bourdieu, 1997, p. 47), along with their personal investment in their parenting skills and human capital (Schutlz, 1977, p. 313), appeared to outweigh any of the advantages that the HSCL programme conferred on disadvantaged parents. In fact a lot of middle class parents had their own 'personal' HSCL teacher from whom they could seek advice and support.

Parents' educational qualifications are form of cultural capital (Bourdieu, 1997, p. 50) and one of the most important predictors of social participation (Putnam, 2000, p. 186). Respondents with lower educational qualifications were the most 'marginalised' (Conaty, 2002) in this research. They received less support than those with higher levels of education (Table 4.13) even from their immediate family. Without a 'certificate of cultural competence' (Bourdieu, 1997, p. 50), these parents may lack the confidence to build friendships with others. They may also exclude themselves because they do not feel at ease in a social setting where they are not familiar with, and proficient in its specific cultural norms (Lamont and Lareau, 1988, p. 159). It is interesting in the light of the various research findings from disadvantaged areas (Ryan, 1994; Conaty, 2002; Eivers, et al., 2004) that those with lower levels of education were also less likely to find their child's class teacher supportive. The HSCL scheme does not appear to have influenced their feelings of exclusion from the school system.

Mothers appeared to have a better school related network than fathers. They were more likely to get support from their friends and to talk to other parents about the school. This is similar to the findings of other research (Bell and Ribbens, 1994, p. 238; Graue et al., 2001, pp. 475-6; McNamara Horvat et al., 2003, p. 14). Fathers, on the other hand, were more likely to get support from their partners. This was linked to family forms with lone parents, who were mainly mothers in this research, less likely to get support from their partners.

Lone parents also got less support from the Church, books, media and their neighbours (Table 4.14). While one can understand them feeling unsupported by their partners and the Catholic Church, it is hard to fathom why they feel that they do not receive the same support from their neighbours, books and the media. It is not clear whether others used their social capital to exclude them (Healy, 2004, p. 6) or they disassociated themselves from representations of the norm (Williams, 2004, p.

18). The stigma of being a lone parent may also prevent them from discussing their problems with others. It may also be that the dilemmas of one-parent families are not dealt with in the media. Lack of time may also prevent them from attending parenting courses and networking with other parents.

Parents with children in the more junior classes were more likely to network with other parents. In the junior classes parents collect children from school and have the opportunity to build up a network of like-minded parents through meeting them in the school yard. Fourth class is when decisions about second level schools are made so getting advice and support from other parents in relation to school choice is important. In sixth class the social networks may be disintegrating. Parents are less likely to bring or collect children from school and may have lost interest in sustaining relationships with people whose children may not be attending the same school next year.

Two-child families received the most support from everyone except from their grandparents (Table 4.15). As they were more likely to be older and middle class, their parents may be too elderly or not near enough to help. One-child and larger families with four plus children received the least support, even from their friends. Those with larger families will be more experienced and may have 'seen it all'. They may be the ones providing the advice and support to others. One-child families may not have the same need for support or they may be more possessive of their children. Others may be reluctant to offer support as it is a big responsibility to mind an only child and a lot of work to mind more than three.

Parental Involvement in the Home Curriculum

Much of the child's learning, Macbeth and Ravn (1994) suggested, takes place outside the school and parents who may be 'missing' (Edwards and Alldred, 2000, p. 452) from the school's perspective may be very active in the home setting. This section explores how parents are involved in the home curriculum (Figure 4.6). It looks at how parents complement the work of school by engaging in educational activities with their children (Bourdieu, 1974). According to Reay (1998, p. 70), parents engage in extensive systematic programmes of generating cultural capital for their children through art, music and other extra-curricular activities. The extra-curricular activities that the respondents' children engage in are also outlined in this section. The variables which influence these aspects of the home curriculum are highlighted.

According to Macbeth (1994, p. 85), the home is the place where language, social skills, moral values and citizenship are taught. Respondents in this research appeared to be very involved in all aspects of the home curriculum. All those who were interviewed had certain 'preset' (Blenkin et al., 1992, pp. 23-4) behaviours and values that they actively encouraged from an early age. Social class influenced their disciplining techniques rather than their goals. Middle class parents ascribed to being 'sensitive, supportive' parents as promoted by educational and psychological experts (Dix, 1991). They had 'no rules as such' (I4MF). By modelling and encouraging 'good' behaviour, they ensured that their children conformed to societal norms.

> I encourage them to be extremely courteous and polite to people. I absolutely wouldn't tolerate children being rude or being aggressive. I'm well capable of giving out to them of course which I try not to actually. I really think that everything when it comes to children is based on example. Children see you being respectful, their parents being respectful to other people in every situation in life ... I suppose I learnt when she was a baby to turn everything in to something that was pleasurable and fun and not to confront her and to encourage and to work a child around to wanting to do the right thing. I do that all the time and that's a skill in itself and I apply that to everything. I will never confront the children in a situation where I know that they are overtired or not going to do it so I won't put down my foot on something unless I know I'm going to win. (I6MM)

Disadvantaged parents emphasised the more traditional role of the 'responsible' (Wyness, 1996, p. 141) parent as demanded by the school, State and society. They had explicit rules and strict routines, which their children were expected to adhere to. They felt that because they had taught and modelled these behaviours from a young age that their children were, on the whole, well behaved.

As outlined in Chapter Four, most participants engaged in a variety of educational activities with their children. They read stories (Figure

4.7) and played with their children at least once a week (Figure 4.8). While practically everyone brought their children on an outing at least once a month (Figure 4.9), only half brought them to the library (Figure 4.10).

Family size appeared to be an important influence in determining the involvement of parents in the home curriculum. Parents with only one child provided a more intensive and varied home curriculum. The majority played with their children daily and took them on weekly outings (Table 4.16). However, they were less likely to bring them to church regularly (Table 4.19). As these parents were more likely to be younger and in paid employment, they would have both the finance and the energy to go places and do things with their children. It may be an indication of the changing trends in Irish society or it may be a 'life style pattern' (Putnam, 2000, p. 73). Parenting practices may change with the birth of the second child (Schultz, 1973, p. S8) with parents having fewer resources to invest in their children. The lack of siblings means that only children are more dependent on their parents. Older siblings can support their parents in rearing, educating and entertaining their younger brothers and sisters (Isherwood and Hammah, 1981). In larger families, the work and cost involved in catering for the basic care needs such as food, clothing and cleaning is multiplied (Fahey and Russell, 2001, p. 57). This may reduce the amount of time and money parents have for educational activities and outings. In addition, the variety of extra-curricular and other social activities, e.g., birthday parties, which children engage in today, can make it difficult to organise family outings and activities to suit everyone's schedule. Parents may also be too busy transporting children from one venue to another to read or play with their children on an individual basis.

Almost two-thirds of respondents brought their children to church at least once a month (Figure 4.11). It was difficult to assess whether this was motivated by personal beliefs or social conformity (Hunt, 2002, p. 60). Only one interviewee felt that giving their child a Catholic education was part of the commitment they made at the child's baptism (I2DM). The others were more ambivalent about the faith and the role of the Church in their children's education. Some parents took their children to church to ensure that they fitted in with the values of the school and were not 'one of those' (I5MM) who did not know how to behave in church. Others felt that it instilled in their children certain attitudes and values. Some, like the minority belief parents in Lodge's (2004, p. 24) study, conformed for fear that their children would be ostracised and bullied by other children. Traditional gender patterns were evident with parents more likely to bring girls to church than boys (Table 4.17).

In addition, parents under thirty were the least likely to attend church (Table 4.18). This is similar to the findings of the Taskforce on Active Citizenship (2007b, p. 15). As this generation would be most affected by the rise of the Celtic Tiger and the decline in the moral authority of the Catholic Church (Keohane and Kuhling, 2004), it is difficult to assess whether this is a life stage or a generational change. Pressure from extended family networks and neighbours, according to Fulton (2000b, p. 164) makes it difficult for parents to break links with the Church. However, this research found that, apart from grandparents, these networks had little influence on church attendance. Younger respondents with supportive parents were more likely to attend church.

The vast majority of children were involved in some form of extra-curricular activity (Figure 4.12). The parents, who were interviewed, felt that it was good for them

> to be involved in other things outside school because there again all they are doing is hanging round the streets, playing with their pals which is grand. They have to socialise and all that sort of stuff but I would like them to do something constructive as well. (I5MM)

Sport was the most popular, followed by computers, art and music. Some children had very full schedules and appeared to be involved in a variety of activities. However, apart from music and computers, children's participation in extra-curricular activities declined as they grew older (Table 4.21).

Similar to Broderick and Shiel's (2000, p. 45) study of fifth class students, traditional views on what were 'appropriate' activities for boys and girls influenced children's participation in extra-curricular activities. Less than half of the girls in the disadvantaged school were involved in sport as compared to three quarters of those from the three other schools

(Table 4.20). Girls were much more likely to be involved in dancing, drama and music, while boys tended to do computers more. These results are interesting because during a planning day in the middle class boys' school, I had a very hard time convincing some members of staff that they could not omit the dancing section of the *Primary School Curriculum* (DES, 1999a) even if they were an all-boys' school. They firmly believed that it was unsuitable for boys.

Similar to research done by Barnardos (2006, p. 17), which showed that the cost of extra-curricular activities impacted on the out-of-school activities children could engage in, there were differences in the variety of extracurricular activities children from middle class and disadvantaged schools engaged in. This was particularly noticeable for sporting and dancing activities. Apart from their disciplining techniques and the variety of extra-curricular activities their children engaged in, there appeared to be no difference between the home curriculum of the middle class and disadvantaged parents. This is similar to the second of the two Annual Parent Surveys for an Early Intervention Strategy Project in eleven Scottish urban authorities, characterised by extensive social disadvantage and educational underachievement (Bastiani, 2000, p. 20). It found that parents were engaged in a wide range of educational activities at home.

Supporting the School at Home

According the DES (1994, p. 5), children and parents must abide by the school's regime. Parents are expected to support the school by ensuring that homework is done and that their children are 'compliant learners' (Hennessey, 2005, pp. 53-4). This section examines how the participants in this research supported the work of the school including the school rules and the curriculum. A lot of this work is informal and invisible. It was only through participant observation that I became aware of how much support I provided to my children's school (Figure 4.13).

Supporting the School Rules

The *Educational Welfare Act 2000* requires parents to ensure that their children comply with the school's Code of Behaviour. Most participants agreed with the DES (1994, p. 5) that they should ensure their children obey their teachers (Figure 4.14) and comply with the school rules.

> I have always told them to do exactly what the teacher says and do not disobey. (I8DM)

While they actively encouraged their children to conform, they also provided a lot of support and encouragement to their children on how to behave at school. This included teaching them how to react when teachers were giving out to them along with trying to ease their fears around many of the school rules. Gender influenced parents' perceptions of the school rules. Mothers were actively engaged in mediating the rules for their children, while the men appeared to be more removed from the school rules and their impact on their children.

The 'power differential' (Fine, 1995, p. 86) between parents and the school was most noticeable in the comments made about the school rules. Most felt that they had little control over the school rules and had no choice but to comply with them.

> We got a list of them when the kids started. You get them and they tell you that they will enforce them and there is no avoiding them. (I8DM)

If parents were unhappy with a particular rule, they had no problem approaching the school and discussing it with the principal. However, they felt that rules could not be changed for one person and parents had just to live with them.

> But I think if there is a school rule you do not like, you just have to talk about it and you have to get used to it. A rule can't be changed for one person. (I2DM)

This may reflect their views on society and citizenship. The school is an institution of the State. One of the goals of the DES (1995, p. 193) is to enable individuals to 'participate fully as citizens in society'. Through its Code of Behaviour, the school inducts children into the norms, values and practices of civil society. Social, Personal and Health Education (SPHE) is used to teach children how to behave in a democracy (DES, 1999c, p. 9).

> Respect – I mean I would see it as an inherent part of the teacher's job is not just in educating them in purely academic sense but educating them as individuals, you know, the kids would have an awareness of what to do, the effect on others in terms of bullying, in terms of even from a more, a ahem, broader perspective ... As well as purely educating them, that they'd get that sense of social awareness ahem, you know, gradually done over a period of years. (I4MF)

The 'public interest' (Levin, 2004, p. 174) is promoted both explicitly through the school rules and implicitly through the 'positive school climate and atmosphere' (DES, 1999c, p. 11). Parents' 'private interests' (Levin, 2004, p. 174) are accommodated only if they conform to the cultural and institutional norms (Lodge, 2004, p. 32).

Sykes (2001, p. 274) suggested that once a parent decides to send their child to a school, an implicit agreement between the home and the school takes place. When enrolling their children, parents have no choice but to recognise the legitimacy of the school rules (Ireland 2000). Their only chance of neutralising their effects on their children lies in submitting to them in order to make use of them (Bourdieu, 1977b, p. 165). As can be seen from this quote, schools use different approaches to remind parents of their obligations to enforce the school rules.

> I can't think of them offhand but I know them but I suppose over the last two or three years, you know, they have been sort of built up because we would got the pack initially, then we would have got, sort of, the constant reminders but I mean, you know, my first reaction was I do not know what the school rules are, because it is not that they are nailed on the front door, it is not that God, these are the school rules, make sure your kids follow those rules, it is not that sort of heavy enforcement policy. (I4MF)

The conflict in today's society between traditionalism and modernisation (Keohane and Kuhling, 2004, p. 11) was reflected in the comments on behaviour. Some felt that schools were 'handling children better' (Q127MB4), with other feeling that 'since they do not smack children they have no respect for teachers, parents or property' (Q22DB4).

Supporting the School's Curriculum

While recognising the complementary nature of the roles, about half the respondents felt that education should be left to teachers who were the experts (Figure 4.15). Those with lower levels of education were more likely to depend on the teacher to educate their children (Table 4.6).

All parents appeared to 'keep a good eye' on what their children were learning at school. They monitored the work done in school by asking their children about their day and by examining the copy books they brought home (Figure 4.16). Like the parents in Murphy's (2002, p. 84) and the NCCA's (2005, p. 208) research, most helped their children with homework daily (Figure 4.17). This kept parents informed of the curriculum and their children's progress.

By being aware of what was going on in school, parents felt that they could help their children cope with problems that arose in school. It also enabled them to 'compensate' (Reay, 1998, p. 66) for what they perceived as gaps in the child's schooling. They did this by helping the child at home or employing tutors.

> There are subjects I look after and subjects he looks after so he'd do anything that has to be done with Maths … I do the other subjects with them – like we have a balance of subjects because there would be a lot of Maths I wouldn't remember, where as he would. Then there'd be stuff that he wouldn't remember and I would so that's how we balance it and if we can't do it, we'd get grinds or tutors or whatever. (I8DM)

However, many parents felt that the schools were reluctant to listen to them and that they had to fight for additional resources for their children.

Like the NCCA's (2005, p. 208) research on the implementation of the revised curriculum, parents were less involved in monitoring their children's learning in the senior classes (Table 4.22). There may be several reasons for this. As children move up the school they are more independent so parents are either discouraged or have less need to monitor their work. Teachers in disadvantaged areas have suggested to me that parents, due to poor literacy and numeracy skills, are unable to help with homework in the senior classes. However, Eivers et al. (2004, p. 59) found that the amount of help given by parents with homework was

negatively associated with the achievement of children in the standardised tests. Similarly, Furstenberg and Hughes (1995, p. 587) found that
parents helping their children with homework was associated with lower
likelihood of labour force participation and stable economic status. They
suggested that parents are more likely to help those with difficulties.

There were also gender differences in whether parents monitored and
supported their children's learning. Mothers, like those in Reay's (1998,
p. 60) research, were more likely to help with homework and look at
school work on a daily basis than fathers.

Supporting the School Financially

While parents, as Cullingford (1996b, p. 57) and Gorard (1997, p. 253)
found in their studies, may not perceive themselves as consumers, much
of their involvement in the education system was as consumers. Not only
did they have to pay for school items such as books, pencils and uniforms (Figure 4.18), they also contributed to the schools' fundraising
efforts along with paying for their children's extracurricular activities.
Some felt that these had got much more expensive over the past six
years. Changes in the curriculum had not only increased the price of
books, but made it difficult to buy second hand books. Barnardos research in 2005 shows that the average costs for basic uniform, sports-
wear, shoes and textbooks for a primary school pupil is €225.60. These
costs exclude expenses during the year (Barnardos, 2006, p. 16).

Middle class and disadvantaged parents differed in their perceptions
of the costs of schools (Table 4.23). While the book rental scheme and a
reduced number of fundraising events should mean that parents in disadvantaged areas paid less, they reported that they paid for school items
more frequently than those in the middle class schools. It may be that
middle class parents pay for items in a lump sum at the beginning for the
year, while disadvantaged pay in instalments over the year. Middle class
parents also appeared to be better able to supplement the quantity and/or
quality of state education by contributing to fundraising, paying for extra-curricular activities and by providing a varied home curriculum
(Lynch and Lodge, 2002; O'Connor, 2003, p. 397). Disadvantaged parents were not in a financial position to do so.

Younger respondents and those with only one child were less likely to contribute to the schools' fundraising efforts. This may be the result of the increase in modern individualism (Keohane and Kuhling, 2004, p. 81) and/or the high cost of living for younger parents.

Conclusion

Participants in this research reflected the dominant culture in Irish society in that the majority were Irish Roman Catholics. However, not all parents returned their questionnaires and it may be that this research reflects the views of either those parents who value education most or had the time available to participate. Fathers and one-child families appear to be under-represented, while lone parents are over-represented. In order to probe whether the findings are analytically 'generalisable' (Yin, 2000 p. 10), they were compared with other research in this area.

Parents took their responsibility as the 'primary educator' of their children very seriously (Ireland, 1937). While sharing part of the task with the teacher, they monitored their children's school work to ensure that they were making progress. While fathers were considered to be just as responsible for their children's education as mothers, mothers appeared to play a more active role. While some felt that men were 'lazy gits' (I2DM) who left most of the work to women, others felt that mothers prevented fathers from playing a more active role.

While all parents had similar ambitions and hopes for their children, social class influenced the social capital and parenting practices of the respondents. Disadvantaged parents feared more for their children's future and had internalised the message that they were solely responsible for their children's education. Middle class parents had a wider support network and were more likely to perceive education as a partnership between home and school. They appeared to be more confident that their children would do well in school and go on to third level education. All parents prioritised 'approachable' schools with good academic reputations. Middle class parents tended to be more proactive about their choice of school with all of them having their children's names down in several second level schools.

The respondents' supportive networks were composed mainly of their family and friends. The class teacher and other parents were also an important source of advice. Parents tended to network informally with other parents who shared their values rather than attending parenting classes or joining groups outside the school. Those with lower levels of education and in one-parent families received the least support. There were also differences due to the social class, gender and the age of the respondents' children.

Parents appeared to be highly involved as educators in the home curriculum with most of their children engaged in some form of extra-curricular activity. Family size, along with the age and gender of the respondents' children (Gorard, 1997, p. 189), influenced the frequency in which they engaged in educational activities with their children.

There were three ways in which parents supported the school at home. They ensured that their children complied with the school rules and obeyed the teacher. They monitored their children's progress and supplemented the work of the school at home. Thirdly, most parents supported the school financially, by paying for school items, giving money to the school and paying for grinds if their children were having difficulties with their school work. A lot of this work is often invisible and unacknowledged even by the parents themselves.

Chapter Seven

DISCUSSION OF FINDINGS: EDUCATION SYSTEM

Introduction

While Chapters Four and Six examined parental involvement in their children's education at home, Chapters Five and Seven focus on home-school partnership. Chapter Five outlined the findings of this research in relation to the involvement of parents in the education system at both local and national level. This chapter discusses these findings.

The first section explores the respondents' perceptions of partnership at national level. The role of the State, Church and parents in children's education is outlined. As parents' educational capital is crucial in helping them negotiate the system, the participants' knowledge of the recent changes in legislation and curriculum is explored in section three. The home-school relationship is probed in section four. Successful relationships require good communication systems. The content, method and effectiveness of the communication between home and school are examined in section five. The final section explores parental engagement as audiences, volunteers and decision-makers in their children's schools. The factors, which influence their involvement, are also discussed.

Partnership at National Level

Parents had little understanding of the process of partnership and policy formation at national level. In fact, they assumed that the State, in particular the Department of Education and Science (DES), was totally responsible for all aspects of their children's education. National policy, as far as parents were concerned was decided by the DES and taken 'as given' (FG2MC) at local level.

As citizens and welfare recipients, most parents felt that the State was not meeting its basic responsibilities towards their children.

> I think they give up very easily on certain schools, certain children and the funding isn't there for a lot of the stuff kids need so to me that is down to them. (I8DM)

Schools, they felt, were not properly resourced. Class sizes were too high in middle class areas and children with learning difficulties were not getting the support they needed. This put additional pressure on parents to monitor their children's progress and ensure that their education was not neglected due to the shortfall in state provision. Others felt that the State could do more as the 'good parent' (Pinkney, 2000, p. 251) or provider to subsidise the costs of education. This included helping parents to defray the costs of extra-curriculum activities. Parents, it appears, are not happy with the State's policy of limiting its responsibility to those most in need and encouraging private market solutions as the norm (Epsing-Anderson, 2002a, p. 15). They felt that it did not support them as parents and was detrimental to the best interests of their children.

All the schools in this research were under the patronage of the Catholic Archbishop of Dublin. Though their children were attending Catholic schools, most of those interviewed were very ambiguous about the governance role of the Catholic Church. They found it very difficult to describe its role.

> Well they [the Church] run this school, they have a hold over, bar the Educational Board or who ever funds it, how it works …
>
> Well I do not know an awful lot about them - may be they do give loads of support …
>
> But isn't that mad, we should know about it because they have the running of the place. (FG1D)

If the goal of Catholic education is to socialise pupils into a tradition and a way of life (Inglis, 1998, p. 6), the schools in this research appeared to be doing a good job. As the Commission on the Family (1998, p. 548) found, there was considerable support for maintaining the Catholic ethos of the school with most parents agreeing that the Catholic values of the school were very important. Regular attendees at church were more supportive of the ethos of the school (Table 5.1). However, even those who were very ambiguous about their faith wanted their children to take part in the schools' religious activities and were careful not to contradict what was taught in school (Lodge, 2004, p. 29).

Some participants questioned the Church's involvement in education in today's increasingly secular, multi-cultural, almost post-Christian (Fullar, 2002, p. 173) society. While parents were enthusiastic about the input of the local clergy in visiting the schools and preparing the children for the sacraments, some felt that the connection between the school and the Church, in particular the local parish, had weakened over the years. The school was no longer used to inform and/or involve parents and children in parish events and activities. Others, due to the recent Church scandals and their own lack of faith, resented the influence of the Church over their children's education. They, like Rodger (1999, p. 320) and Tuohy (2005, p. 122), wondered how realistic it was to expect schools, especially those with an increasing number of non-Catholic pupils, to continue to emphasise Catholic traditions and beliefs. This had an influence on their relationship with the school.

The Minister for Education, according to the *Education Act 1998,* must make all reasonable efforts to consult with national associations of parents on all aspects of national policy (Ireland, 1998, p. 12). Most participants in this research were unaware of this (National Council for Curriculum and Assessment (NCCA), 2005, p. 215) and felt that parents as a group had very little influence at national level. While participants could list the various methods that can be used to protest, most had little confidence that parents' views were listened to or acted on.

> We do not have influence. To ask me as a parent, how can I ensure. I can't ensure. I can make quiet protests. Unless we collectively get together ... but by and large everybody's working now, mortgages are huge ... they haven't got time to be protesting against the State... you can draw up a petition and go around to every door and you sign your name and you hand it in 'There's a 100 people down in [the local area] think that it is

wrong to be teaching German in the [disadvantaged] school'.
'Well yeah, that's okay but we are still teaching German'. Where
do you go? We do not have any influence. (I1DGF)

Historically, the institutional authority of both Church and State exercised a powerful control over the citizenry and inhibited questioning and dissent. The women in Hilliard's (2003) study reacted in two ways. Some passively accepted things the way they were and did what was expected of them. Others adopted a strategy of deliberate distancing and avoided complying with certain requirements. Passivity was a notable feature in the interviewees' replies to the question on parental influence on educational policy. Most felt that there was no point in complaining or protesting as their concerns would not be addressed. Even the most active parents were prepared to accept certain issues 'as is' (FG2M) and comply with the boundaries as defined by the State.

Educational Capital at National Level

Over the past six years, the majority of participants had noticed various changes at local level (Table 5.2). Changes in curriculum and attitudes towards parents were the two items that were mentioned most. Most of the changes noticed were specific to the local schools such as additional educational activities and programmes along with building improvements.

The vast majority of parents were very aware of their responsibilities under the *Education Welfare Act 2000* (Figure 5.1). They knew that the school had to report them to the Education Welfare Officer (EWO) if their children missed twenty days of school and that they could be taken to court for non-attendance. Respondents were also aware that they were entitled to the schools' Code of Behaviour. This is probably due to the fact that the *Education Welfare Act 2000* concentrates mainly on attendance and the National Educational Welfare Board (NEWB) is responsible for its implementation. Not only does it keep parents informed of their obligations under the Act through leaflets and the media, it follows up on non-attendance reported by the schools. In addition, schools themselves remind parents of their obligations under the Act.

According to Riddell (2003, p. 194), very few parents are informed of their rights beyond the legal minimum. This was obvious in relation to the *Education Act 1998* (Figures 5.2, 5.3). About three-quarters knew that they were entitled to see their children's records and take a Section 29 Appeal if the school refused to enrol their child. The same number was also aware that the parents were represented on the Board of Management (BOM) and that the BOM had to keep parents informed of all school matters. Only half knew that they had to be consulted by the BOM and that they were entitled to access the school's financial accounts. Several factors were responsible for this information deficit. The *Education Act 1998* is a complex piece of legislation, which covers a wide range of educational issues. In addition, different agencies are responsible for the implementation of different sections of the Act. There was no information leaflet produced which summarised the Act for parents and outlined their rights and the rights of their children. The School Development Planning Support (SDPS) (2004) leaflet just highlights their involvement in the development of the school plan. In addition, schools may not be particularly interested in informing parents of their rights.

Despite the respondents' awareness of curriculum changes and the in-service days, slightly less than half knew that a revised curriculum had been introduced in Irish primary schools (Figure 5.5). Furthermore, their knowledge of the content of the curriculum was very slight with most perceiving it as something over which they had little influence. Most were quite happy to leave it up to the teachers as long as they were 'sort of competent and up to the job' (I4MF). Apart from an introductory booklet (DES 2000a) when the curriculum was first introduced, there had been no other communication with parents on a national level. Following the NCCA's (2005) review of the implementation of the revised curriculum, a DVD was issued to all parents (NCCA, 2006a, p. 7). However, this did not arrive in schools until the questionnaires and interviews were finished. The last focus group were the only ones to have received it. These participants welcomed it, especially as it would tell them what their child was 'learning in each subject at each class level of primary school' (NCCA, 2006a, p. 7). Parents' awareness of the introduction of the revised curriculum may have increased since receiving the DVD.

It appears that there is an information deficit at national level. While the media highlights the agenda of teachers' unions and issues of resources, there is little debate about the purposes of education and the impact of the policy changes on schools and children. In addition, while teachers have the opportunity to discuss national policy on planning days and at staff meetings, there is no similar forum for parents. While the DES asks that copies of circulars and other documentation are made available to parents, this does not happen on a systematic basis. Parents, whose Parents Associations are affiliated to the National Parents Council Primary (NPCP), are probably the best informed as they receive a regular newsletter. However, not all schools are affiliated to the NPCP. Even when 'all them brochures and things' (FG1D) come home, they may not even be read, let alone have an impact on parents' knowledge. As a result, parents may only notice the changes that impact on them personally (Moos et al., 1998, p. 66). Part of the problem is that nobody has overall responsibility for informing parents of changes to national polices or monitoring that schools pass on the information. As a result, parents are dependent on their social capital, the goodwill of the school and their children's memory to keep them informed.

It is important to remember that lack of knowledge or educational capital does not stop people from being effective parents. According to Michael (2004, p. 437), there are three discourses of ignorance: 'can't'; 'do not need to' and 'do not want to' and the motivation behind each of them is very different. In the case of parents in this research, 'do not need to' appeared to be the underlying factor. Over a third stated that parents did not need a copy of the school plan (Figure 5.4), despite their entitlement to it under the *Education Act 1998*. Despite being fully aware of their entitlement to the Code of Behaviour (Figure 5.1) just over half had a copy. This may be an indication of 'passive acceptance' (Hilliard 2003, p. 188) of welfare recipients or the 'complicitous silence' (Bourdieu, 1977b, p. 188) of supporters, who implicitly accepted the school rules. Even parent 'educators' may be like those in Riddell's study (2003, p. 194) and trust teachers as professionals to do the right thing. Alternatively, it could be that the multi-dimensional part parents play in their children's lives (Wolfendale, 1996, p. 3) leads them to prioritise their children's more immediate needs and their relationship with the school over more abstract rights.

Several variables, particularly social class and educational qualifications (Tables 5.3, 5.4) influenced the respondents' educational capital. The longer they and their children were in the education system the more educational capital they acquired. Older parents (Table 5.5) and those with children in the senior classes and secondary school were more likely to be aware of their rights and responsibilities under the legislation along with the introduction of the revised curriculum.

Home–School Relationships

Positive home-school relationships are necessary if parents, teachers and the school are to work in partnership. Unlike the participants in Hanafin and Lynch's (2002, p. 44) study, most parents in this research felt that they had a good relationship with their children's school (Figure 5.6) and felt welcome there. Many commented on the change in attitude towards them over the last six years. They perceived the school to be more 'approachable' with parents being encouraged to become more involved in various activities. Most felt that they could talk to the teachers and that they were listened to. They were also sympathetic to the difficulties teachers faced daily in trying to teach the curriculum, while at the same time meeting the learning needs of the children.

> You have got to get through the curriculum. You've got to watch the special needs and deal with 30 different personalities every day. (FG1D)

As Reay (1998, p. 71) found in her research, the dynamics of power appeared to influence home-school relationship. Surveillance or 'ear to the ground' (FG2M) was a key element in the home-school relationship. Parents monitored their children's schools very carefully. Before enrolling their children they discussed the school with others and watched the behaviour of the children attending the school. This helped them to decide if the school was suitable for their children. They were also vigilant in monitoring their children's learning in school (Vincent, 2001, p. 351). By discussing the school day with their children and checking their copies and workbooks (Figure 4.16), they assessed their children's progress and whether they needed additional help. In addition, their social networks and involvement in school activities ensured that they had enough information about the operation of the school to act as an advocate for their children, when issues arose (Vincent, 2001, p. 357).

Schools control parents' access to the building, personnel, resources and information. Being aware that their relationship with the school was very much on the school's terms, parents prioritised choosing 'approachable' schools for their children. As a result they felt comfortable about making a complaint (Figure 5.6) but were careful not to damage their relationship with school when doing so. Most tried to deal with problem at the lowest level possible beginning with the child and would only approach the BOM and the DES if all else failed. However, there were other parents that went directly to the DES. This was to inform themselves of national policy and their rights before approaching the school. Others asked a teacher from another school.

Some parents, because of past experiences, felt uncomfortable about approaching the school. As Cullingford (1996a, p. 5) suggested there were impenetrable barriers, which prevented parents feeling totally comfortable in the school environment. Parents felt that they were encroaching on professional territory and 'not nearly qualified enough' (I3MM) to bring issues to the teachers' attention.

> Well that's my feeling about the school anyway ... They very very much want to be in control of that and you are just the parent ... and it is probably that it just a feeling, I do not know, but that's the sense I get, you're not invited in, we do this kind of thing, we're the educators and you just stay back. (I3MM)

Those, who tried to 'modify the school's provision' (Reay, 1998, p. 68) for their children, met with mixed results. In some cases, the school eventually provided the additional resources, while in other cases the school refused to acknowledge that there was a problem. Parents were left feeling that their fears and concerns were ignored (Mulkerrins, 2005, p. 66) and that they were effectively excluded from the process of educating their child (Coleman, 1998, p. 13).

> Do not feel that teachers always listen to what you have to say as a parent. Have felt quite helpless to help my child to get a place in a resource class. Have paid for grinds because there was no space. I really felt his life was being wasted. (Q150MB2)

When help from the school and the DES is not forthcoming, they have to 'compensate' (Reay, 1998, p. 66) for the school's lack of resources by either helping their children at home or paying for grinds.

Other research found that middle class parents had a better relationship with the school than disadvantaged parents (Hanafin and Lynch, 2002, p. 41). This was not evident in this research. The majority of respondents, regardless of what school their children attended, had a good relationship with the teachers. While some parents found it difficult to approach teachers or make a complaint, this was not confined to any one type of school.

Communication is a vital part of any relationship. A good home-school relationship can be defined as one where parents feel that they are listened to by teachers and can make a complaint. Respondents who spoke to their child's teacher daily (Table 5.7) and read the notes sent home weekly (Table 5.8) had a better relationship with the school as compared to those who were less active in communicating with the school.

Gender was also influential. Mothers were more active than fathers in communicating with the school. They had more frequent contact with the principal (Table 5.6) and their children's teachers. In addition, mothers had a different perspective on their relationship with the school. Fathers appeared to see the school as a service provider and could outline very clearly their expectations of the teachers. Mothers, on the other hand, saw the work of the teacher as an extension of their work at home. The majority had great praise for the work of the school and the support of teachers when they and their children were going through difficult personal circumstances. They appeared to have more 'moral affective' relationships (Bourdieu, 1977b, p. 19) with the school.

In today's society, parental involvement in their children's education could almost be called a religion. As seen in Chapter Four, it unites parents into a group leading a common life (Durkheim, 1971, p. 44). Not only do they think in the same way about what it means to be a 'good' parent but they translate these ideas into common practices, which influence their relationship with the school. Like the parents in Cullingford's (1996a, p. 5) research, those who were supportive of the Catholic values of the school and attended church weekly had a better relationship with the school (Tables 5.9, 5.10). Monitoring children's school work and helping out in the school (Table 5.11) also had a positive effect on home-school relationships. It is not clear whether the minority, whose values differ from the norms of the school, were passive (Hilliard, 2003, p. 44), silenced (Devine et al., 2004, p. 246) or detached from the school and its activities (Vincent, 1996, p. 149). In addition, the school, as Hughes et al. (1994, p. 164) suggested, may resist these parents becoming involved in making decisions about their children's schooling.

Home–School Communication

From my observations, home-school communication revolved mainly around school events, information and money (Figure 5.7). Occasionally parents are required to act as advocates for their children and intervene to support them. The frequency of this communication was dependent on the time of the year and the children's ages. In addition, the school was used by others to communicate with their parent body (Figure 5.8). These included the Parents Association, the Church, statutory agencies such as the Health Service Executive, Dublin City Council and groups advertising extra-curricular activities.

Written communication was the schools' preferred means of communication (Figure 5.10). This, as the Organisation for Economic Co-operation and Development (OECD) (1997, p. 148) found, tended to be one-way. From my observations, the school sent home a note on average every third day over the course of the school year. In contrast, less than half the parents wrote to the school once a month. Like in Hughes et al.'s (1994, p. 169) study, this communication was of a fairly limited nature and tended to concentrate on requests for help along with information about school activities and events (Figure 5.9). Very few notes informed parents about the curriculum or matters of educational importance, which meant that parents, like those in de Abreu and Cline's (2005, p. 709) study had very limited access to what their children were studying in school. Despite the limited nature of this communication, respondents who read notes more frequently had a better relationship with the school (Table 5.8) and felt more involved in the school decision-making processes (Table 5.17).

Verbal communication also had a positive influence on home-school relationships (Table 5.7). Along with disadvantaged parents (Table 5.12), younger parents and those with children in the junior classes met the teacher more frequently. As they are more likely to accompany their children to and from school, they have more opportunities to meet the teacher informally. Since older children are more independent, respondents with children in the senior classes and secondary school have to rely on written communication.

Schools also used parent-teacher meetings and end-of-year reports to inform parents about their children's progress. However, children played a major role in keeping parents abreast of what was happening in school (Epstein and Seyong, 1995). Most of those who were interviewed discussed the school day with their children and observed the 'demeanour and motivation of their children towards school activities' (Bastiani, 1989, p. 38). They also used their child's homework, test results along with their school work to keep themselves informed on what their child was doing in school.

Some parents, like those in Bridgemohan et al.'s (2005, p. 7) study, felt that children were undependable. To keep themselves informed, they had to network and get involved with the school.

> My opinion is that if you are not there or you're not at the meetings, you can't know, because your child is not going to tell you. They are only going to tell you the things that are important to them – like so and so had two apples for his lunch – but sure that's no good. (FG2M)

It appears that they were aware, as Edwards and Alldred (2000, p. 446) found, that children can control communication between home and school by deciding what information is passed on or withheld. By getting involved personally they had access to this information.

Most participants felt that the school kept them informed of school events and activities (Figure 5.11).

> O very informed, there is a torrent of notes coming out, ahem you know, and the newsletter every week or two, so I think we would be very aware of what's going on. (I4MF)

Many parents were proactive in ensuring that they knew what was happening by helping out in the school and examining their children's copies and workbooks. Some, however, were less than happy with the school's communication system. They felt upset that they had missed out on certain events due to the school's failure to communicate with them.

> You do not know what they are doing. [My child] had a session with a little music festival they had over in Tallaght. Well I knew nothing about that until [she] asked me for the €2 for the bus... She looked for a cap off me another time. Again, 'What do you want the cap for?' 'Oh, we are going over to-morrow to do ...' – like a Feis or something but I would have loved to have known that. They told me then 'Oh, the parents can go'. I work but if I had known I would have went. (I3MM)

Most respondents knew how their child was progressing along with the standard of teaching and learning in the school (Figure 5.12). Like the parents interviewed by the NCCA (2005), they thought that schools needed to be proactive in keeping parents informed of their children's progress and curriculum changes (Figure 5.13). This included the results of the standardised tests. Some felt there was a need for more regular communication than the annual parent-teacher meeting and problem-orientated approach at present (Bridgemohan et al., 2005, p. 10).

The dynamic of power infused all aspects of home-school communication. The schools 'controlled' (I3MM) the amount of information parents received. Parents' cultural capital, their knowledge of the 'questions to ask' (FN 13-03-06) influenced their interactions with the school and the amount of information they received. Many respondents were hesitant in approaching the school for fear of 'antagonising people' (FN 13-03-06). Parents appeared to accede to the DES's right to decide on the 'subject matter to be taught and the manner of teaching' (Department of Education, 1994, p. 5). Apart from their right to withdraw their children from religious instruction, they felt that they had no business interfering in the curriculum as taught in the school. Nevertheless, parents got confused and anxious about major changes, which they were not informed about (Vincent, 1996, p. 152).

Parental Involvement in the School

This section examines the involvement of parents in their children's school. It looks at how the respondents participated in their children's schools by attending events, helping out with school activities and getting involved in decision-making and governance.

Audience and Volunteers

All the parents in this research were involved in their children's schools. As can be seen in Chapter Five, this was limited, for most participants, to what one interviewee (I4MF) described as the 'set pieces' (Figure 5.14). These included attending parent-teacher meetings and events such as plays, concerts and games. Events such as talks and classes organised by the school or activities organised by the Parents Association, which did not directly involve their own children and the class teacher, were not as popular. There appeared to be an almost implicit consensus (Bourdieu, 1977b) among parents and teachers that these rituals fulfilled the basic requirement for being an 'interested' (Hanafin and Lynch, 2002, p. 38) and 'conscientious' parent (NCCA, 2005, p. 226).This allowed schools to control their contact with parents (Burke, 1992, pp. 189-90) and parents to limit their involvement in the school.

When it came to actually volunteering, the numbers involved were much lower than for attending events (Figure 5.15). While just over a quarter helped out in the school, less than a fifth helped out in their children's classrooms and organised fundraising and other events in the school. Most had a preferred activity (Table 5.13). These finding are similar to those of the Central Statistics Office (CSO) (2007b, p. 29) and the Taskforce on Active Citizenship (2007b, p. 5) and the figures provided by Home School Community Liaison (HSCL) scheme on the number of parents who helped out in disadvantaged schools (Conaty, 2006, pp. 131-4). However, there is a considerable discrepancy between my findings and those of Archer and Shortt's (2003, p. 81) evaluation of the HSCL scheme. Using a questionnaire sent to the HSCL coordinators and their principals, they found that 50 per cent of parents helped with classroom activities and 84 per cent helped with school activities to some extent. This may be the result of a different research methodology or the over reporting by principals and the HSCL coordinators of the involvement of parents in school activities.

Although most parents did not put themselves forward as volunteers, they appeared to be quite happy to help out when asked. Like in Murphy's (2002, p. 84) research in a Gaelscoil, they were most likely to get involved when it directly concerned or benefited their own child. As with volunteers in the community (Molloy, 2005, p. 136), lack of time and energy due to other demands were cited as the reasons why parents did not get involved more. The fear that the group was a clique and would not be welcoming was off-putting to some. In contrast to Donaghue's (2002, p. 71) research, where participants did not volunteer because they had either never thought about it or had never been asked, most of the respondents in this research felt that the schools had given them 'every opportunity to get involved' (Q24DB2).

School Decision-making and Governance

Unlike Murphy's (2002, p. 86) research in a Gaelscoil, where over a quarter of parents were involved in either the Parents Association and/or BOM, very few respondents were members of the Parents Association and/or the BOM. Like those in Wyness's (1996, p. 139) study, there was a spectrum of opinion, which 'flowed from a reticence to get involved – they had neither the time nor the inclination – to a complete rejection of the principle of parental intrusion into the school'. Most of the respondents were like the parents in the research done by Vincent (2001, p. 251). While they monitored their children's learning carefully, perhaps even questioned some of the school's policies, they were not prepared to challenge the school directly or take action unless it affected their own children's education.

Like those in other research (Hanafin and Lynch, 2002, p. 40; Mulkerrins, 2005, pp. 113-4), most respondents felt that parents had very little say over school related events and policies (Figure 5.16). However, home-school relationships and communication influenced their perceptions. Frequent attendees and volunteers (Table 5.15) felt more included in the decision-making processes. In addition, parents who read the notes sent home (Table 5.17) and spoke to the teacher regularly tended to feel more included in the school organisation. Active participation, it appears, fosters inclusion and partnership. It was interesting that members of the Parents Association felt that they had more of a say in the operation of the school than BOM members (Table 5.16). The limited representation of parents and the more formal structures of the BOM may undermine the parents' contributions to the decision-making processes.

The lack of school-based structures means that parents' voices are not included in the decision-making and planning process in a systematic and continuous way (DES, 2006b, p. 80). While those interviewed gave examples of the parent body being consulted on issues such as uniforms and healthy lunches, most respondents felt that they had little say even in those decisions. Normal practice, according to my observations as SDPS facilitator and the DES's research on school planning (DES, 2006b; 2006c), is for teachers to discuss and agree on policies, which are then disseminated to parents as appropriate. Most of those interviewed felt that they would comment on policies sent home by the school but that they 'just never get the opportunity really' (I3MM). It appears that while schools may consult with parents on particular issues, it is not systematic enough to allow the parent body as a whole to express their opinions on a variety of issues at regular intervals (DES, 2006b, p. 80).

Some respondents suggested that their lack of involvement in school governance was their own fault because they had not got involved with either the BOM or the Parents Association. However, there was also a recognition from even the most involved parents in this study that certain issues, such as curriculum implementation, were off limits (DES, 2006b, p. 81) and that often lip-service was paid to their suggestions. In addition, they tended, like the school boards and governing bodies in Munn's (1998, p. 388) study, to be guided by the expertise of the principal. The fear of being 'wrong' and/or appearing 'stupid' (FG2M) held them back from both expressing their views and insisting that their ideas be implemented in the school.

Nevertheless, most respondents felt that they could make a complaint (Figure 5.6) and were quite happy to deal with issues that arose on an individual basis with either the class teacher or the principal. They did not appear to agree with the parents in Mulkerrins' study (2005, pp. 113-4) that the schools 'exploited, manipulated and patronised them and rarely consulted with them in a meaningful way'. It appears that parents in this study, like many Irish citizens, prefer to rely on individual representation rather than collective action to address their grievances (O'Sullivan, 1992). While this approach was very effective for parents as individuals, it may have curbed collective involvement in the Parents Association, BOM and other school activities.

In Irish politics there is a relationship between the sense of economic well-being of the electorate and the popularity of the government (Mair, 1992, p. 376). The same may be true of the parents in this research. The majority were satisfied with the schools and felt that the teachers were doing a good job. Like the parents in Coleman's (1998, p. 147) research in England, they were conscious of the difficulties teachers face daily and were reluctant to interfere as long as they were happy that the teacher was 'sort of competent and up to the job' (I4MF). Happy as long as they felt that their children's learning needs were being met, they were not interested in getting involved with decision-making processes within the school. While they may have privately questioned some of the schools' decisions and practices, very few were prepared to challenge the schools (Vincent, 2001, p. 351) unless it concerned their own child. In these cases, individual representation (O'Sullivan, 1992, p. 466) was perceived as being the most effective way to address their grievances. If that failed they were prepared either to move their child to another school or supplement the school's provision by helping the child at home or paying for grinds (Reay, 1998, p. 67). This is in line with the 'individualistic consumerism' (Bottery, 2005, p. 277) of modern society.

The clientelist relationship in Irish society between politicians and citizens was reflected in the relationship parents had with the school. All the parents had easy access to the principal and expected that their concerns would be listened to and dealt with. From the principal's point of view, they were in touch with the views of parents and got feedback on the organisation of the school. Its disadvantage was that the emphasis was on individual specific issues rather than on whole school policies and approaches. It also prioritised day-to-day rather than long-term issues. This is similar to the participants in the YES (Your Education System) process, who found it difficult to shift their perspectives from their immediate concerns to the longer-term view of the development of education system (Kellaghan and McGee. 2005. p. 21). They also tended to focus on the needs of a particular sector or group of students rather than the needs of the system as a whole.

Factors Influencing Parental Involvement in Their Children's Schools

Being an active citizen implies that one is an aware and responsible member of a community (Taskforce on Active Citizenship, 2007c, p. 1). Active citizens support and get involved in community activities along with playing their part in making decisions on issues that affect themselves and others. The findings of this research are very similar to the statistical evidence available about active citizenship in Ireland (Taskforce on Active Citizenship, 2007b) both in relation to volunteering and participants' attitudes towards decision-making.

At the centre of what it means to be an active citizen in a democracy, according to the Taskforce on Active Citizenship (2007a, p. 11), are values, conversations and belonging. While respondents cited lack of time and energy as being the reason why parents did not get involved with their children's schools, analysis of the questionnaires illustrated the impact of shared values and norms in the social networks that surround the school. The parents who shared the Catholic values of the school were not only more involved (Table 4.20), but were also more likely to feel that they had a say in the decision-making and governance structures within the school (Table 5.14). There was no difference between the middle class and disadvantaged schools in this respect. The parents who were most involved in each of the schools attended church weekly. This is not an isolated finding. Research has consistently shown that there is clear evidence of higher involvement and volunteering among the more frequent church-goers (Putnam, 2000, p. 67; Taskforce on Active Citizenship, 2007b, p. 15).

Those who did not share the educational values of the school and had lower levels of education were also 'marginalised' (Conaty, 2002). Respondents who had only a primary education were the least likely to access support from any source, even the class teacher (Table 4.13). This detachment from society was reflected in their lack of involvement in school activities (Table 5.19). Not alone did those with lower educational qualifications not volunteer for various activities both inside and outside the school, they were also the least likely to attend the 'set pieces'

(I4MF) such as parent-teacher meetings and school events. Their self-confidence to engage with the education system may be diminished by their own negative experience of the education system and 'the fear they felt in school' (Ryan, 1994, p. 135). In addition, their lower 'cultural capital' (Bourdieu, 1997, p. 47) may mean that these parents do not have the knowledge and language to discuss their children's education with more educated professionals (Eden, 2001, p. 98).

Interestingly, lone parents, who do not conform to the norm of a 'good' Catholic family, also appeared to be 'marginalised' (MacGiolla Phádraig, 2005, p. 64). They had lower social capital and were less likely to get involved in school activities (Table 5.21). Of course, lack of time (Servon, 2003 p. 14) and childcare may be the reason rather than 'feelings of difference' (Bell and Ribbens, 1994, p. 252). Without a partner to share the tasks involved with parenting, it is difficult to access courses and activities, particularly if they are held outside school hours.

The concern expressed by some that getting involved in school activities would be 'like walking in to a clique' (I8DM) appears justified. Social capital perpetuated exclusivity and a social network in these schools in which identity determined membership (Healy, 2004, p. 6). However, there is no evidence to suggest that the schools were deliberately excluding other parents (Lodge, 2004, p. 27). It seems as if assumptions about the homogeneity of Irish society (Devine et al., 2004, p. 246) and the continuous reinforcement of collective beliefs (Bourdieu, 1977b) by the schools sent implicit messages on the requirements for active parental involvement in the school. As Healy (2004, p. 12) suggested, the 'rules of engagement' [his apostrophes] were 'informal, tacit and possibly not even consciously acknowledged or codified'.

Both the Taskforce on Active Citizenship (2007b, p. 5) and the CSO (2007b, p. 29) noted also gender differences in the pattern of engagement with community groups. Women were more involved in Church, charitable and community/resident associations, while men tended to be involved more in sports and political organisations. This was reflected in my observations of my children's extra-curricular activities with fathers being more involved in their children's sporting activities. The fathers in Doucet's (2006, p. 700) study were similar. Like the grandfather in this research, they felt uncomfortable in women-centred venues such as playgrounds and schools, where they felt mothers were keeping a suspicious 'watchful eye on them' (Doucet, 2006, p. 703). From my observations, fathers have to engage in consistent self-monitoring when children are in their care so that they are not leaving themselves open to accusations of child abuse (Corcoran, 2005, p. 147). This makes them reluctant to get involved in school activities, especially in girls' schools (I2DG).

Fathers' working time arrangements may have meant that they had less time and were not available during the school-day when many of these activities take place. The CSO (2007b, p. 26) found that men left much earlier for work with women dominating the time slots between 8.00 and 9.00 am. Similarly, fathers in this study were less likely to attend school events such as plays, concerts, games and parent-teacher meetings, which are held during the day. However, there were no significant gender differences in attendance at the school activities, which were held at night. Fathers were also as likely as mothers to be involved in helping out in the school, especially in organising the fundraising and other events. However, they were less likely to help out in the classroom. Interestingly, the men who were interviewed had different perspectives on parental involvement than mothers. They felt that parents, not having the 'big picture' (I2DG), should leave the school alone to get on with the job of educating their children. While parents should support the school at home, they should only approach the school if they felt that the child was experiencing difficulties or if the teacher was incompetent and not doing their job (I4MF).

Like in the NCCA's (2005, p. 206) research, the disadvantaged parents were more likely to help out in the school and the classroom (Table 5.18). It appears that the HSCL scheme may have made a difference to the involvement of parents as volunteers and audiences in these schools. However, middle class parents were more likely to organise fundraising and other events in the school. They also attended activities run by the Parents Association more frequently. While these activities, as the NCCA (2005, p. 208) suggested, may 'not involve parents being in regular contact with the class teacher and learning from him/her about new ways of supporting children's own learning', their wider support network outside the school may have compensated for their lack of involvement in the school.

There was little difference between the schools in the involvement of parents in their decision making processes. In fact, the parents in the middle class schools could be said to have more of a say as they were more likely to help organise school events. Involving parents in school decision-making and governance is not one of the aims of the HSCL schemes (DES, 1999d) nor is it a priority with the HSCL coordinators (Archer and Shortt, 2003, p. 61). The HSCL programme appears to concentrate on 'service delivery' (Fine, 1997, p. 464) and 'changing parenting practices' (Clarke, 2006, p. 701).

As the SDPS facilitator for the schools, I was involved in helping the two boys' schools draw up three year plans. Both schools sent out a questionnaire to all parents asking them to review what was working well and what changes and improvements they felt were needed in the school. While the replies from the parents were similar, the principal of the disadvantaged school organised the questionnaire and parents did not attend the planning day. In contrast, the Parents Association organised the questionnaire in the middle class school and three parents attended the planning day. At the end of the day, one parent checked that the parents' priorities were addressed. This ensured that parents were not dependent on the goodwill of the teaching staff to ensure that their views and issues were taken into consideration. It appears that a Parents Association may be a more effective way of ensuring that parents are represented and have a voice than a HSCL teacher.

As other research (Donaghue, 2002, p. 69; MacGiolla Phádraig, 2005, p. 62; Taskforce on Active Citizenship, 2006b, p. 5) found, older parents were more likely to volunteer to help out in school activities (Table 5.23). Having been involved with the education system for longer, they have accumulated knowledge over the years and may have seen the benefits of parental involvement. They may also have internalised the norms for being a 'good' parent and may feel guilty that they did not get involved sooner. Having resisted the calls for help in the junior classes when child care was more of an issue, they may now have the time and the inclination to get involved. They may also have become aware of the educational capital that other parents accrued by being involved in school activities.

Unlike other research (Ryan, 1994, p. 26; Murphy, 2002, pp. 88-90; DES, 2005a, p. 63; NCCA, 2005, p. 208), parents in this study, who had children in second and fourth classes, were the most active in helping out in the school (Table 5.24). If parents are targeted by the Parents Associations and the HSCL coordinators as they enrol their children in the school, it is surprising that so few senior infant parents are involved. It may be that at second class, parents are much more familiar with the school, know the staff and have made friends with other parents. This increases their self-confidence to get involved. In addition, their children will be in the school for another four years and will reap the benefits of their efforts. In sixth class, the children are moving on to secondary school so parents have little incentive to get involved. As they were also less likely to talk to other parents about the school, it appears as if they have disengaged from the school and its community.

Parents of only children were less interested in getting involved in school activities (Table 5.22). This may be because their engagement with the school is of a shorter time-frame than that of larger families. As their contribution may not benefit their own child (I3MM), their vested interest in the schools may be less than those with larger families. In their 'cost-benefit calculus' (Servon, 2003, p. 18) it may appear that engaging in the home curriculum is more beneficial to their child. Time may also be an issue as parents with only one child were more likely to be in one-parent families and paid employment. It is unclear whether this is a life style stage or an indication of a move towards egalitarian individualism and consumerism in Irish society.

Conclusion

This chapter looked at parental involvement in the education system at both national and local level. At national level, participants had little understanding of the partnership process. They felt that the State and the DES made all the important educational decisions. Parents, they felt, had little influence on these decisions. While supportive of the Catholic ethos of the school, they were ambiguous about the role of the Church in school governance. In general, they were quite passive about the education system. While wishing that the State would put more resources in to the system, they accepted it for what it is and did what they could for their own children. Most felt that there was little point in protesting as their issues would not be addressed.

Parents were very aware of their responsibilities under the *Education Welfare Act 2000,* mainly because of the work of the NEWB and the schools. They were less aware of their rights under the *Education Act 1998* and the introduction of the revised curriculum. There is no systematic effort made at national level to inform parents of the curriculum and their entitlements in relation to the education system. Respondents' educational capital appears to increase the longer they are engaged with the system. Social class and education qualifications also impacted on the educational capital of the respondents.

While the majority of the research respondents felt that they had a very good relationship with the school, there was a power dynamic (Reay, 1998, p. 71) at play. Some felt very uncomfortable entering the professional territory of the teachers. While parents, in general, felt that they could make a complaint, they were very careful to manage this process so that they did not damage their relationship with the school. Some, who had raised issues, felt that their concerns had not been listened to or addressed. While good home-school communication had a positive impact, participants who adhered to the schools' educational and religious values had a better rapport with the school. Gender influenced the respondents' perceptions of the home-school relationship. Men saw the school as a service provider, while women saw it as an extension of their mothering work and had a more personal relationship with it.

Home-school communication mainly focused on information about events and requests for money. While occasionally parents acted as an advocate for their children, curriculum issues were rarely addressed. Written communication was the preferred means of communication with the school sending home notes at least once or twice a week. Disadvantaged parents and those with children in the junior classes met the teacher more frequently. The power differential was obvious in communication between home and school with the school controlling parents' access to information about their children.

While most parents attended parent-teacher meetings and school events, only a minority got involved in volunteering and governance. This minority, unlike other parents, were more likely to perceive that they had a say in school decisions and policies. Lack of time and fear of cliques were the reasons given by the interviewees as to why parents did not get involved in the school more. However, from the questionnaires, it appeared that those who do not conform to the religious and educational norms of the school were less likely to be involved. Gender influenced both how participants got involved in the school and their views on 'appropriate' parental involvement in their children's schooling. While parents in the disadvantaged schools were more likely to help out in the school, they were less likely to organise school events and fundraising. This may have given them less of a say in school decisions. Older parents with larger families were the most likely to be involved as volunteers and decision-makers.

Chapter Eight

CONCLUSION AND RECOMMENDATIONS

Introduction

This case study evaluated the implementation of national policy of home-school partnership in five primary schools in North Dublin. The policy aspirations, as outlined in the *Education Act 1998*, the *Education Welfare Act 2000* and the *Primary School Curriculum* (Department of Education and Science (DES), 1999a) and other documentation, was compared with the perceptions and experience of parents whose children attended these schools. The following four indicators were used to explore how the participants were involved in their children's education, both at home and at school:

- Open, caring, respectful relationships

- Home-school communication

- Parental involvement in the home curriculum

- Parental involvement in the school.

These four indicators match the policy as outlined in *Looking at our Schools* (DES, 2003b) and the categories of parental involvement, as identified by the literature (Epstein, 1992, p. 1145; Esptein and Seyong, 1995, p. 122; Organisation for Economic Co-operation and Development (OECD), 1997, p. 19). These are detailed in Chapter Two. These indicators, while very suitable for exploring parental involvement in their children's education, limited partnership to that of a relationship between individual parents and the school. They omitted the role of cultural capital (Bourdieu, 1997, p. 47) and national policy for involving parents in the education system as a whole.

The following research questions, which are outlined in more detail in Chapters One and Two, were devised using these indicators:

- How were case study participants involved in their children's education both at home and in school?

- What kind of a relationship did participants have with the school?

- What type of home-school communication system existed?

As the policy was implemented differently in middle class and disadvantaged schools, the following variables were also explored:

- What difference did social class make to parental involvement in their children's education?

- What influence had other variables, such as family status, religion, gender, age, on parental involvement both at home and school?

The overall research question asked:

- How was the national policy of partnership between parents, schools and teachers in supporting and planning for the best possible education for children both at home and at school being implemented in these schools?

Five schools, three middle class and two disadvantaged, were chosen to participate from the database of schools I worked with as a School Development Planning Support (SDPS) facilitator. One of the middle class schools was the local school, which my daughters attended. It was used to develop the research questions and to supplement the data from the other four schools.

As described in Chapter Three, triangulation (Wolff et al., 1993, p. 130) clarified the ways parents were involved in their children's education. Participant observation, through my roles as a parent and as a SDPS facilitator, gave me an introduction to the local language, the daily routines and the power structures (Kvale, 1996, p. 96). It allowed me to formulate relevant research questions and ensure that I had a sense of what the participants in this research were talking about. Structured observations of my own interactions with my children and their school were used to supplement the data from the other research methods. Questionnaires were used to examine the knowledge, beliefs and behaviour of a large number of parents in four of the case study schools. Interviews and focus groups were used to supplement the information from the questionnaires and to gather more in-depth information about parents' attitudes to and involvement in their children's education and schooling.

The research findings were outlined in Chapters Four and Five. Chapter Four outlined the involvement of parents in their children's education at home. Chapter Five described parental involvement in their children's schooling at local level. Participants' perceptions and knowledge of the stakeholders, policy, legislation and curriculum at national level were also probed. These findings were discussed in Chapter Seven.

This chapter explores the themes as developed in Chapter One in the context of findings from this research. Home-school relationships and communication systems underpin each of the themes. Section one examines the role that parents play in their children's education. It focuses on what the participants perceived as their priorities. Section two discusses the values and identities of the participants and the impact they have on their involvement in their children's education. The implementation of the national policy of home-school partnership is evaluated in section three. The implications of the research findings for national policy are outlined. Section four summarises the conclusions from this research, while the recommendations for home-school partnership at both local and national level is outlined in section five.

As this is a case study consisting of five schools, its results cannot be generalised to the school population as a whole. However, as outlined in Chapter 6, the results will be compared with other research findings in the same area.

Parental Involvement in Their Children's Education

In Chapter One, four broad headings were used for the purposes of this research to describe the parents' role in their children's education. They were educator, supporter, consumer and welfare recipient. Parents do not consciously choose their preferred role. Most of the time, they operate at an instinctive level while choosing a role that meets their perceived needs. Their identities and values, which are examined in section two, implicitly influence the stance they take on their children's education.

Educators lead and manage their children's learning as they proceed through the education system. They will ensure that the school complements their home curriculum. Supporters perceive their role as solely supporting the work of the school and will follow the school's agenda unless it impacts adversely on their children's well-being. Consumers, on the other hand, choose and pay for an educational service, which they will monitor to ensure that it is meeting their children's needs. Finally, the welfare recipients are dependent on the school and the State to help them meet their children's educational needs. They lack the confidence and the skills to question the school's provision for their children. In practice, these roles are intertwined as parents pragmatically adopt the one that best meets their children's learning needs and their own immediate interests. This section examines the participants' involvement in their children's education both at home and school using these descriptors. Their relationship with the school, in particular their method of communication, is also explored.

Educators

The majority of the participants perceived themselves as educators and they were heavily involved in their children's education. As seen in Chapter Four, most of this work took place incidentally at home through the home curriculum. They read to their children, played games with them, took them on outings and enrolled them in a variety of extra-curricular activities. Educators also took their responsibilities for 'cooperating with and supporting the school' (Department of Education, 1995, p. 9; 1996, p. 14) seriously. They ensured that their children attended school and conformed to the school rules. While educators regarded their children's formal education as a collaborative effort between home and school, they felt that it was too important to leave to teachers, particularly if their children were to realise their 'full potential' (DES, 1999a, p. 7) in the education system. These parents fulfilled their 'special role' (Department of Education 1995, p. 9; 1996, p. 14) by monitoring the work of the school and by supplementing it, if necessary, at home.

Parents' 'cultural capital' (Bourdieu, 1997, p. 47) was a vital asset in this role. Educators used it to monitor their children's progress and their schools, both present and future, and ensure that their children's academic and social needs were being met. Cultural capital was accumulated through informal networks, involvement in school activities, developing their human capital through parenting courses (Schultz, 1977, p. 318) and accessing information through the media. Personal contact, especially with those whose opinions they trusted, was perceived as the most effective source of information. In this way, educators acquired the knowledge and confidence to deal with the education system.

Educators had a sense of entitlement (Vincent, 2001, p. 348) in relation to their constitutional prerogative as the primary educators of their children (Ireland, 1937). They had no problem taking action in order to enhance their children's opportunities or if they felt that their children's needs were not being met at school. This included seeking additional support for their children at school, supplementing the work of the school at home and/or paying for grinds or extra-curricular activities. Though educators choose 'approachable' schools in order to ensure that their concerns would be listened to, they were also prepared to change schools if the school did not respond to their complaints. They had the confidence and knowledge to engage with the education system and ensure that it met their children's educational needs (Reay, 1998, p. 70).

As can be seen from the above, there was a consensus between the DES (1995, p. 9) and the educators in this research as to the role of parents in their children's education. There was also agreement around the goals of education. Educators' hopes for their children were very much in line with the DES's mission statement (1995, p. 193) While they wished their children to develop into happy, well-behaved citizens, educators also wanted their children to go to college and get a 'good job' (I7DM).

Educators saw themselves as the 'primary educators' (Ireland, 1937) of their children and were uneasy about the present partnership processes. They felt that the present structures needed to be improved to allow 'the systematic and continuous involvement of parents in the planning process' (DES, 2006b, p. 80), particularly in relation to curricular changes and their children's progress.

Supporters

All the parents in this research supported their children's schools, though some were more active than others. They felt responsible for ensuring that their children attended school, wore the correct uniform and had the appropriate books, pencils and copies. In addition, most parents supported the school ethos and rules publicly, if not privately, and felt that their children should obey their teachers. They also contributed to the schools' fundraising efforts, helped their children with homework and attended parent-teacher meetings and other school events. By complying with these practices or 'rituals' (Durkeim, 1971, p. 44), supporters fulfilled the basic requirement for being a 'good' parent as defined by the DES and Irish society.

Most parents, due to work and other commitments, were silent supporters. They helped their child at home, but remained detached from the school. The more active supporters, who helped out in the school or got involved in school governance, only did so when asked by the school or when they thought it might benefit their child's education. In some cases, 'support' could be defined as an extension of the educator role. Involvement was used to improve their educational capital and ensure that their concerns were addressed.

Supporters had a good relationship with the school and were confident that their issues would be addressed. However, they also accepted the status quo and recognised that the school would not always be able to meet their demands. While attempts to modify the school's provision in relation to their own children met with mixed results, supporters were very reluctant to change schools. They applied the 'good enough' standard to schools (Furstenberg et al., 1999, pp. 225-6) and focused on the here and now rather than the future.

Supporters relied on the school to educate their children and saw no reason to intervene unless there was a problem. Being aware of the difficulties teachers faced daily, they valued and appreciated their work. They were quite happy with the partnership model as outlined by the DES (1994, p. 5), Irish National Teachers' Organisation (INTO, 1997) and the Catholic Primary School Managers' Association (CPMSA, 2004, p. 17), whereby professional and financial matters relating to the school were left to the BOM and the teachers.

Consumers

'Consumers' are those whose 'prime investment' (Wolfendale, 1996, p. 35) in their own children takes precedence. They view the school as a service provider and see no reason to get involved with its activities unless it directly benefits their own children. Being aware of the quality and cost of the service provided, consumers will complain if it is not delivered as promised.

Participants in this research, whether they liked it or not, had to act as consumers in order to supplement the education system. All parents paid for school items along with regularly contributing to the schools' fundraising efforts. They also supplemented the school curriculum at home by paying for extra-curricular activities and, when necessary, for grinds. Some participants were resentful when the school refused to provide additional support for their children, leaving them with little choice but to augment the schools' provision out of their own resources.

Like many other consumers, parents planned their children's education from an early age and were active choosers when deciding on their children's schools. However, this could be seen as an extension of their 'educator' role. Despite the information deficit (Kellaghan and McGee, 2005, p. 15), parents used their social capital (Bourdieu, 1997, p. 51) to find a school with a good reputation. If their choice of school was not meeting their children's needs, they were prepared to move their children to another school.

Consumers prefer to pay others to do the decision-making and the work rather than get personally involved (Irvin and Stansbury, 2004, pp. 58-9). Many parents in the research held similar attitudes towards their involvement in the school. They did not get involved unless there were 'tangible benefits' (National Centre for Partnership and Performance, 2002, p. 32) to their own children. They were unconcerned about being excluded from the decision-making processes as they felt that they could use the complaint procedure if necessary. This was done on an individual rather than a collective basis. Consumers favoured the DES's (1998a; 1998b; 2005c) partnership model, where parents are clients and customers of both the schools and the DES and can expect to be provided with a quality service.

Welfare Recipients

The term 'welfare recipient' appeared initially to be inappropriate in this research as most parents took responsibility for and got involved in their children's education. There was no evidence that the constant stream of expert advice on how to be a 'good' parent undermined their confidence or made them dependent on outside professionals (McKeown et al., 1998, p. 80). In fact, very few relied on the professional services, apart from the class teachers, for support and advice in rearing and educating their children. Opinion was equally divided over whether children's education should be left to the teachers as the 'experts'. While most perceived their children's education to be a collaborative effort, a minority felt that teachers were solely responsible for children's numeracy, literacy and socialisation skills.

However, most were welfare recipients in their acceptance of 'public patriarchy' (Walby, 1994), whereby the State took responsibility for children's education. All the participants availed of the State education system and depended on the State to provide resources, define the curriculum and ensure standards in the schools. While they were critical of the State's failures in this regard, participants saw no role for themselves in changing national policy. They were unaware of the partnership process, in particular the role of National Parents' Council Primary (NPCP), at national level. As far as the research respondents were concerned, national education policy, particularly the curriculum, was determined by the DES and therefore off-limits to parents.

Parents were also dependent on the school for information about their children's progress, the curriculum and national education policy. This was compounded by the practices of the NPCP and other national agencies to use the school as a means of communicating with parents. Much of this communication did not reach parents (Kilfeather, 2003). This information deficit left a lot of parents unaware of their rights and the curriculum being taught in the schools. Some used their social capital (Bourdieu, 1997, p. 51) to access this information from other parents and 'teacher' friends. Others used the media, the Internet and parenting courses to keep themselves informed. However, there were others who were quite happy to depend on the school. As welfare recipients, these parents wondered if they needed to know more about national policy and the curriculum, especially if the teachers looked as if they knew what they were doing and the school appeared to be a happy, ordered place (Taylor, 1997, p. 119).

Most participants, even those who acted as educators in the home, tended to act as welfare recipients in the school. Preserving the home-school relationship took precedence over asserting their parental rights. These parents felt uncomfortable entering the professional territory of the teachers and were very aware of the power differential (Reay, 1998) with most believing that they had very little say over school activities and policies. As welfare recipients, parents were inclined to be 'passive' (Hilliard, 2003) and conform to the norms of the school unless the issue impacted directly on their own children. Some of those who did complain felt that their concerns were either shelved or dismissed. This minority were angry that they had to fight for services to which they felt, based on their observations of their children's needs and progress, their children were entitled. It appears from this research that the implicit message that parents got from the State and schools was that their children's formal education was to be left solely to the teachers who were the experts.

Parental Roles

These headings: educator, supporter, consumer and welfare recipient, proved very useful in describing parental involvement in their children's education. Not only did they uncover the underlying motivations of parents, they also illustrated how these motivations influenced parental actions, particularly their interactions with their children's schools.

Parents tended to act as educators at home and welfare recipients at school. Even though they supplemented the school's funding, the information deficit made it difficult for them to act as consumers in the true sense of the word. Most parents complied with the expectations of the State and supported the work of the school. The majority were passive, while a few were actively involved in their children's schools. This was mainly on an individual basis with parents primarily focused on the benefits to their own children.

Influence of Parental Identities and Values

While on the surface, most of the participants appeared to belong to the dominant 'status group' (Collins, 1977, p. 125) which was white, Catholic and Irish, they were not homogenous. The way they got involved in their children's education reflected the increasing diversity of Irish society and the changing cultural and social norms. Chapter One examined the impact of the citizenship, social class, gender, religion and other family factors on parents and their identities as individuals. This section explores the influence of these factors on the respondents in this research.

Citizenship

Nearly all the respondents were Irish citizens and this was reflected in their attitude towards the school. Like the relationship between citizens and the political parties (Mair, 1992, p. 376), there was a strong link between perceptions of children's social and academic well-being and the popularity of the school. Once they felt that their children were happy and learning, parents were satisfied to let the teachers get on with it. As with the findings of the Taskforce on Active Citizenship (2007b) and the 2006 Census (Central Statistics Office, 2007b, p. 29), only a minority were willing to get involved with the school. Older parents and frequent church-goers were the most likely to volunteer, while those with lower levels of education were the least likely to get involved.

Like with politicians, parents had easy access to the principal and the teachers. Most had no problem talking to the teachers and felt that they were listened to. This tradition of clientelism (Keohane and Kuhling, 2005, p. 50) meant that parents were quite happy to rely on individual representation rather than collective action to address their grievances (O'Sullivan, 1992, p. 466). Like those who participated in the Your Education System (YES) process (Kellaghan and McGee, 2005, p. 21), parents' focused on their own immediate personal concerns rather than long-term whole school priorities. This may be a reflection of the increase in consumerism in society.

Traces of the past, when the power of both Church and State inhibited questioning and dissent (Hilliard, 2003, p. 31), were also apparent. Most parents accepted the school rules and believed that children should obey their teachers. Fully aware that they were dependent on the school to educate their children, they felt uncomfortable questioning the school's approach for fear of alienating the teachers. A minority who had raised issues with the school found it difficult to get their concerns addressed. Unlike at national level, there was no systematic approach to involving parents in decision-making at local level (DES, 2006b, p. 80). Only a small minority were involved with the Parents Association and the Board of Management (BOM) and even these felt that certain areas such as curriculum were out-of-bounds.

Some parents preferred to phone the DES before approaching the school. This, as Keohane and Kuhling (2004, p. 51) argued, may be seen as the emergence of modernisation, where the principles of accountability and transparency are chosen over the tradition of clientelism and brokerage. It was also perceived as a neutral way of accessing power/ knowledge that ensures that the relationship with the school is maintained and that their concerns are addressed.

Gender

The tensions between traditional patriarchal familism policy paradigm and the more modern egalitarian individualism (Fahey, 1998) were apparent in this research. While participants, especially those in two-parent families, accepted that fathers had a responsibility for their children's education, there were mixed views on how willing fathers were to accept this responsibility. Family forms, social class along with employment and education levels influenced these views with over half the respondents to the questionnaires feeling that mothers were primarily responsible for their children's education.

The fathers who participated in this research felt just as responsible for their children's education as the mothers. However, as other researchers (Reay, 1998, p. 60; O'Brien, 2005, p. 239; Graue et al., 2001) suggested, mothers appeared to be more involved in the day-to-day business of educating their children. They were more likely to monitor their school work and network with other parents and the principal. This is similar to other research, which found that mothers did the majority of networking, with fathers playing a more marginal role (Bell and Ribbens, 1994, p. 238; McNamara Horvat et al., 2003, p. 14). However, it was suggested that fathers might find it difficult to fit into these mother-dominated networks, especially when they are viewed suspiciously (Doucet, 2006, p. 704).

In addition, fathers had a different attitude to school than mothers. They were more inclined to view it as a service provider where one did not get involved unless there was a problem. Mothers, on the other hand, perceived the role of the teacher and parent to be complementary and felt that a supportive home-school relationship benefited their children. Employment levels, along with traditional views of the appropriate gender roles, appeared to influence the involvement of fathers in their children's education. However, they perceived an increased role for themselves in supplementing the work of the school as their children grew older.

Social Class

As stated in Chapter One, social class was determined by the school the respondents' children attended. Both the disadvantaged schools in this research were in DEIS Band 1 Urban, which meant that they were two of the 150 Irish primary schools with the highest level of disadvantage (DES, 2005d, p. 78). The parents in the middle class schools were more likely to be in two-parent families, paid employment and have third level qualifications. The majority of fathers who responded to the questionnaire were from the middle class schools.

Other research found that middle class parents had a better relationship with the school than disadvantaged parents (Lareau, 1997, p. 709; Hanafin and Lynch, 2002, p. 41). This was not evident in this research. The majority of respondents, regardless of what school their children attended, had a good relationship with the teachers. Adherence to the Catholic values of the school and active engagement with the school had more influence on home-school relationships than social class.

There was also nothing to indicate that middle class parents were treated more favourably than disadvantaged parents. While a minority of parents found it difficult to approach teachers or make a complaint, this was not confined to any one type of school. In fact, the disadvantaged parents appeared to have more frequent contact with the school. They talked to the teacher more often and were more likely to help out in the classroom and school. This was similar to Reay's (1998, p. 62) and the National Council for Curriculum and Assessment's (NCCA) (2005, p.

206) findings. It appears that the Home School Community Liaison (HSCL) scheme may have made a difference to both the involvement of parents as audiences and volunteers in these disadvantaged schools. However, it could be said that middle class parents were more involved in the decision-making processes as they were more involved in organising school events.

Social class did have an influence on the respondents' 'cultural capital' (Bourdieu, 1997, p. 47), parenting practices and their aspirations for their children. Not only did middle class parents have the financial capital to supplement the work of the school, they also had more educational capital and a wider support network. Disadvantaged parents appeared to favour the traditional 'responsible' parent (Wyness, 1996 p. 14). While having the same aspirations as middle class parents, they had very specific fears about the influence of the 'street' on their children's educational prospects. Like those in Furstenberg et al.'s (1999) study, disadvantaged parents employed a range of preventative strategies to reduce their children's exposure to various types of dangerous circumstances. These included a high degree of monitoring their children's behaviour and that of their friends. However, they tended to adopt a more 'wait-and-see' fatalism about their children's education (Gewirtz et al., 1995, p. 44). Middle class parents, in contrast, favoured the sensitive supportive parent (Dix, 1991). They had implicit flexible rules and elaborate code of communication and negotiation (De Regt and Weenink, 2005, pp. 60-3). Their fears for their children were very vague and they actively shaped their children's educational career from an early age (Reay, 2003, p. 56).

Nolan and Whelan (1999, p. 117) identified two contrasting groups in the literature on disadvantage. One adhered to mainstream norms, while the other is more marginalised. In this study, the group with the lower levels of education appeared to be the most 'marginalised' (Conaty, 2002) regardless of what school their children attended. Respondents with higher levels of education perceived their children's education to be a shared enterprise between home and school. Not only did they have more social and educational capital, but they were more inclined to attend school events, volunteer as helpers and organisers, and get involved in decision-making within the school. While those with lower levels of education felt more responsibility for their children's education, they also relied more on the teacher in the areas of literacy, numeracy and socialisation. They were also the least likely to receive support from any quarter. It is unclear whether this was due to their lack of social skills and confidence to engage with the education system or whether they did not share the educational norms and values of the school and other parents. While there is a relationship between educational qualifications and social class (Bourdieu, 1977a), it appears that education levels of parents have a far greater impact on parental involvement in their children's education than the parents' social class.

Religious Values

The five schools were under the patronage of the Catholic archbishop of Dublin and three-quarters of the respondents to the questionnaire supported the Catholic values of the school. While it appears that there is considerable support for retaining the Catholic ethos of schools (Commission on the Family, 1998, p. 548), the degree to which parents adhered to the Catholic ethos influenced their relationship with the school. Practising Catholics felt more welcome in the school. They were more involved in school activities and appeared to feel a greater sense of 'entitlement' (Vincent, 2001, p. 348) to engage with decision-making and governance within the school. Practising Catholics were also unusually active social capitalists outside the school (Putnam, 2000, p. 67) in that they were more likely to be a member of a group and attend talks and classes for parents outside the school.

There was no evidence to suggest that those whose values differed from the school were deliberately discriminated against or excluded. However, rituals, such as homework, the sacraments, parents' meetings, confirmed and reinforced the collective norms and values of the school (Durkheim, 1971, p. 427). These permeated the Code of Behaviour, which formed an implicit home-school agreement. In addition, the assumption of homogeneity (Lodge et al., 2004, p. 5) and the continuation of Church paternalism, whereby the rights and duties of parents, the school and the Church were considered to be complementary (O'Sullivan, 1992, p. 465), made it difficult for parents to challenge the status quo.

Parents' reaction to the power differential (Reay, 1998, p. 71) varied depending on their relationship with the school. Aware that they lacked the ability to influence the system at national and local level, most parents, as Bourdieu (1977b, p. 5) suggested, submitted to the norms of the school in order to use them to their advantage. Some, usually those whose values were similar to those of the school, got involved in school activities to increase their educational capital and ensure that their individual concerns were addressed (Coleman, 1998, p. 24). Others tended to be passive (Hilliard, 2003, p. 44) supporters. They accepted things the way they were and ensured that their children conformed to the school ethos and rules. Those, whose complaints were ignored by the school, felt silenced (Devine et al., 2004, p. 246). Many of those whose beliefs differed from the norm maintained an independent stance from the school and its activities (Vincent, 1996, p. 149). Despite privately questioning the Church's role in education, they complied publicly with the Catholic ethos for fear that their children would be ostracised or bullied by other children (Lodge, 2004, p. 24).

Family or Lifestyle Factors

Partnership, as Hornby (2000, p. 20) suggested, requires a long-term commitment. The short time-frame that their child is in the system may make it unproductive for parents to get involved. The length of time that change can take may mean that a child has left the school before the changes are implemented. This may be why family-size had such an impact on parental involvement in schools. One-child families focused more on the home curriculum rather than developing social networks and getting involved in the school. This, of course, was of immediate benefit to their individual child. One-child families were also less likely to uphold the Catholic ethos of the school and to contribute to the school's fundraising efforts. As most of the parents with only one child were under thirty, it was unclear whether this was a life stage or a generational difference (Putnam, 2000). Older parents had more educational capital and similar to other research they were more likely to volunteer with school activities (Taskforce on Active Citizenship, 2007b, p. 5; CSO, 2007b, p. 29).

Parents also behaved differently depending on the gender and age of their children (Gorard, 1997, p. 189). As in other research girls were more supportive of their parents (Evertsson, 2006). Boys were more likely to participate in sport and computers rather than music, art and dancing. They were also less likely to be brought to church than girls. Respondents with older children in the senior classes and secondary school had more educational capital than those with younger children. With their children moving towards increasing levels of independence and responsibility (Heightman, 1992, p. 21), they were less involved in networking and the home curriculum. Parents of children in the junior classes, on the other hand, had a wider support network, more contact with the class teacher and a more extensive home curriculum. They were also more likely to help with homework and examine their children's copybooks and workbooks.

As children grow increasingly independent, they may limit their parents' involvement in their education (Edwards and Alldred, 2000, p. 448). This may be why, contrary to other research (Ryan, 1994, p. 26; Murphy, 2002, pp. 88-90; DES, 2005a, p. 63; NCCA, 2005, p. 208), parents of children in second and fourth classes were more involved with the school. It may have been their only way of keeping themselves informed. While realising the advantages of being involved, they may also feel comfortable enough to volunteer their services.

While being a lone parent is not reducible to class-related factors (Nolan and Whelan, 1999, p. 112), they were also marginalised in that they had less of a social network and were less likely to help out in the school. It is not clear whether this was due to them holding different values from the school or because they were particularly 'time-poor' (Servon, 2003, p. 14) compared to other parents. However, like in Ho Sui-Chu and Willms's study (1996, p. 137), there was no difference in the involvement of lone parents in the home curriculum. In this context, it is interesting that they felt more responsible for their children's education than those in two-parent families who perceived it to be the joint responsibility of both home and school.

Influence of Values and Beliefs

Parents' involvement in their children's education varied according to their values and beliefs. Like most Irish citizens, parents focused on the needs of their own children and preferred to rely on individual representation rather than collective action. Those who supported the religious and educational norms of the school were more likely to get involved with the school. Both gender and family size influenced the participants' involvement in the home curriculum and the school. However, as in other research (Dronkers, 1994, p. 186; Craig, 2006, p. 563; Crozier and Davies, 2006, p. 681), the participants' educational levels appeared to have a greater influence on their parenting practices than either social class or gender.

National Policy of Home–School Partnership

The term 'partnership', while generally regarded as a formal agreement between two or more parties that will provide them with mutual benefits (Levin, 2004, p. 171), can embrace a wide range of concepts. In Chapter One, educational partnership was defined as

> The relationship between parents, the school, the State and the Catholic Church in supporting and planning for the best possible education for children both at home and at school.

This section examines, from the perspective of parents, the implementation of the national policy of home-school partnership at both local and national level.

Partnership at Local Level

As Skeggs (1994, p. 84) suggested, those with the power at local level can decide whether or not to implement policies. There was no evidence to suggest that the case study schools were resistant to the idea of parental involvement. In fact, many participants remarked that the schools had become more approachable and more open to the involvement of parents over the last six years. However, it should be recognised that this was just one national policy among a host of others that these schools were required to implement. With most parents quite happy about the amount of involvement they had, especially since the schools were very open to dealing with their individual concerns, there was little incentive for the schools to initiate a major reform of their current practice in this area.

There were differences between the actual policy and the policy-in-use (Crump, 1992, p. 419) in the schools. The traditional form of silent partnership (Lareau, 1997, p. 706) was most evident in this research. While parents were actively involved in their children's education outside the school, their involvement within the school was limited to clearly defined partnership rituals (Durkheim, 1971, p. 427). These included helping with homework and attending school events. Only a minority of parents were active partners and felt that they had a say in school events and polices.

Views varied among the participants as to how involved they needed to be in their children's schooling. Most interviewees were fairly happy to maintain their existing individual relationship with their children's teachers and help out occasionally when asked. They were quite willing to leave professional matters to the teachers and were not really interested in getting involved in decision-making and governance.

However, there may have been 'unspoken' (Bourdieu, 1977b) forces at work. Analysis of the questionnaires highlighted that those who volunteered shared the religious values of the schools. These were more likely to have a better relationship with the school and to feel that they had a say in school events and policies. It is not clear why the 'others' did not get involved. Those with different religious values may have either chosen to remain detached from the school or they may not feel 'entitled' (Vincent, 2001, p. 360) to intervene in the operation of the school. Those with lower levels of education tended to be the most 'marginalised' (Conaty, 2002) and may have lacked the confidence and cultural capital (Bourdieu, 1997, p. 47) to contest the schools' way of doing things.

Home-school communication is an essential element of national policy. Written communication appeared to be the preferred means of communication, though parents with children in the disadvantaged schools and junior classes were more likely to talk to the teachers. Most participants were satisfied with the amount of information they received from the school. They felt that they were kept informed of their children's progress and the operation of the school. Participants were also very aware of the implications of the *Education Welfare Act 2000*. All the schools had grievance/appeal procedures in place and most respondents felt that they could make a complaint, if necessary.

However, there were gaps in their knowledge about the *Education Act 1998* and the introduction of the revised curriculum. While aware of some changes to the curriculum, less than half the respondents knew that the curriculum had been revised. Their knowledge of the roles and responsibilities of the BOM was vague and very few knew that they were entitled to see the school's financial accounts. In addition, respondents' understanding of both the concept and the content of the school plan was limited. While assistance was sought for school activities, there was little evidence that the schools involved parents in organisational and curricular reviews. However, as noted in Chapter Seven, this issue is being addressed due to the disadvantaged schools' obligation to devise a three-year plan as part of the DEIS Action Plan (DES, 2005d) and following a Whole School Evaluation (WSE) in the middle class boys' school.

It appears that while the schools kept parents informed of personal local issues, they did not alert them to changes in national policy. It may be, as Furstenberg et al. (1999, p. 228) suggested, that schools deal with children for such a brief span that they have neither the time nor the resources to keep them informed. Overload is an issue for many schools. In my experience as an SDPS facilitator, schools are too busy keeping up-to-date with the developments in national policy to even consider the needs of parents in relation to these changes. In any case, parents appeared to be more interested in the progress of their own children than in national policy (Moos et al., 1998, p. 72). However, as Hargreaves (2000, pp. 220-21) pointed out, if parents do not understand the changes being made, it is more difficult for them to support their children at home.

Home-school partnership, as it operated in these schools, consisted of parents supporting their children's learning informally at home and teachers providing the formal education at school. As part of this agreement, teachers kept parents informed of their children's progress along with school policies and activities. Parents, for their part, provided the teachers with 'school trained' (Wyness, 1996, p. 141) children. They also contributed to fundraising and helped out when asked. However, none of the five schools had established a process whereby teachers and parents could engage in structured and continuous dialogue about organisational and curricular policies (DES, 2003b; DES, 2006b p. 80). As a result, parents had little or no influence on the operation of school.

The HSCL scheme in the two disadvantaged schools aims to develop the parents as the primary educator and promote partnership between teachers and parents (Conaty, 2002, p. 29). The three middle class schools were relying on the efforts of the BOMs, principals and the Parents Associations. It is difficult to assess the difference the HSCL scheme had made to parents using previous evaluations. Feedback is normally obtained from the HSCL teachers and principals and the number of parents who availed of the various supports is not readily available (Archer and Shortt, 2003; Conaty, 2006, p. 131). While it may be that the 'most marginalised' parents (Conaty, 2002) did not return their questionnaires in this research, the HSCL service also acknowledges that it is difficult to elicit a response from these families (Purcell, 2006, p. 9).

As Archer and Shortt (2003, p. 111) found, the HSCL scheme appeared to improve home-school relationships. Parents in the disadvantaged schools had more contact with the teachers and helped out more in the school. However, only a small minority of parents found the HSCL teacher a useful source of support and advice. Like the middle class parents, they were more likely to rely on the class teacher. However, the scheme does not appear to address the educational capital of parents and equip them with the knowledge needed to make informed decisions about their children's future education. Middle class parents were not only far more aware of the educational changes over the last six years, but they were also more aware, through their social networks, of how the system works. They not only had the economic resources to provide a wide variety of extra curricular activities for their children, but they also had the 'cultural capital' (Bourdieu, 1997, p. 47) to consider and plan for their children's future educational needs.

Partnership at National Level

All the interviewees were aware of the role of the State and the DES in regulating and funding schools. They were perceived as being solely responsible for the education system and parents depended on them to ensure that their children received a quality education that was up to international standards (Department of Education, 1995, p. 193). They favoured welfare rather than private provision and felt that the State was not doing enough to support families. While interviewees felt that the State was not meeting its responsibilities towards their children, particularly in the area of special needs and class size, they also felt powerless to address these issues. Complaining was pointless as they would not be listened to. The State's emphasis on the human capital model meant that parents perceived the needs of parents and children as being subservient to serving the needs of business and high-tech industry (Walshe, 1999, p. 6).

Interviewees had no concept of the partnership process at national level and felt that parents had very little say in the curriculum and other DES policies. While the NPCP represents parents at national level, those who were interviewed were unaware, not only of its role, but also of its existence. There was no recognition that the NPCP was an influential national organisation, which would make representations on their behalf or advise them on educational matters. Parents rang the DES if they had a problem rather than the NPCP. It remains to be seen if the revised structures as envisaged in the NPCP's Strategic Plan (2007a) will make a difference to parental involvement at national level.

As with the NPCP, there was no awareness of the role of the Church in school management and governance. This highlights the change in the Church's status in today's society. From an era of total control and domination, the school was no longer linked with the Church in the minds of the interviewees. No one saw the rights of parents and the Church to be complementary and some questioned the Church's right to be involved in education, particularly in the light of recent scandals.

Active partnership requires information. The last decade has been a time of immense change in Irish Education. New legislation and a re-vised curriculum have been introduced. Chapter Five, which examined the participants' knowledge of these changes, highlighted the information deficit at national level. While the National Education Welfare Board (NEWB) and the schools keep parents informed of their responsibilities under the *Education Welfare Act 2000*, there is no similar body to inform parents of their rights, particularly in relation to the *Education Act 1998*. The NCCA has begun to address the deficit in relation to the curriculum with the introduction of the DVD and a dedicated area of their website addressed to parents.

While the use of the schools as channels of communication with parents may be cost-effective, there is plenty of evidence to suggest that it may not be the most effective means of communication. Not only does the NEWB send its brochures directly to parents using the children's allowance database, but, being aware that its clientele is constantly changing, it sends them at regular intervals. This ensures that the information reaches parents directly.

Finally, partnership requires active engagement by all of the partners. Parents in this research were very much focused on the local immediate issues that related specifically to their own children. They were prepared to trust their children's teachers and had little interest in long-term national concerns. As suggested by the INTO (1997, p. 9) and the CPSMA (2004, p. 17), parents were quite happy to leave professional and financial matters to others. The culture of clientelism and history of passivity prevented them from questioning the status quo at both national and local level. While parents were very happy to support the school in educating their children, they prioritised their own individual private planning for their children's education over getting involved in the school's SDP processes.

Conclusion

This section evaluated the research findings in relation to the implementation of the national policy of home-school partnership in five primary schools in North Dublin. As this is only a small sample of the total parent and school population, these results may not be generalisable to other schools.

The model of partnership adopted implicitly reflects the power and practices of the dominant group, which in this case is the State and the DES. Partnership is described in official documents as a set of relationships based on the pursuit of common goals, trust and a problem-solving approach, where the government retains the ultimate responsibility for decision-making (Department of the Taoiseach, 2006, p. 74). The main emphasis is on involving parents in policy development and the provision of education services (DES, 2005c, p. 15; DES, 2006a, p. 26).

Research Question 1: How were case study participants involved in their children's education both at home and at school?

As seen in Chapters Four and Six, they were heavily involved in their children's education at home. They read to their children, took them on outings and did all the educational work that is expected of 'good' parents. Involvement in their children's schools, which was outlined in

Chapters Five and Seven, was a different matter. While the majority supported their children's school work and attended school events, only a minority volunteered or got involved in school governance. Participants appeared to prefer helping out informally rather than joining the Parents Association or the BOM. Most parents felt that they were well informed about their children's progress either by the teacher or by monitoring their children's learning. However, they had little information about the curriculum and were not involved in policy formation in any systematic way.

Service delivery rather than policy development was the prime focus of parental involvement. While parents acted as educators at home, they operated as supporters, consumers and welfare recipients in the school. Most adopted whichever role suited their children's immediate interests.

Research Question 2: What kind of relationship did participants have with the school?

As seen in Chapters Five and Seven, most parents had a very good relationship with the school. They felt that they were welcome in the school, that they could talk to the teachers and make a complaint when necessary. However, there were some impenetrable factors (Cullingford, 1996a, p. 5) which prevented parents from feeling comfortable about raising issues with the teachers with only a minority feeling that they had a say in school policies and events. Frequent home-school communication and adherence to the values of the school enhanced the relationship between parents and the school.

Research Question 3: What type of home-school communication system existed?

Parent-teacher meetings, notes, end-of-year reports along with children's anecdotes were the main means of communication between home and school. This tended to be one-way and centred on organisational rather than curriculum issues. With both sides only making contact when an issue arose, it also tended to be problem-orientated. Written communication was the norm, though in the disadvantaged schools and the junior classes, parents met the class teacher more frequently.

With most parents monitoring their children's learning by helping with homework and checking copies and workbooks, they felt that they knew both the standard of learning in the school and their children's progress. However, this did not keep them up-to-date on curriculum and national policy changes.

Research Question 4: What was the difference in how parents from middle class and disadvantaged schools got involved in their children's education?

While disadvantaged parents had more frequent contact with the teachers and helped out more in the school, the 'cultural capital' (Bourdieu, 1997, p. 47) of the middle class parents appeared to outweigh any of the advantages that the HSCL scheme conferred on disadvantaged parents. Being more future orientated, middle class parents actively shaped their children's educational career from an early age. Disadvantaged parents appeared to hold more traditional views on child rearing and the appropriate parenting roles. The dangers of the 'street' and their lack of educational capital resulted in a more resigned attitude towards their children's educational outcomes. The most 'marginalised' (Conaty, 2002) parents were those with lower levels of education.

Research Question 5: What influence had other variables such as family status, religion, gender and age on parental involvement both at home and at school?

While the majority of participants supported the Catholic values of the school, practising Catholics were more likely to get involved with the school and have a say in school policies and events.

While the fathers who participated in this research felt just as responsible for their children's education as mothers, traditional gender practices and attitudes remained. Mothers appeared to be more active and 'hands-on' in their involvement in their children's education, especially at school. 'Maternal gatekeeping' (Allen and Hawkins, 1999), child protection issues along with education and employment levels were cited as the reasons why fathers were not involved more.

One-child families and those with younger children were more actively involved in the home curriculum. Those with larger families supported the school more. Older parents had more educational capital. In addition, like those in two-parent families, they had a better social network and were more likely to get involved in the school.

Research Question 6: How was the national policy of partnership being implemented in these schools?

In Chapter One partnership was defined as the relationship between parents, the school, the State and the Catholic Church in supporting and planning for the best possible education for children both at home and at school. This definition, like much of the national policy on parental involvement, is expressed in broad symbolic terms.

Parents in this research appeared to keep their side of the bargain in that they nurtured a learning environment, co-operated with and supported the school and other educational partners, and fulfilled their special role in the development of their child as best they could (Department of Education, 1995, p. 9). They also ensured that their children complied with the school rules (Ireland, 2000).

Participants felt that their children's schooling was a partnership between home and school. Home-school relationships were very positive with most parents feeling that the schools were doing a very good job under difficult circumstances. The majority felt that they were informed of school activities and their children's progress. However, while class teachers were an important source of support and advice, parents still felt it necessary to monitor their children's school work to ensure that the teachers were doing their job and that their children were learning.

Home-school partnership in planning for children's learning was not evident in this research. Most parents were involved in the schools as spectators rather than volunteers and decision-makers. While they could raise issues with the principals and teachers as individuals, the majority did not feel that parents had a say in whole-school decisions and policies. The power structures within the schools prevented the full implementation of this aspect of the policy (Foucault, 2000, p. 18). Home-school collaboration focused mainly on the peripheral and uncontested areas of school life (Blenkin et al., 1992, p. 52). 'Involved' parents tended to conform to the religious and educational values of the school. As the schools' SDP structures could not accommodate the systematic and continuous involvement of parents in planning process, parents were usually informed about decision after they had been made (DES, 2006b). Lacking the educational capital to challenge these decisions, most parents deferred to the teachers' professional expertise and judgement (DES, 2006b, p. 51).

While the power differential between home and school was influential, the interest of parents in their own individual child (Wolfendale, 1996, p. 35) also prevented the successful implementation of the policy. The majority of participants prioritised the home-curriculum and supporting their own children's learning over helping out in the school. This was particularly evident in one-child families. Consequently, the increase in secular consumerism and the number of one-child families (CSO, 2007a, p. 20) may have major implications for the national policy of parental involvement.

In the future, schools may not be able to rely on the financial contributions and unpaid labour of parents to supplement the resources provided by State. If, like the parents of only children in this research, parents focus solely on their private objectives for their own individual child, they will not be interested in supporting the 'public goals' of education (Levin, 2004, p. 172) and getting involved with their children's schools. In an increasingly consumerist society, the school may be viewed as a service provider, which is accountable to parents to provide international standards of performance and delivery (DES, 1998b, p. 8). This may lead to impersonal, adversarial and fragile relationships between home and school.

The changes in the Church-State relationship were evident in this research. With the increasing diversity of the school population, monopoly Catholicism (Fulton, 2000a, p. 13) no longer appeared to exist. While participants valued the Catholic ethos of the schools, the Church was not perceived as a partner in their children's education. Most of those interviewed questioned the role of the Church in school governance and ownership. This finding is particularly relevant in the light of the current debate on school patronage.

The State, on the other hand, had moved from a subsidiary role (Inglis, 1998, p. 57) to one of domination, as far as the interviewees were concerned. They were quite happy with this highly centralised model, once the DES was prepared to monitor teaching standards and fund their children's education. It was interesting that while the DES perceived parents as consumers (DES, 1998a), parents perceived the State's provision for their children's education as part of their entitlements as citizens of a welfare state. Some interviewees considered the State neglectful in that they felt that it did not take its responsibilities seriously and provide the necessary resources to ensure that the education system was of the highest quality as measured by international standards (Department of Education, 1995, p. 193).

Interviewees were unaware of the partnership process at national level and felt that parents had little say over national policy. While networking with other parents at local level was an important source of support and advice for parents, they were unable to identify the contribution of the NPCP to the partnership process.

Policy evaluation, according to Dye (1995, p. 320) is about learning about the consequences of public policy. The key objectives of this policy were to ensure that parents were involved in their children's learning as well as school decision-making and governance. In this research, which is only based on a small sample of the total parent population, there were major gaps between the rhetoric of national policy and the reality in schools (Cussen, 1995, p. 51).

However, while the national policy of home-school partnership may have been only partially successful, its symbolic (Dye, 1995, p. 323) or 'feel-good' (Ó Cinnéide, 2003, p. 330) function of giving legitimacy to parental involvement in their children's schooling was important. As a result, parents felt that schools had become more open and approachable over the last six years. With parents prioritising their private interests over the public goals of education (Levin, 2004, p. 174), this tended to be on an individualistic clientelistic basis. It appears from this research that Ireland has some way to go before it has one of the 'most parent-participative systems in the world' (OECD, 1997, p. 141).

Recommendations

The recommendations, as outlined here, are those of the researcher and are based on the findings of this case study of five schools in North Dublin. If future research finds that these results apply to the total population of schools and parents, then the following recommendations need to be implemented at local and national level for the national policy of parental involvement in their children's education to be effective.

Parental Involvement in School Planning

- School-based structures, which can 'accommodate the systematic and continuous involvement of parents in the planning process' (DES, 2006b, p. 80), are needed. At present, only a minority, whose values correspond with those of the school, are involved in the planning process and this tends to be on an irregular and once-off basis.

- Additional resources at both national and local level are needed if all parents are to be involved in the SDP process. This will include additional personnel and funding at local level to enable schools to establish planning structures that will allow all parents to engage in ongoing review and action planning on curriculum and organisational issues. The SDPS service will need to be expanded so that facilitators can support these structures and processes.

- The WSE process needs to be reviewed to give all parents the opportunity to contribute. At present, only the parents' representatives on the BOM and the officers of Parents Associations, which are affiliated to the NPCP, are invited to meet with the inspectorate at the pre-evaluation stage. Only the teachers and the BOM (DES, 2006a, p. 12) attend the post-evaluation meeting. This not only limits the parents' contribution to the WSE and SDP process but also their educational capital. As seen from this research it also excludes those who values differ from that of the school.

Improving Parents' Educational Capital

- The DES needs to address how parents can be kept informed of the various changes at national level which will impact on their children's education. While the NCCA and the NEWB keep parents informed about the curriculum and their responsibilities under the *Education Welfare Act 2000*, there is no similar body to inform parents of their rights, particularly in relation to the *Education Act 1998*.

- The HSCL scheme needs to address the educational capital of disadvantaged and 'marginalised' (Conaty, 2002) parents and equip them with the knowledge needed to make informed decisions about their children's future education. A programme is needed to help parents plan for the future educational needs of their children.

- The Parent Section of the DES's website needs to be updated to make it more informative and user-friendly for parents. It also needs a link to the WSE reports, which is easily accessible for parents.

- Not only does the NPCP need to involve parents more in the partnership process at national level, they also need to be proactive in highlighting for parents the changes in national education policy and their implications for children's education and schooling.

Professional Supports

- Specific training for the BOMs, principals and Parents Associations is needed in how they can involve all parents in the schools' activities and SDP processes. Particular attention should be given to the impact of the ethos of the school on the participation of parents in school activities.

- Both teacher education and continuous professional development needs to include modules on involving parents in their children's education. The headings, educator, supporter, consumer and welfare recipient, as used in this research, would be very useful in examining the home-school relationship and the power differential that exists between teachers and parents. The connection between the home-school communication system and parental perceptions that they are both welcome in the school and have a say in school policies and events needs to be highlighted.

- Circular 24/91 *Parents as Partners in Education* (Department of Education 1991) needs to be updated to include a clear definition of partnership along with the rights and responsibilities of the stakeholders as outlined in the legislation and official documentation.

BIBLIOGRAPHY

Abrahamson, P., Boje, T.P. and Greve, B. (2005) *Welfare and Families in Europe*, Aldershot, Harts: Ashgate Publishing

Alder, P.A. and Alder, P. (1998) Observational Techniques, in Denzin, N.K. and Lincoln, Y.S. [Eds.] *Collecting and Interpreting Qualitative Materials*, Thousand Oaks, Ca.: Sage

Alder, E.S. and Clarke, R. (2003) *It's Done: An invitation to social research*, (2nd Ed.), Belmont, Ca.: Wadsworth/Thomson Learning

Allen, S. M. and Hawkins, A.J. (1999) Maternal Gatekeeping: Mothers' beliefs and behaviours that inhibit greater father involvement in family work, *Journal of Marriage and the Family*, Vol. 61, No. 1, February, pp. 199-212

Ali, S., Campbell, K., Branley, D. and James, R. (2004) Politics, Identities and Research, in Seale, C. [Eds.] *Researching Society and Culture* (2nd Ed.) London: Sage

Ali, S. and Kelly, M. (2004) Ethics and Social Research, in Seale, C. [Eds.] (2004) *Researching Society and Culture* [2nd Ed.] London: Sage

Anderson, G.L., Herr, K. and Nihlen, A.S. (1994) *Studying your Own School: An educator's guide to qualitative practitioner research*, Thousand Oaks, Ca.: Corwin Press

Andrews, P. S.J. (2005) Retreat of the Father, in Jesuit Centre for Faith and Justice *Catholic Social Teaching in Action*, Dublin: Columbia Press

Archer, P. and Shortt, F. (2003) *Review of the Home/School/Community Scheme*, Dublin: Educational Research Centre, St Patrick's College

Babbie, E. (1990) *Survey Research Methods*, (2nd Ed.), Belmont, Ca.: Wadsworth

Ball, S. (2003) Social Justice in the Lead: Are we all libertarians?, in Vincent. C. *Social Justice, Education and Identity*, London: Routledge Falmer

Barnardos (2006) *School Report 2006*, Dublin: Barnardos

Bascia, N. and Hargreaves, A. (2000) Teaching and Leading on the Sharp Edge pf Change, in Bascia, N. and Hargreaves, A. [Eds.] *The Sharp Edge of Educational Reform: Teaching, leading and the realities of reform*, London; Routledge Falmer

Bastiani, J. (1989) *Working with Parents: A whole-school approach*, Windsor: NFER-Nelson

Bastiani, J. (2000) 'I know it works!...Actually proving it is the problem!': Examining the contribution of parents to pupil progress and school effectiveness, in Wolfendale, S. and Bastiani, J. [Eds] *The Contribution of Parents to School Effectiveness,* London: David Fulton

Bell, L. and Ribbens, J. (1994) Isolated Housewives and Complex Maternal Worlds: The significance of social contacts between women with young children in industrial societies, *The Sociological Review,* Vol. 42, No. 2, May 1994, pp. 227-261

Bhreathnach, N. (1995) Foreword, in Department of Education *Charting our Education Future: White paper on education,* Dublin: Stationery Office

Black, T.R. (2002) *Understanding Social Science Research,* London: Sage

Blenkin, G.M., Edwards, G. and Kelly, A.V. (1992) *Change and the Curriculum,* London: Paul Chapman

Bloch, M.N. (2003) Global/Local Analyses of the Construction of "Family-Child" Welfare in Bloch, M.N., Holmlund, K., Moqvist, I. and Popkewitz, T.S. [Eds.] *Governing Children, Families and Education:. Restructuring the welfare state,* New York: Palgrave Macmillan

Booth, D.J. (1992) *A First Course in Statistics: Foundation instruction: Right start textbooks* (2nd Ed.) London: DP Publications

Bosetti, L. (2004) Determinants of School Choice: Understanding how parents choose elementary schools in Alberta, *Journal of Education Policy,* Vol. 19, No. 4, July, pp. 387-405

Bottery, M. (2005) The Individualization of Consumption: A Trojan horse in the destruction of the public sector? *Educational Management Administration and Leadership,* Vol. 33, No. 3, pp. 267-288

Bourdieu, P. (1974) The School as a Conservative Force: Scholastic and cultural inequalities (translated by J.C. Whitehouse), in Eggleston, J. [Ed.] *Contemporary Research in the Sociology of Education,* New York: Harper and Row

Bourdieu, P. (1977a) Cultural Reproduction and Social Reproduction, in Karabel, J. and Hallsey, A.H. [Eds.] *Power and Ideology in Education,* New York: Oxford University Press

Bourdieu, P. (1977b) *Outline of a Theory of Practice,* Cambridge: Cambridge University Press [Translated by Richard Nice]

Bourdieu, P. (1997) The Forms of Capital, in Hasley, A.H., Lauder, H., Brown, P. and Wells S. [Eds.] (1997) *Education, Culture, Economy and Society,* Oxford: Oxford University Press

Bourdieu, P. and De Saint-Martin, M. (1974) Scholastic Excellence and the Values of the Educational System (translated by J.C. Whitehouse), in Eggleston, J. [Ed.] *Contemporary Research in the Sociology of Education,* New York: Harper and Row

Bourque, L and Fielder, E.P. (1995) *How to Conduct Self-administered and Mail Surveys,* Thousand Oaks, Ca.: Sage.

Bridgemohan, R., van Wyk, N. and van Staden, C. (2005) Home-School Communication in the Early Childhood Development Phase, *Education,* Fall, Vol. 126, Issue 1, pp. 60-77

http://search.epnet.com/login.aspx?direct=true&db=pbh&an=18359995   site   viewed
07/02/06

Broderick, D. and Shiel, G. (2000) *Diet and Activity Patterns of Children in Primary Schools in Ireland,* Dublin: St Patrick's College, Drumcondra

Brooks, R. (2004) 'My mum would be as pleased as punch if I actually went, but my dad seems a bit more particular about it': Paternal involvement in young people's higher education choices, *British Educational Research Journal,* Vol. 30, No. 4, August, pp. 495-514

Burgos, R.B. (2004) Partnership as a Floating and Empty Signifier within Educational Policies: The Mexican case, in Franklin, B.M., Bloch, M.N. and Popkewitz, T.S. [Eds.] *Educational Partnerships and the State: The paradoxes of governing schools, children and families,* New York: Palgrave Macmillan

Burke, A. (1992) The Teacher-Parent Relationship, in *Oideas,* Fómhair, Vol. 39, pp. 189-193

Carlen, P., Gleeson, D. and Wardhaugh, J. (1992) *Truancy: the politics of compulsory schooling,* Buckingham: Open University

Catholic Primary School Managers Association (2004) *Management Board Members' Handbook,* Dublin: Veritas

Central Statistics Office (2007a) *Census 2006 Principal Demographic Results,* Dublin: Stationery Office, http://www.cso.ie/census/Census2006Results.htm (Site viewed 6th May 2007)

Central Statistics Office (2007b) *Census 2006 Principal Socio-economic Results,* Dublin: Stationery   Office,   http://www.cso.ie/census/Census2006Results/   PSER/PSER%20 complete.pdf (Site viewed 3rd July 2007)

Chomsky, N (1987) *on Power and Ideology,* New York: Black Rose Books

Clancy, P. (1995) Education in the Republic of Ireland: The project of modernity? in Clancy, P.; Drudy, S., Lynch, K., O'Dowd, L. [Eds] *Irish Society: Sociological perspectives,* Dublin: Institute of Public Administration

Clancy, P. (1999) Education Policy in Quinn, S., Kennedy, P., O'Donnell A. and Kiely, G. (1999) *Contemporary Irish Social Policy,* Dublin: University College Dublin Press

Clarke, K. (2006) Childhood, Parenting and Early Intervention: A critical examination of the Sure Start national programme, *Critical Social Policy,* Vol. 26, No. 4, November, pp. 669-721

Coffey, A. (1999) *The Ethnographic Self Fieldwork and the Representation of Identity,* London: Sage

Cohen, L., Manion, L. and Morrison, K. (2000) *Research Methods in Education,* [5th Ed.], London: Routledge

Coleman, P. (1998) *Parent, Student and Teacher Collaboration: The power of three,* London: Paul Chapman

Colgan, A. (2003) *The Future of NPC – the Future of Education: Planning together for Change: A strategy for the future of NPC.* National Parents Council Primary Annual Delegate Conference 2003 www.npcp.ie site viewed 1/7/04

Collins, R. (1977) Functional and Conflict Theories of Educational Stratification, in Karabel, J. and Halsey, A.H. [Eds.] *Power and Ideology in Education,* New York: Oxford University Press

Commission on the Family (1998) *Strengthening Families for Life: Final Report to the Minister for Social, Community and Family Affairs,* Dublin; Stationery Office

Compston, H. (2002) The Politics of Policy Concertation in the 1990s: The role of ideas, in Berger, S. and Compston, H. [Eds.] *Partnership in Western Europe: Lessons for the 21st Century,* New York: Berghahn Books

Conaty, C. (2002) *Including All: Home school and community: United in education,* Dublin: Veritas

Conaty, C. (2006) Statistical Data, in HSCL *The Home, School, Community Liaison Scheme in Ireland: From vision to best practice,* Dublin: DES

Connelly, E. (2007) *The Institutionalisation of Anti-Poverty and Social Exclusion Policy in Irish Social Partnership,* Dublin: Poverty Research Initiative funded by Combat Povertyhttp://www.cpa.ie/publications/workingpapers.2007-01_wp_The Institutionalisa-tionOfAnti-PovertyAndSocialExclusionPolicyInIrishSocial Partnership.pdf

Coolahan, J (1981) *Irish Education: Its history and structure,* Dublin: Institute of Public Administration

Coolahan, J. (1989) Educational Policy for National Schools 1960-1985, in Mulcahy, D.G. and O'Sullivan, D. [Eds.] *Irish Educational Policy: Process and substance,* Dublin: Institution of Public Administration

Coolahan, J. [Ed.] (1994) *Report on the National Education Convention,* Dublin: The National Education Convention Secretariat.

Coolahan, J. (1995) Policy Formulation and Implementation: Overview of the Irish context in Coolahan, J. [Ed.] *Issues and Strategies in the Implementation of Educational Policy: Proceedings of Bicentenary Conference,* Maynooth: Education Department, St Patrick's College

Corcoran, M.P. (2005) Portrait of the 'Absent' Father: The impact of non-residency on developing and maintaining a fathering role, *Irish Journal of Sociology,* Vol. 14, No. 2, pp. 134-154

Craig, L. (2006) Parental Education: Time in paid work and time with children: An Australian time-diary analysis, *The British Journal of Sociology,* Vo. 57, No. 4, December 2006, pp. 553-575

Cresswell, J.W. (2003) *Research Design. Qualitative and Quantitative Approaches,* (2nd Ed.) Thousand Oaks, Ca.: Sage

Croll, P. (2004) Families, Social Capital and Educational Outcomes, *British Journal of Educational Studies,* Vol. 52, No. 4, December 2004, pp. 390-416

Crozier, G. and Davies, J. (2006) Family Matters: A discussion of the Bangladeshi and Pakistani extended family and community in supporting the children's education, *The Sociological Review*, Vol. 54, No. 4, November, pp. 678-695

Crump, S.J. (1992) Pragmatic Policy Development: Problems and solutions in educational policy making, *Journal of Education Policy*, Vol. 7, No. 4, pp. 415-425

Cuban, L. (2003) *Why is it so Hard to get Good Schools?*, New York: Teachers College Press

Cullingford, C. (1996a) The Role of Parents in the Education System, in Cullingford, C. [Ed] *Parents, Education and the State*, Aldershot: Arena

Cullingford, C. (1996b) Parents' Views of the Education System, in Cullingford, C. [Ed] *Parents, Education and the State*, Aldershot: Arena

Cussen, O. (1995) A Policy Advisor's Perspective, in Coolahan, J. [Ed.] *Issues and Strategies in the Implementation of Educational Policy: Proceedings of Bicentenary Conference*, Maynooth: Education Department, St Patrick's College

Daly, M. (2000) Feminist Research Methodology: The case of Ireland, in Byrne, A. and Lentin, R. [Eds.] *(Re)searching Women: Feminist research methodologies in social sciences in Ireland*, Dublin: Institute of Public Administration

Daly, M. and Yeates, N. (2003) Common Origins, Different Paths: Adaptation and change in social security in Britain and Ireland, *Policy and Politics*, Vol. 31, No. 1, pp. 85-97

Darlington, Y. and Scott, D. (2002) *Qualitative Research in Practice. Stories from the field*, Buckingham; Open University Press

David, M.E. (1993) *Parents, Gender and Education Reform*, Cambridge: Polity Press

David, M.E. (2004) Partnerships and Parents: Issues of sex and gender in policy and practice, in Franklin, B.M., Bloch, M.N. and Popkewitz, T.S. [Eds.] *Educational Partnerships and the State: The paradoxes of governing schools, children and families*, New York: Palgrave Macmillan

De Abreau, G. and Cline, T. (2005) Parents' representations of their children's mathematics learning in multiethnic primary schools, *British Educational Research Journal*, Vol.31, No. 6, December 2005, pp. 697-722

De Graaf, N.D., De Graaf, P.M. and Kraaykamp, G. (2000) Parental Cultural Capital and Educational Attainment in the Netherlands: A Refinement of the Cultural Capital Perspective, *Sociology of Education*, Vol. 73, No. 2, April p.. 92-111

Dennis, J.P. (2002) The McDonaldization of the Family, in Ritzer, G. [Ed.] *McDonaldization. The Reader*, Thousand Oaks, Ca.: Sage

De Paor, R (2003) *A Policy Analysis of the 1990 Revised Primary Curriculum in the Republic of Ireland*, (Unpublished) Doctor in Philosophy, Thesis, Leeds Metropolitan University

Department of Education (Ireland) (1971) *Curaclam na Bunscoile*, Dublin: Stationery Office

Department of Education (Ireland) (1991) *Parents as Partners in Education* Circular 24/91

Department of Education (Ireland) (1994) *School Attendance / Truancy Report,* Dublin: Stationery Office

Department of Education (Ireland) (1995) *Charting our Education Future: White paper on education,* Dublin: Stationery Office

Department of Education (Ireland) (1996) *Implementing the Agenda for Change,* Dublin: Stationery Office

Department of Education and Science (Ireland) (1998a), *Customer Service Statement,* Dublin: Stationery Office

Department of Education and Science (Ireland) (1998b), *Strategy Statement: Implementation of the Public Service Management Act, 1997,* Dublin: Stationery Office

Department of Education and Science (Ireland) (1999a) *Primary School Curriculum: Introduction,* Dublin: Stationery Office.

Department of Education and Science (Ireland) (1999b) *Developing a School Plan: Guidelines for primary schools,* Dublin: Stationery Office.

Department of Education and Science (Ireland) (1999c) *Primary School Curriculum: Social, personal and health education,* Dublin: Stationery Office.

Department of Education and Science (Ireland) (1999d) *Home School Community Liaison,* Dublin: Stationery Office.

Department of Education and Science (Ireland) (1999e) *Primary School Curriculum. Social, Personal and Health Education Teacher Guidelines,* Dublin: Stationery Office.

Department of Education and Science (Ireland) (2000a) *Primary School Curriculum: Your child's learning: Guidelines for parents,* Dublin: Stationery Office

Department of Education and Science (Ireland) (2000b) *Fifty School Reports: What Inspectors Say: Quality of educational provision in primary schools,* Dublin: Stationery Office

Department of Education and Science (Ireland) (2003a) *School Development Planning Initiative: National Progress Report 2002,* Dublin: Stationery Office

Department of Education and Science (Ireland) (2003b) *Looking at our School: An aid to self-evaluation in primary school,* Dublin: Stationery Office

Department of Education and Science (Ireland) (2005a) *Literacy and Numeracy in Disadvantaged Schools: Challenges for teachers and learners: An evaluation by the Inspectorate of the Department of Education and Science,* Dublin: Stationery Office

Department of Education and Science (Ireland) (2005b) *An Evaluation of Curriculum Implementation in Primary Schools: English, Mathematics and Visual Arts,* Dublin: Stationery Office

Department of Education and Science (Ireland) (2005c) *Statement of Strategy 2005-2007,* Dublin: Stationery Office

Department of Education and Science (Ireland) (2005d) *DEIS (Delivering Equality of Opportunity in Schools): An Action Plan for Educational Inclusion,* Dublin: Stationery Office

Department of Education and Science (Ireland) (2006a) *A Guide to Whole-School Evaluation in Primary Schools* Dublin: Stationery Office

Department of Education and Science (Ireland) (2006b) *An Evaluation of Planning in Thirty Primary Schools* Dublin: Stationery Office

Department of Education and Science (Ireland) (2006c) *Cooperative School Evaluation Project CSEP: A study of the development of non-curricular school policies in a school development planning context,* Dublin: Stationery Office

Department of the Taoiseach (2006) *Towards 2016: Ten-year framework: Social partnership agreement 2006-20015,* Dublin: Stationery Office, http://www.taoiseach.gov.ie/attached_files?Pdf%20files/Towards2016PartnershipAgree ment.pdf sited viewed: 08-08-2007

De Regt, A. and Weenink, D. (2005) When Negotiation Fails: Private education as a disciplinary strategy, *Journal of Education Policy,* Vol. 20, No. 1, January, pp. 59-80

De Vaus, D (2002a) *Analyzing Social Science Data: 50 Key problems in data analysis,* London: Sage

De Vaus, D. (2002b) *Surveys in Social Research* (5th Ed), London: Routledge

Devine, D., Lodge, A. and Deegan, J. (2004) Activating Voices through Practice: Democracy, care and consultation in the primary school, in Deegan, J. Devine, D. and Lodge, A. [Eds.] *Primary Voices: Equality, diversity and childhood in Irish primary schools,* Dublin: Institute of Public Administration

Dix, T. (1991) The Affective Organisation of Parenting: Adaptive and maladaptive processes, *Psychological Bulletin,* Vol. 110, No. 1, July, pp. 3-25

Donaghue, F. (2002) Civic Expression: The value of volunteering, in Bohan, H. and Kennedy, G. [Eds.] *Is the Future my Responsibility? Our Society in the new Millennium,* Dublin: Veritas

Doucet, A. (2006) 'Estrogen-filled Worlds': Fathers as primary caregivers and embodiment, *The Sociological Review,* Vo. 54, No. 4, November, pp. 696-716

Dronkers, J. (1994) The Changing Effects of Lone Parent Families on the Educational Attainment of their Children in a European Welfare State, *Sociology,* Vo. 28, No. 1, February, pp. 171-191

Drudy, S. and Lynch, K. (1993) *Schools and Society in Ireland,* Dublin: Gill and Macmillan

Duncan, W. (1993) The Constitutional Protection of Parental Rights: A discussion of the advantages and disadvantages of according fundamental status to parental rights and duties in Eekelarr, J. and Sarcevic, P. [Eds] *Parenthood in Modern Society: Legal and social issues for the twenty-first century,* Dondrecht: Martinus Nijhoff

Durkheim, E. (1971) *The Elementary Forms of the Religious Life by Émile Durkheim, translated from the French by Joseph Ward Swan ,* London: George Allen & Unwin

Dye, T. R. (1995) *Understanding Public Policy* (8th Ed.), Englewood Cliffs, NJ: Prentice Hall

Eden, D. (2001) Who Controls the Teachers? Overt and covert controls in schools, *Educational Management and Administration*, Vol. 29, No. 1, pp. 97-111

Edwards, R. and Alldred, P. (2000) A Typology of Parental Involvement in Education Centering on Children and Young People: Negotiating familialisation, institutionalisation, individualism, *British Journal of Sociology of Education*, Vol. 21, No. 3, pp. 435-455

Egan, E. (1998) *An Analyses of Key Issues in Planning a Strategy for the Implementation of the Revised Primary Curriculum,* (Unpublished) Master in Science in Educational Management, Thesis TCD

Eichelberger, R. T. (1989) *Disciplined Inquiry: Understanding and doing educational research,* White Plains, N.Y.: Longman

Eivers, E., Shiel, G and Shortt, F. (2004) *Reading Literacy in Disadvantaged Primary Schools,* Dublin: Educational Research Centre

Ellis, C. and Bochner, A.P. (2003) Autoethnography, Personal Narrative, Reflexivity, in Denzin, N.K. and Lincoln, Y.S. [Eds.] *Collecting and Interpreting Qualitative Materials,* (2nd Ed.) Thousand Oaks, Ca.: Sage

Epstein, J.L. (1992) School and Family Partnerships, in Alkin, M.C., Linden, M., Noel and Ray, K. [Eds.] *Encyclopaedia of Educational Research,* (6th Ed.), New York; Macmillan

Epstein, J.L. and Seyong, L. (1995) National Patterns of School and Family Connections in Middle Grades, in Ryan, B.A., Adams, G.R., Gullotta, T., Weissberg, R.P. and Hampton, R.L. [Eds.] *The Family-School Connection: Theory, research and practice,* Thousand Oaks, California: Sage

Esping-Anderson, G. (2002a) Towards the Good Society Once Again?, in Esping-Anderson, G., Hemerijck, A. and Myles, J. [Eds.] *Why We need a New Welfare State,* Oxford: Oxford University Press

Esping-Anderson, G. (2002b) A Child-Centred Social Investment Strategy, in Esping-Anderson, G., Gallie, D., Hemerijck, A. and Myles, J. [Eds.] *Why We need a New Welfare State,* Oxford: Oxford University Press

Evertsson, M. (2006) The Reproduction of Gender: Housework and attitudes towards gender equality in the house among Swedish boys and girls, *The British Journal of Sociology,* Vol. 57, Issue 3, September, pp. 415-436

Fahey, T. (1992) Catholicism, in Goldthorpe, J.H. and Whelan, C.T. [Ed.] *The Development of Industrial Society in Ireland,* Oxford: British Academy and Oxford University Press

Fahey, T. (1995) Family and Household in Ireland, in Clancy, P.; Drudy, S., Lynch, K., O'Dowd, L. [Eds.] *Irish Society: Sociological perspectives,* Dublin: Institute of Public Administration

Fahey, T. (1998) Family Policy in Ireland, in Commission on the Family *Strengthening Families for Life: Final Report to the Minister for Social, Community and Family Affairs,* Dublin: Stationery Office

Fahey, T. and Russell, H. (2001) *Family Formation in Ireland: Trends, data needs and implications: Report to the Family Affairs Unit, Department of Social, Community and Family Affairs,* Dublin: Economic and Social Research Institute

Feiler, A., Greenhough, P., Winter, J. with Salway, L. and Scanlan, M. (2006) Getting Engaged: Possibilities and problems for home-school knowledge exchange, *Educational Review,* Vol.58, No. 4, November, pp. 451-469

Fine-Davis, M., Fagnani, J., Giovannini, D., Højgaard, L., Clarke, H. (2004) *Fathers and Mothers: Dilemmas of the work-life balance: A comparative study in four European countries,* Dordrecht: Kluwer Academic Publications

Fine, M. (1995) The Politics of who's "at risk" in Swadener, B.B. and Lubeck, S. [Eds.] *Children and Families "at promise": Deconstructing the discourse of risk,* Albany, New York: State University of New York

Fine, M. (1997) [Ap]parents Involvement: Reflections on parents, power and urban schools, in Hasley, A.H., Lauder, H., Brown, P. and Well, A.M. [Eds.] *Education: Culture, economy and society,* Oxford: Oxford University Press

Fink, A. (1995) *Evaluation for Education and Psychology,* Thousand Oaks, Ca.: Sage

Fleming, J. and Boeck, T. (2005) Can Social Capital be a Framework for Participative Evaluation of Community Health Work?, in Taylor, D. and Balloch, S. [Eds.] *The Politics of Evaluation: Participation and policy implementation,* Bristol; The Polity Press

Fletcher, C. (1999) Parents, Teachers and Governors Myth: Parents don't care, in O'Hagan, B. [Ed.] *Modern Educational Myths: The future of democratic comprehensive education,* London: Kogan Page

Flick, U. (1998) *An Introduction to Qualitative Research,* London: Sage

Flouri, E. and Buchanan, A. (2004) Early Father's and Mother's Involvement and Child's Later Educational Outcomes, *British Journal of Educational Psychology,* Vol. 74, Part 2, June, pp. 141-153

Fontana, S. and Frey, J.H. (2003) The Interview: From structured questions to negotiated text in Denzin, N.K. and Lincoln, Y.S. [Eds.] *Collecting and Interpreting Qualitative Materials,* (2nd Ed.) Thousand Oaks, Ca.: Sage

Forde Brennan, P. (2003) Chairperson's Address, National Parents Council Primary Annual Delegate Conference 2003 www.npcp.ie site viewed 1/7/04

Foster, J.J. (2001) *Data Analysis Using SPSS for Windows New Edition: Versions 8-10,* London: Sage

Foucault, M. (2000) The Subject and Power, in Nash, K. [Ed.] *Readings in Contemporary Political Sociology,* Oxford: Blackwell

Franklin, A. and Madge, N. (2000) *In Our View: Children, teenagers and parents talk about services for young people,* London: National Children's Bureau

Fuller, L. (2002) *Irish Catholicism since 1950: The undoing of a culture,* Dublin: Gill and Macmillan

Fulton, J. (2000a) Young Adults, Contemporary Society and Catholics in Fulton, J., Abela, A.M., Borowik, I., Dowling, T., Marler, P.C., Tomas, L. [Eds.] *Young Catholics at the New Millennium: The religion and morality of young adults in western countries,* Dublin: University College Dublin Press

Fulton, J. (2000b) Young Adult Catholics at the Millennium, in Fulton, J., Abela, A.M., Borowik, I., Dowling, T., Marler, P.C., Tomas, L. [Eds.] *Young Catholics at the New Millennium. The religion and morality of young adults in western countries,* Dublin: University College Dublin Press

Furstenberg, F.F. Jr. and Hughes, M.E (1995) Social Capital and Successful Development Among At-risk Youth, *Journal of Marriage and the Family,* Vol. 57, August, pp. 580-592

Furstenberg, F. F. Jr., Cook, T.D., Eccles, J., Elder, G.H. Jr. and Sameroff, A. (1999) *Managing to Make it: Urban families and adolescent success,* Chicago: University of Chicago Press

Gaire, E. and Mahon, O. (2005) *Primary Options: How to choose the right school for your child and much more!,* Dublin: The Liffey Press

Garanzine, M. S.J. (2000) Dealing with Narcisstic Families: Lessons for educational leadership in parents and child guidance, in Hunt, T.C., Oldenski, T.E. SM, Wallace, T.J. [Eds.] *Catholic School Leadership: An invitation to lead,* London: Falmer

Geist, C. (2005) The Welfare State and the Home: Regime difference in the domestic division of labour, *European Sociological Review,* Vol. 21, No. 1, February, pp. 23-40

Gewirtz, S., Ball, S.J. and Bowe, R. (1995) *Markets, Choice and Equity in Education,* Buckingham: Open University

Giddens, A. (2001) *Sociology,* (4th Ed), Cambridge: Polity Press

Glover, D. (1992) Community Perceptions of the Strengths of Individual Schools: The basis of 'judgement', *Educational Management and Administration,* Vol. 20, No. 4, pp. 223-230

Gorard, S. (1997) *School Choice in an Established Market,* Aldershot: Ashgate

Gorard, S. (2001) *Quantitative Methods in Education: The Role of Numbers Made Easy,* London: Continuum

Graue, M.E., Kroeger, J. and Prager, D (2001) A Bakhtinian Analysis of Particular Home-School Relations, *American Educational Research Journal Washington,* Fall, Vol. 38, Issue 3, pp. 467-499 http://proquest.umi.com/pqdweb?did=316486991

Gray, D.E. (2004) *Doing Research in the Real World,* London: Sage

Green, A. (1997) *Education, Globalization and the Nation State,* London: Macmillan Press

Greenberg, R.C. and Walberg, H.L. (1998) The Diogenes Effect: Why program evaluations fail, in Wong, K.K. (1998) *Advances in Educational Policy, Volume 4,* Stanford, Connecticut: JAI Press

Hanafin, J. and Lynch, A. (2002) Peripheral Voices: Parental involvement, social class and educational disadvantage, *British Journal of Sociology of Education,* Vol. 23, No. 1, March, pp. 35-49

Hantrais, L. (2004) *Family Policy Matters: Responding to family change in Europe*, Bristol: Polity Press

Hargreaves, A. (2000) Professionals and Parents. A Social Movement for Educational Change?, in Bascia, N. and Hargreaves, A. [Eds.] *The Sharp Edge of Educational Reform: Teaching, leading and the realities of reform*, London; Routledge Falmer

Harris, J. (1989) The Policy-making role of the Department of Education, in Mulcahy, D.G. and O'Sullivan, D. (1989) *Irish Education Policy: Process and substance*, Dublin: Institute of Public Administration

Healy, T. (2004) Social Capital: Old hat or new insight?, *Irish Journal of Sociology*, Vol. 13, No. 1, pp. 5-28

Heeney, M. (2006) The Way Forward, in Home School Community Liaison *The Home, School, Community Liaison Scheme in Ireland: From vision to best practice*, Dublin: DES

Heightman, S. (1992) Parenthood, in Burgess, T. [Ed.] *Accountability in Schools*, Harlow, Essex: Longman

Held, D. (1989) *Political Theory and the Modern State*, Cambridge: Polity Press

Hennessey, C. (2005) *Implementation of Change in an Irish Primary School: A case study* (unpublished) Masters in Education, Joint Faculty of Education, St. Patrick's College, Dublin City University

Herbert, D. (2003) *Religion and Civil Society: Rethinking public religion in the contemporary world*, Aldershot: Ashgate

Heywood, A. (1997) *Politics*, London: Macmillan Press

Hilliard, B. (2003) The Catholic Church and Married Women's Sexuality: Habitus change in the late 20th Century Ireland, *Irish Journal of* Sociology Vol. 12, No. 2, pp. 28-49

Hornby, G. (2000) *Improving Parental Involvement*, London: Continuum

Hornsby-Smith, M.P. (1992) Social and Religious Transformation, in Goldthorpe, J.H. and Whelan, C.T. [Eds] *The Development of Industrial Society in Ireland*, Oxford: British Academy and Oxford University Press

Ho Sui-Chu, E. and Willms, J.D. (1996) Effects of Parental Involvement on Eight-Grade Achievement, *Sociology of Education*, Vol. 69, April, pp.126-141

Hughes, M. (1994) Researching Parents after the 1988 Education Reform Act, in Halpin, D. and Troyna, B. [Eds.] *Researching Educational Policy: Ethical and methodological issues*, London: Falmer Press

Hughes, M. and Greenhough, P. (2006) Boxes, Bags and Videotape: Enhancing home-school communication through knowledge exchange activities, *Educational Review*, Vol. 58, No. 4, November, pp. 471-487

Hughes, M., Wikeley, F and Nash, T. (1994) *Parents and their Children's Schools*, Oxford: Blackwell

Hunt, S.J. (2002) *Religion in Western Society*, Basingstoke, Hampshire: Palgrave

Hunter, J. B. (1991) Which School? A study of parents' choice of secondary school, *Educational Research*, Vol. 33, No. 1, Spring, pp. 31-41

Hyland, A. (1995) The Role of the Family in Education: The Irish story, in Feheney, M.J. [Ed.] *Education and the Family,* Dublin: Veritas

Illich, I. (1973) *Deschooling Society,* Middlesex: Penguin Education

Inglis, T. (1998) *Moral Monopoly: The rise and fall of the Catholic Church in modern Ireland,* Dublin: University College Dublin Press

Inglis, T. (2000) Irish Civil Society: From church to media domination in Inglis, T., Mach, Z., Mazanek, R. [Eds.] *Religion and Politics: East-west contrasts from contemporary Europe,* Dublin: University College Dublin Press

Ireland (1926) *School Attendance Act 1926,* Dublin: Stationery Office

Ireland (1937) *Bunreacht na hEireann* 1937, Dublin: Stationery Office

Ireland (1991) Child Care Act 1991, Dublin: Stationery Office

Ireland (1992) *Education for a Changing World Green Paper,* Dublin: Stationery Office

Ireland (1998) *Education Act 1998,* Dublin: Stationery Office

Ireland (2000) *Education Welfare Act 2000,* Dublin: Stationery Office

Irish National Teacher's Organisation (1993) *Among School Children: The INTO response to the Green Paper: Education for a Changing World: A policy statement,* Dublin: INTO

Irish National Teacher's Organisation (1997) *Parental Involvement: Possibilities for partnership,* Dublin: INTO

Irish National Teacher's Organisation (2005) *School Evaluation: Including proceedings of INTO Consultative Conference on Education, Kilkenny, November 2005,* Dublin: INTO

Irvin, R.A. and Stansbury, J. (2004) Citizen Participation in Decision Making: Is it worth the effort, *Public Administration Review,* Vol. 64, No. 1, January / February, pp. 55-64

Isherwood, G. B. and Hammah, C. K. (1981) Home and School Factors and the Quality of School Life in Canadian High Schools, in Epstein, J.L. [Ed.] *The Quality of School Life,* Lexington, Mass.: Lexington Books

Kellaghan, T. (1989) The Interface of Research, Evaluation and Policy in Irish Education, in Mulcahy, D.G. and O'Sullivan, D. [Eds.] *Irish Educational Policy: Process and substance,* Dublin: Institution of Public Administration

Kelleghan, T. and McGee, P. (2005) *Your Education System: A report on the response to the invitation to participate in creating a shared vision for Irish education into the future,* Dublin: Educational Research Centre

Keohane, K. and Kuhling, C. (2004) *Collision Culture: Transformations in everyday life in Ireland,* Dublin: Liffey Press

Kilfeather, F. (2003) Chief Executives Address: National Parents Council – Primary, Annual Delegate Conference 2003 www.npcp.ie viewed 1/7/04

Kilfeather, F. (2005) The National Parents Council, in Gaire, E. and Mahon, O. *Primary Options: How to choose the right school for your child and much more!*, Dublin: Liberty Press

Kilfeather, F. (2006) *National Parents Council Primary Annual Report 2005*, Dublin: National Parents Council Primary

Kvale, S. (1996) *Interviews: An introduction to qualitative research interviewing*, Thousand Oaks, California: Sage

Lamont, M. and Lareau, A. (1988) Cultural Capital: Allusions, gaps and Glissandos in recent theoretical developments, *Sociological Theory*, Vol. 6 pp. 153-68

Lareau, A. (1997) Social-Class Differences in Family-School Relationships: The importance of cultural capital, in Hasley, A.H., Lauder, H., Brown, P. and Well, A.M. [Eds.] *Education: Culture, economy and society*, Oxford: Oxford University Press

Lareau, A. and McNamara Horvat, E. (1999) Moments of Social Inclusion and Exclusion: Race, Class and Culture Capital in Family-School Relationships, *Sociology of Education*, Vol. 72, January, pp. 37-53

Leonard, M. (2004) Teenage Girls and Housework in Irish Society, *Irish Journal of Sociology*, Vol. 13, No. 1, pp. 73-87

Leonard, M. (2005) *Why Europe will run the 21st Century*, London: Fourth Estate

Levin, H.M. (2004) The Public-Private Nexus in Education, in Franklin, B.M., Bloch, M.N. and Popkewitz, T.S. [Eds.] *Educational Partnerships and the State: The paradoxes of governing schools, children and families*, New York: Palgrave Macmillan

Library Association of Ireland (2002) *The Borrowers at School: A Report on primary school libraries*, Dublin: Library Association of Ireland

Lodge, A. (2004) Denial, Tolerance or Recognition of Difference? The experience of minority belief parents in the denominational primary system, in Deegan, J. Devine, D. and Lodge, A. [Eds.] *Primary Voices: Equality, diversity and childhood in Irish primary schools*, Dublin: Institute of Public Administration

Lodge, A., Devine, D. and Deegan, J. (2004) Equality, Diversity and Childhood in Irish Primary Schools, in Deegan, J. Devine, D. and Lodge, A. [Eds.] *Primary Voices: Equality, diversity and childhood in Irish primary schools*, Dublin: Institute of Public Administration

Lopez, G.R. (2001) Redefining Parental Involvement: Lessons from high-performing migrant-impacted schools, *American Educational Research Journal Washington*, Summer, Vol. 38, Issue 2, pp. 253-289 http://proquest.umi.com/pqdweb?did=187561551 site viewed 25/02/05

Lynch, K (1999) *Equality in Education*, Dublin: Gill and Macmillan

Lynch, K. and Lodge, A. (2002) *Equality and Power in Schools: Redistribution, recognition and representation*, London: Routledge Falmer

MacBeath, J. (1999) *Schools Must Speak for Themselves: The case for school self-evaluation*, London: Routledge.

McCullagh, J. Canon (2005) Protestant Primary Schools, in Gaire, E. and Mahon, O. *Primary Options: How to choose the right school for your child and much more!*, Dublin: Liberty Press

Mac Giolla Phádraig (2005) Parents' Associations: Co-operatives or cliques: An investigation of the extent to which parents' associations exist and to which parents join them, *Oideas*, Vol. 51, Spring, pp. 55-70

McGuire, M. (2002) *Religion: The social context*, (5th Ed.), Belmont, California: Wadsworth Thomson Learning

McKeown, K., Ferguson, H. and Rooney, D. (1998) *Changing Fathers? Fatherhood and family life in modern Ireland*, Cork: Collins Press

McKeown, K (2001) *Fathers and Families: Research and reflection on key questions*, Dublin: Department of Health and Children

McKernan, J. (1996) *Curriculum Action Research: A handbook of methods and resources for the reflective practioner*, (2nd Ed.), London: Kogan Page

McManus, L. (2004) Respect for Democratic Politicians in Steady Decline, in Mulholland, J. [Ed.] *Political Choice and Democratic Freedom in Ireland: 40 Leading Irish thinkers*, Donegal: Mac Gill Summer School

McNamara Horvat, E., Weininger, E.B., Lareau, A. (2003) From Social Ties to Social Capital: Class differences in the relations between school and parent networks, *American Educational Research Journal Washington*, Spring, Vol. 40, Issue 2, pp. 319-351 http://proquest.umi.com/pqdweb?did=411228391

McWilliams, D. (2006) *The Pope's Children: Ireland's new elite*, Dublin: Gill and Macmilliam

Macbeth, A. (1994) Expectations about Parents in Education, in Macbeth, A. and Ravn, B. [Eds] *Expectations about Parents in Education: European perspectives*, Glasgow: European Parents' Association; Computing Services (University of Glasgow)

Macbeth, A. and Ravn (1994) Expectations about Parents in Education, in Macbeth, A. and Ravn, B. [Eds] *Expectations about Parents in Education: European perspectives*, Glasgow: European Parents' Association; Computing Services (University of Glasgow),

Macbeth, A. (1995) Partnership between Parents and Teachers in Education, in Macbeth, A., McCreath, D., Aitchison, J. [Eds.] *Collaborate or Compete? Educational partnerships in a market economy*, London: Falmer Press

Madriz, E. (2003) Focus Groups in Feminist Research in Denzin, N.K. and Lincoln, Y.S. [Eds.] *Collecting and Interpreting Qualitative Materials*, (2nd Ed.) Thousand Oaks, Ca.: Sage

Mair, P. (1992) The Absence of Class Politics, in Goldthorpe, J.H. and Whelan, C.T. [Eds.] *The Development of Industrial Society in Ireland*, Oxford: British Academy and Oxford University Press

Mangaoang, D. (2005) Educate Together Schools, in Gaire, E. and Mahon, O. *Primary Options: How to choose the right school for your child and much more!*, Dublin: Liberty Press

Martin, M. (1997) *Report to the Minister for Education Niamh Bhreathnach, T.D. on Discipline in Schools,* Dublin: Stationery Office

May, T. (2001) *Social Research Issues, Methods and Process* (3rd Ed) Buckingham: Open University Press

Michael, M. (2004) When things go wrong, in Seale, C. [Ed.] (2004) *Researching Society and Culture,* (2nd Ed.) London: Sage

Milbourne, L. (2005) Children, Families and Inter-agency Work: Experiences of partnership work in primary education settings, *British Educational Research Journal,* Vol. 31, No. 6, December 2005, pp. 675-695

Miles, M.B. and Huberman, A.M. (1994) *An Expanded Sourcebook: Qualitative data analysis,* (2nd Ed.) Thousand Oaks, Ca.: Sage.

Mintzberg, H. (1996) Managing Government: Governing management, *Harvard Business Review,* May-June 1996, pp. 75-83

Molloy, C. (2005) Solidarity in Catholic Social Teaching, in Jesuit Centre for Faith and Justice in *Catholic Social Teaching in Action,* Dublin: Columba Press

Moos, L. and Dempster, N. (1998) Some Comparative Learnings from the Study, in Mac Beath J. [Ed.] *Effective School Leadership: Responding to change,* London: Paul Chapman

Moos, L, Mahony, P. and Reeves, J. (1998) What Teachers, Parents, Governors and Pupils want from their Heads, in Mac Beath J. [Ed.] *Effective School Leadership: Responding to change,* London: Paul Chapman

Mulkerrins, D. (2005) *Home School Community Liaison Co-ordinators: Tackling inequality in education? A case study in a North Dublin area,* (Unpublished) M.Ed. Thesis St Patrick's College, Dublin City University

Munn, P. (1998) Parental Influence on School Policy: Some evidence from research, *Journal of Education Policy,* Vol. 13, No. 3, pp. 379-394

Murphy, M (2002) *An Evaluation of Parental Involvement in Early Childhood Education in an Irish Primary School,* (Unpublished) M.St. Thesis TCD

National Centre for Partnership and Performance (2003) *Achieving High Performance: Partnership works: The international evidence,* Forum on the Workplace of the Future, Research Series, No.1, http://www.ncpp.ie/dynamic/doc/Partnership%20Works.pdf (Site viewed: 08-08-2007)

National Council for Curriculum and Assessment (2005) *Primary Curriculum Review: Phase 1: Final Report,* Dublin: NCCA

National Council for Curriculum and Assessment (2006a) Engaging Parents, *info@ncca,* January, Issue 2, p. 7

National Council for Curriculum and Assessment (2006b) Communicating with Parents, *info@ncca,* September, Issue 4, p. 13

National Education Welfare Board (2004) *Don't let your child miss out!,* Dublin: NEWB

National Education Welfare Board (2005) *Annual Report 2005,* Dublin: NEWB, http://www.nemb.ie/downloads/pdf/annualreport05_eng.pdf (Site viewed 09-08-2007)

National Education Welfare Board (2006) *Press Releases 27 March 2006 NEWB Takes First Case to Court,* Dublin: NEWB http://www.newb.ie/news/pressreleases/ 27_03_06.asp (Site viewed 01-01-2008)

National Parents Council Primary (2004) *Working Effectively as a Parent Association: Guidelines for Parent Associations,* Dublin : NPCP.

National Parents Council Primary (2006) *Annual Report 2006 National Parents Council Primary,* Dublin: NPCP

National Parents Council Primary (2007a) *Strategic Plan 2007 National Parents Council Primary,* Dublin: NPCP

National Parents Council Primary (2007b) *Home Page* www.npc.ie (site viewed 03-08-2007)

Neuman W.L. (2004) *Basics of Social Research: Qualitative and quantitative approaches,* Boston: Pearson Education

Nic Ghiolla Phádraig, M. (1995) The Power of the Catholic Church in the Republic of Ireland, in Clancy, P.; Drudy, S., Lynch, K., O'Dowd, L. [Eds] *Irish Society: Sociological perspectives,* Dublin: Institute of Public Administration

Nolan, B. and Whelan, C.T. (1999) *Loading the Dice: A study of cumulative disadvantage,* Dublin: Oak Tree Press

Oakes, J., Stuart Wells, A. Yonezawa, S. and Ray, Y. (2000) Change Agentry and the Quest for Equity: Lessons from detracking schools, in Bascia, N. and Hargreaves, A. [Eds.] *The Sharp Edge of Educational Reform: Teaching, leading and the realities of reform,* London; Routledge Falmer

O'Brien, M. (2005) Mothers as Educational Workers: Mothers' emotional work at their children's transfer to second-level education, *Irish Educational Studies,* Vol. 24, No. 2-3, September, pp. 223-242

Ó Buachalla, S. (1988) *Education Policy in Twentieth Century Ireland,* Dublin: Wolfhound Press

Ó Cinnéide, S. (2003) Democracy and the Constitution, *Administration,* Vol. 51, No. 1-2, Spring/Summer, pp. 326-340

O'Connell, P.J. and Rottman, D.J. (1992) The Welfare State, in Goldthorpe, J.H. and Whelan, C.T. [Eds.] *The Development of Industrial Society in Ireland: The Third Joint Meeting of the Royal Irish Academy and the British Academy,* Oxford: Oxford University Press for the British Academy

O'Connor, D. Fr. (2005) Catholic Primary Schools, in Gaire, E. and Mahon, O. *Primary Options: How to choose the right school for your child and much more!,* Dublin: Liberty Press

O'Connor, J.S. (2003) Welfare State Development in the Context of European Integration and Economic Convergence: Situating Ireland within the European Union context, *Policy and Politics,* Vol. 31, No.3, pp. 387-404

O' Donnell, R. and Thomas, D. (2002) Ireland in the 1990s: Policy concertation triumphant, in Berger, S. and Compston, H. [Eds.] *Partnership in Western Europe: Lessons for the 21st Century,* New York: Berghahn Books

O'Halloran, A. (2004) The Privatisation of Citizenship? Exploring frameworks for membership of the Irish polity, *Administration,* Vol. 52, No. 1, Spring, pp. 19-34

O'Leary, Z (2004) *The Essential Guide to Doing Research,* London: Sage

O'Mahony, E. and Prunty, M. (2007) *Active Citizenship in Faith-based Communities: A report from focus groups,* Dublin: Secretariat of the Task force on Active Citizenship, www.activecitizenship.ie (sited viewed 10/04/2007)

O'Malley, F. (2004) Reducing the Number of TDs would Enhance our Democracy, in Mulholland, J. [Ed.] *Political Choice and Democratic Freedom in Ireland: 40 Leading Irish Thinkers,* Donegal: Mac Gill Summer School

Oplatka, I (2004) The Characteristics of the School Organisation and the Constraints on Market Ideology in Education: An institutional view, *The Journal of Education Policy,* Vol. 19, No.2, March, pp. 143-161

Organisation for Economic Co-operation and Development (1965) *Investment in Education,* Paris: Centre for Educational Research and Innovation

Organisation for Economic Co-operation and Development (1991) *Review of the National Policies for Education, Ireland,* Paris: Centre for Educational Research and Innovation

Organisation for Economic Co-operation and Development (1997) *Parents as Partners in Schooling,* Paris: Centre for Educational Research and Innovation

Osnowitz, D. (2005) Managing Time in Domestic Space: Home-based contractors and household work, *Gender and Society,* Vol. 19, No. 1, February, pp. 83-103

O'Sullivan, D. (1989) The Ideational Base of Irish Educational Policy, in Mulcahy, D.G. and O'Sullivan, D. [Eds.] *Irish Educational Policy: Process and Substance,* Dublin: Institution of Public Administration

O'Sullivan, D. (1992) Cultural Strangers and Educational Change: The OECD Report *Investment in Education* and Irish Educational Policy, *Journal of Education Policy,* Vol. 7, No. 5, pp. 445-469

O'Toole, J. (1999) So whose Curriculum is it anyway?, *InTouch,* Issue No. 16, October, p. 3

Ozga, J. and Gewirtz, S. (1994) Sex, Lies and Audiotapes: Interviewing the education policy elite, in Halpin, D. and Troyna, B. (Eds.) *Researching Education Policy: Ethical and methodological issues,* London: Falmer Press

Peillon, M. (1995) Interest Groups and the State in the Republic of Ireland, in Clancy, P., Drudy, S., Lynch, K., O'Dowd, L. [Eds] *Irish Society: Sociological perspectives,* Dublin: Institute of Public Administration

Peterson, R.A. (2000) *Constructing Effective Questionnaires,* London: Sage

Pinkney, S. (2000) Children as Welfare Subjects in Restructured Social Policy, in Lewis, G., Gewirtz, S., Clarke, J. [Eds.] *Rethinking Social Policy,* Milton Keynes: Open University

Pollard, J. (2001) *Bridging the Gap: Connecting with questioning Catholics,* Dublin: Columba Press

Primary Education Review Body (1990) *Report of the Primary Education Review Body,* Dublin: Stationary Office

Purcell, J. (2006) *Comptroller and Auditor General Report on Value for Money Examination: Department of Education and Science: Educational disadvantage initiatives in the primary sector,* Dublin: Stationary Office

Putnam, R.D. (2000) *Bowling Alone: The collapse and revival in American community,* New York: Touchstone

Quinton, D. (2004) *Supporting Parents: Messages from research,* London: Jessica Kingsley Publications

Reay, D. (1998) Cultural Reproduction! Mothers involvement in their children's primary schooling, in Grenfell, M. and James, D. with Hodkinson, P., Reay, D. and Robbins, D. *Bourdieu and Education: Acts of practical theory,* London: Falmer Press

Reay, D. (2003) Shifting Class Identities? Social class and the transition to higher education, in Vincent, C. [Ed.] *Social Justice, Education and Identity,* London: RoutledgeFalmer

Redmond, A. and Heanue, M. (2000) Aspects of Society in Central Statistics Office and Redmond, A. [Ed.] T*his was then, this is now. Change in Ireland, 1949-1999,* Dublin: Stationary Office

Reid, L. (2004) Winning Hand? The Challenges Facing the Ministers, *The Irish Times Weekend Review*, Saturday, October 2, p. 3

Review Body on the Primary Curriculum (1990) *Report of the Review Body on the Primary Curriculum,* Dublin: Department of Education

Richardson, V. (2004) Young Mothers, in Kennedy, P. [Ed.] *Motherhood in Ireland,* Dublin : Mercier Press

Riddell, S. (2003) Special Educational Needs and Procedural Justice in England and Scotland, in Vincent, C. [Ed.] *Social Justice, Education and Identity,* London: RoutledgeFalmer

Ritzer, G. (2004) *The McDonaldization of Society.* (Revised New Century Edition), Thousand Oaks, Ca.: Sage

Robson, C. (1993) *Real World Research: A resource for social scientists and practitioner researchers,* Oxford: Blackwell

Rodger, A.R. (1999) Catholic Education: Authority and engagement, in Conroy, J.C. (1999) *Catholic Education: Inside out outside in,* Dublin: Veritas

Rossi, P.H., Freeman, H.E. and Lipsey, M.W. (1999) *Evaluation: A systematic approach,* (6th Ed), Thousand Oaks, CA: Sage

Ryan, S. (1994) *Home-School-Community-Liaison Scheme: Final evaluation report*, Dublin: Educational Research Centre

Ruane, J.M. (2005) *Essential Research Methods: A Guide to social science research*, Maldern, MA: Backwell

Scannell, Y. (1988) The Constitution and the Role of Women, in Farrell, B. [Ed.] *De Valera's Constitution and Ours: Thomas Davis Lectures*, Dublin: Gill and Macmillan

School Completion Programme (2004) *The School Completion Programme: Incorporating the 8-15 Early School Leaver Initiative and the "Stay in School" Retention Initiative*, Dublin: SCP

School Completion Programme (2005) *Guidelines towards Best Practice*, Dublin: SCP

School Development Planning Support (Primary) (2004) *School Development Planning at Primary Level: Information for parents*, Dublin: SDPS

Schultz, T.W. (1973) The Value of Children: An economic perspective, *Journal of Political Economy*, Vol. 81, No. 2, Part 2, (March-April) pp. S2-S13

Schultz, T. W. (1977) Investment in Human Capital, in Karabel, J. and Halsey, A.H. [Eds.] *Power and Ideology in Education*, New York: Oxford University Press

Servon, L.J. (2003) Social Capital, Identity Politics, and Social Change, in Body-Gendrot, S. and Gittell, M. [Eds.] *Social Capital and Social Citizenship*, Lanham, Maryland: Lexington Books

Silverman, D. (2004) Research and Social Policy, in Seale, C. [Ed.] *Researching Society and Culture*, (2nd Ed.) London: Sage

Simpson, D. and Cieslik, M. (2002) Education Action Zones, Empowerment and Parents, *Educational Research*, Vol. 44, No. 2, Summer, pp. 119-128

Simpson, M. and Tuson, J. (2003) *Using Observation in Small-Scale Research: A beginner's guide* (Revised Edition) Glasgow: SCRE University of Glasgow

Sin, C.H. (2005) Seeking Informed Consent: Reflections on research practice, *Sociology*, Vol. 39. No. 2, April, pp. 277- 294

Skeggs, B. (1994) The Constraints of Neutrality, in Halpin, D. and Troyna, B. [Eds.] *Researching Education Policy: Ethical and methodological issues*, London: Falmer Press

Smedley, D. (1995) Marketing Secondary Schools to Parents – Some lessons from the research on parental choice, *Educational Management and Administration*, Vol. 23, No. 2, pp. 96-103

Smith, N.J. (2004) Deconstructing 'Globalisation'in Ireland, *Policy and Politics*, Vol. 32, No. 4, pp. 503-9

Snik, G., De Jong, J. and Van Haaften, W. (2004) Preventative Intervention in Families at Risk: The limits of liberalism, *Journal of Philosophy of Education*, Vol. 38, No. 2, pp. 181-193

Society of St Vincent De Paul (2003) Learning to make do won't do – A survey on educational disadvantage, *Solas*, March/April, p.2

Sugrue, C. (2004) Whose Curriculum is it anyway? Power, politics and possibilities in the construction of the Revised Primary Curriculum in Sugrue, C. [Ed.] *Curriculum and Ideology: Irish experiences: International perspectives,* Dublin: Liffey Press

Sugrue, C. and Gleeson, J. (2004) Signposts and Silences: Situating the local within the global in Sugrue, C. [Ed.] (2004) *Curriculum and Ideology: Irish experiences: International perspectives,* Dublin: Liffey Press

Sykes, G. (2001) Home-School Agreements: A tool for parental control or for partnership?, *Educational Psychology in Practice,* Vol 17, No.3, pp. 273-286

Taskforce on Active Citizenship (2007a) *The Concept of Active Citizenship,* Dublin: Secretariat of the Task force on Active Citizenship, www.activecitizenship.ie (sited viewed 10/04/2007)

Taskforce on Active Citizenship (2007b) *Statistical Evidence on Active Citizenship in Ireland,* Dublin: Secretariat of the Task force on Active Citizenship, www.activecitizenship.ie (sited viewed 10/04/2007)

Taskforce on Active Citizenship (2007c) *Report of the Taskforce on Active Citizenship,* Dublin: Secretariat of the Task force on Active Citizenship, www.activecitizenship.ie (sited viewed 10/04/2007)

Taylor, F. (1997) Governors, Parents and Primary Schools, in Cullingford, C. [Ed.] *The Politics of Primary Education,* Buckingham: Open University Press

Taylor, G. (2005) *Negotiated Governance and Public Policy in Ireland,* Manchester: Manchester University Press

Taylor, S., Rizvi, F., Lingard, B. and Henry, M. (1997) *Educational Policy and the Politics of Change,* London: Routledge

Thomas, L. (2006) *The Family and the Political Self,* New York: Cambridge University Press

Tomanović, S. (2003) Negotiating Children's Participation and Autonomy within Families, in *The International Journal of Children's Rights,* Vol. 11, No. 1, pp. 51-71

Tovey, H. and Share, P. (2003) *A Sociology of Ireland,* (2nd Ed), Dublin: Gill and Macmillan

Tuohy, D. (2005) Catholic Social Teaching in Education, in Jesuit Centre for Faith and Justice *Catholic Social Teaching in Action,* Dublin: Columba Press

Vincent, C. (1996) *Parents and Teachers: Power and participation,* London: Falmer Press

Vincent, C. (2001) Social Class and Parental Agency, *Journal of Education Policy,* Vol. 16, No. 4, pp. 347-364

Vulliamy, G and Webb, R. (2003) Supporting Disaffected Pupils: Perspectives from the pupils, their parents and their teachers, *Educational Research,* Vol. 45, No. 3, Winter, pp. 275-286

Walby, S. (1994) Is Citizenship Gendered?, *Sociology,* Vol. 28, No. 2, pp. 379-395

Walshe, J. (1999) *A New Partnership in Education: From consultation to legislation in the nineties,* Dublin: Institute of Public Administration

Walters, W. (1997) The 'Active Society': New designs for social policy, *Policy and Politics,* Volume 25, No. 3, pp. 221 - 234

Ward, E. (2007) Minister Hanafin Launches National Educational Welfare Board's Parents' Information Leaflet: Parental involvement in children's education is the key to the achievement of childhood dreams, *The National Educational Welfare Board Press Release March 13th 2007* http://www.nemb.ie/news/pressreleases/13_03_07.asp (Site viewed 08/08/2007)

Waters, M. (2000) Inequality after Class, in Nash, K. [Ed.] *Readings in Contemporary Political Sociology,* Oxford: Blackwell

Weiss, H.B., Mayer, E., Kreider, H., Vaughan, M., et al (2003) Making it Work: Low-income working mothers' involvement in their children's education, *American Educational Research Journal Washington,* Winter, Vol. 40, Issue 4, pp. 879-901 http://proquest.umi.com/pqdweb?did=573058921

West, A. (1992) Factors Affecting Choice of School for Middle Class Parents: Implications for marketing, *Educational Management and Administration,* Vol. 20, No. 4, pp. 212-221

Williams, F. (2004) *Rethinking Families,* London: Calouste Gulbenkian Foundation

Williams, J., Collins, C. and ERSI (1998) Childcare Arrangements in Ireland – A Report to the Commission on the Family June 1997, in Commission on the Family *Strengthening Families for Life: Final Report to the Minister for Social, Community and Family Affairs,* Dublin; Stationery Office

Williams, K. (2005) *Faith and the Nation: Religion, culture and schooling in Ireland,* Dublin: Dominican Publications

Wolfendale, S. (1996) The Relationship between Parental Involvement and Educational Achievement, in Cullingford, C. [Ed.] *Parents, Education and the State,* Aldershot: Arena

Wolff, B., Knodel, J., Sittitrai, W. (1993) Focus Groups and Surveys as Complementary Research Methods: A case example, in Morgan, D.L. [Ed.] *Successful Focus Groups: Advancing the state of the art,* Newbury Pk., California: Sage

Wyness, M.G. (1994) Keeping Tabs on an Uncivil Society: Positive parental control, *Sociology,* Vol. 28, No. 1, February, pp. 193-209

Wyness, MG (1996) *School, Welfare and Parental Responsibility,* London: Falmer Press

Yin, R.K. (2003) *Case Study Research: Design and methods* (3rd Ed.) Thousand Oaks, Ca.: Sage

Zappone, K (2002) *Achieving Equality in Children's Education,* National Forum Primary Education: Ending Disadvantage July 1-5 2002 St Patrick's College, Drumcondra